JOURNALISM IN AN AGE OF TERROR

The Reuters Institute for the Study of Journalism at the University of Oxford aims to serve as the leading international forum for a productive engagement between scholars from a wide range of disciplines and practitioners of journalism. As part of this mission, we publish work by academics, journalists, and media industry professionals focusing on some of the most important issues facing journalism around the world today.

All our books are reviewed by both our Editorial Committee and expert readers. Our books, however, remain the work of authors writing in their individual capacities, not a collective expression of views from the Institute.

EDITORIAL COMMITTEE

The Reuters Institute would like to acknowledge the assistance of Stephen Grey and Jean Seaton as editorial advisers on behalf of the Institute.

JOURNALISM IN AN AGE OF TERROR

COVERING AND UNCOVERING THE SECRET STATE

JOHN LLOYD

Published by I.B.Tauris & Co. Ltd in association with
the Reuters Institute for the Study of Journalism, University of Oxford

Published in 2017 by
I.B.Tauris & Co. Ltd
London • New York
www.ibtauris.com

ISBN (HB): 978 1 78453 790 6
ISBN (PB): 978 1 78453 708 1
eISBN: 978 1 78672 111 2
ePDF: 978 1 78673 111 1

A full CIP record for this book is available from the British Library
A full CIP record is available from the Library of Congress

Library of Congress Catalog Card Number: available

Typeset by Riverside Publishing Solutions, Salisbury, SP4 6NQ
Printed and bound in Great Britain by T.J. International, Padstow, Cornwall

Contents

Preface: Divided by a Common Commitment to Democracy

The two trades of espionage and journalism are often said to be close. Both observe behaviour, seek the substance of issues hidden or denied, and construct narratives and analyses based on their research. In fact, the two are divided by a larger issue, large not just for journalism, but for the public it aspires to serve. Journalism seeks audiences, often as wide as possible, or at least as numerous as possible within a particular niche. The secret services, however, serve a strictly limited number of 'customers,' always including the head of the government, together with a small selection of senior ministers and officials, and a few others in the intelligence networks.

And therein lies the basic tension between them. For, in democratic societies – three of those covered in the book which follows – the intelligence agencies' central task is to secure the state against external or internal threats to the democratic polity. Journalism makes a similar claim: that its free activity is a necessary pillar of a democratic order.

Journalism defaults to publication; the intelligence agencies to secrecy. Both argue that these opposing methods of working are necessary in the liberal democratic state. It is in this clash of views, which can be extreme and bitter, that the relationship between the secret services and the news media resides. The relationship is a vital one. Journalism is an erratic and often overstated tool for the preservation of democracy, but an active and, at certain times, crucial one.

I have been fortunate to be able to talk, on the record, to former heads of the external intelligence services of the US, France and the UK: all are revealing about the relationships they had, and which they wish the services to have, with the news media. This is the first time they have addressed, at length, the subject of news media relations.

The work is a comparative one – in keeping both with the policy of the Reuters Institute for the Study of Journalism, and on the understanding that these three agencies are the most important in the present confrontation with jihadist terrorism. Their policies and actions – especially those of the most powerful by far, in the US – dictate the largest part of the Western response to the terrorist organisations, led, as this is written, by the so-called Islamic State (IS).

Each of the three intelligence agencies have quite distinctive histories. They are also independent of each other, and often have quite scratchy relationships – true even between the US and UK agencies, which have been close since World War II and are the founding members of the Five Eyes group of Anglophone countries: the US, UK, Australia, Canada and New Zealand. France has ever been an independently minded member of Western alliances: General de Gaulle pulled the country out of the NATO command structure (though France had been a founder member of the Alliance); in 2009, President Sarkozy rejoined, while keeping its nuclear deterrent independent. Its secret services were similarly independent, but are much closer now, in part because of the growing need to share information against a global threat aimed at Western European states – in 2015/16, particularly at France.

* * *

The immediate prompt for this book has been the mass leaks from the US National Security Agency (NSA), organised by Edward Snowden in 2013. Snowden was a former CIA employee and latterly private consultant contracted to the NSA. The subsequent publication of a selection of these files – said to number as many as 1.7 million, of which some 200,000 may have been passed to journalists – was hailed as exposing extensive deceit on the part of the US and UK governments in the concealment of their bulk collection of data from the communications of their citizens (as well as foreigners). Snowden has said he did not read them, but that 'I've evaluated all of the documents that are in the archive … I do understand what I turned over.'[1]

Bulk collection, ramped up sharply on the orders of the US administration after 9/11, allowed the NSA to collect and examine the communications metadata – the details of the message, not its content – of hundreds of millions of people, both foreign and American: the latter having been explicitly protected against such surveillance before the attack. Other national listening centres, especially the UK's Government Communications

Headquarters (GCHQ) which works closely with the NSA, have similar programmes with an equally large reach.

The revelations were said, powerfully by the journalists who most closely collaborated with Snowden on their publication, to mark a new kind of journalism. This new journalism is one where leaks from governments, corporations and institutions of all kinds, are now explicitly sought on the grounds that documents and policy memoranda allow a much deeper appreciation of the true nature and practices of major centres of power than mainstream, including investigative, journalism.

Thus Snowden, and before his actions, Julian Assange's Wikileaks, have exploded one bomb – that of their revelations. They have left others beneath both trades in the frame here – intelligence gathering and journalism. Under the first, the fear of further mass leaks and a further erosion of trust inflict perhaps more long-lasting damage than that suffered by Snowden's raids. For journalism, there is now a method of illuminating what is going on which trumps the standard process of investigative journalism – radical whistleblowing, which puts the real stuff in the hands of the public, relegating the journalists to the secondary, though vital role of curation.

What secrecy is necessary? How far can the agencies go in securing the public's trust – also necessary to their operation – without betraying their own activities? Philip Bobbitt expressed the dilemma as 'the most difficult intelligence challenge of all ... how to develop rules that will effectively empower the secret state that protects us without compromising our commitment to the rule of law'.[2]

For journalism, the challenge of Assange/Snowden is that of deciding what is and what is not fit to be published – one which events have always posed to editors, but now more urgently press upon them. Can an editor, unversed in what is and what is not a harmful revelation, assume the position of one deciding for the public (which in the internet age is global) what they should see – overriding the fears of agencies and governments? If news organisations now seek the real stuff of internal decisions and arguments, what new relationship does that dictate between news organisations and the state?

Governments have sought to keep secret more than just the activities of the secret services. They have wished to retain the right to have private debates about choices – private, because policies must be canvassed which may, when isolated, sound extreme, or damaging to one part of the government, or to society. Disclosure, they believe, would choke off free discussion within government and between it and the services themselves.

Governments will also wish to test if hostile states or groups can be brought into negotiations. Premature disclosure could force both sides to deny any intention to talk and diminish the chances of an end to conflict. Finally, governments will commit to actions which, if revealed before begun, could place those engaged in the actions in jeopardy. The obvious case is during conflict. Should journalists – either through investigations of their own or leaks from another – reveal these?

Such decisions are hard because, as noted above, journalism defaults – and must default – to publication. These decisions are not new; but the internet is, and sharpens these dilemmas because of the greater ease with which material is leaked, and the speed at which revelations go global. Journalism must default to publication because to do otherwise is to lose its compass. This is not to pretend that journalism, even of the most serious kind, always investigates the right issues well, always unmasks the true villains and always grasps complexity. It often misses on all of these; or does not even try.

But discovering and illuminating issues which bear upon the democratic nature or lack thereof within government and the civility or lack thereof within society cannot be properly done if there is not a powerful urge to reveal. The perceived need for security, as the historian Christopher Andrew has noted, is a large part of history: it is also a large part of the present. Only when the urge to publish is confronted with good reasons for withholding publication, themselves bearing on democratic policy and civil society, can a well-founded (though not necessarily correct) decision be made on whether or not to go ahead, and quite possibly be damned.

* * *

Note: In the case of the UK, the two main agencies are officially called the Secret Intelligence Service (for external intelligence) and the Secret Service (for internal intelligence). They are also, more often, called respectively MI6 and MI5, their old names, derived from Military Intelligence (Department) 5 and 6. I have used the latter throughout, except when quoting from an interview, paper or book which uses the former.

Acknowledgements

As the impresario Max Bialystock remarked in *The Producers*, 'Must have checkies. Can't produce plays without checkies'. Nor can you produce books. Most of the checkies for this book came from David Ure, a very good and sharp-minded friend to the Reuters Institute from its beginning in 2006.

At the Institute, thanks especially to Alex Reid, who shepherded the book through many of its stages; to Director David Levy, Director of Research Rasmus Kleis Nielsen and members of the Editorial Committee for advice and encouragement, especially to Professor Jean Seaton, an editorial committee member who, with Stephen Grey, read over the first draft and was generous in suggestions; and to Kate Hanneford-Smith, the Institute's administrator, and Louise Allcock. James Dawson assisted greatly with research.

At I.B.Tauris, founder and Chairman Iradj Bagherzade encouraged what had been conceived as an essay to grow into a book, and even bought lunch to signify how serious was his commitment; the intelligence and attention of Senior Editor Joanna Godfrey was as usual deployed on it, as was the fine-tuning of the text by Senior Production Editor Sara Magness.

Thanks to all the many interviewees in the UK, the US and France. I have named all I could, and I am very grateful to them for what in some cases was considerable time spent; others who didn't want to be mentioned also contributed time and patience, and are also thanked.

1

Fictions Before Facts

Discussion of the intelligence services 'is left to inquisitive journalists, disgruntled professionals and imaginative fiction writers – categories that confusingly overlap.'
(Michael Howard, Review of *Her Majesty's Secret Service*, *New York Times*, 16 February 1986[1])

Journalism has not had much measure of the secret services until recently, and even now, it cannot have but a partial measure. All journalism about anything, even at its best, is a sketch of the observably and verifiably real, but in matters of security and espionage, the sketch is very sketchy indeed.

The peer-approved stance of a journalist is that of an outsider, with no potentially corrupting links to the subjects covered: it encourages a necessary scepticism, though it also denies useful knowledge of the real experience of and the pressures on the subjects, whether they are a government, the military, a bureaucracy, a political party or a family. Sidney Blumenthal left the coveted post of political editor of the *New Yorker* to become an aide to Bill Clinton and later wrote that 'the decisive moment had arrived when I became a whole-hearted participant. Being on the outside in whatever capacity was never the same as being in.'[2] People who have 'been in' can provide a rich resource for journalists when they write their memoirs or speak of their experiences; they can also be helpful contacts when they are in.

But 'being in', or even 'being close', is impossible in the coverage of the secret services, since they must themselves keep the core of their activities, the business end of espionage and counter-espionage, secret. This is especially so before and during operations, but also after, since they all believe that knowledge of the individuals and tradecraft used in operations, even of many years past, will be useful to the enemy and potentially deadly to friends.

The relationship between hacks and spooks has been fraught, fevered and often mythical: it may be that it cannot fundamentally change (see an attempt to argue it can change, at least a little, in my Conclusion). The CIA's 'secrecy would always conflict with the openness of American democracy', writes one of the agency's severest journalist-critics, and quotes Dean Acheson, US Secretary of State (1949–53), as saying of the fledgling service that he had warned the President (Truman) that, as set up, 'neither he nor the National Security Council nor anyone else would be in a position to know what it was doing or to control it.'[3] Secrecy in such a critically important part of the state's activities – one which, in the twenty-first century, has grown immensely from an already impressive size, especially in the great powers of the US, China and Russia, but also in the agencies of Europe – necessarily conflicts with democratic practice anywhere, and most of all with the most insistent claim of journalism to hold power to account.

The services have existed in organised and semi-acknowledged form since the late nineteenth century; though spying and spymasters were common enough in most states and cultures from medieval times. In Britain, writers/journalists were early hired as spies – a tradition which lasted deep into the twentieth century. The dramatist Christopher Marlowe is thought likely to have been a spy in Elizabethan times, working for Sir Francis Walsingham, known later as Elizabeth's spymaster.[4] Daniel Defoe was employed to spy on the anti-unionist forces in Scotland before the successful vote on Union in 1707 – a job made easier by the author's Presbyterianism, and perhaps, from the author of *Robinson Crusoe*, by his imagination.

Espionage was early entwined with fiction, a constant and continuing adjunct to the craft. The coupling has a sinister side, evident in the instant effectiveness and enduring popularity among anti-Semites of 'The Protocols of the Elders of Zion', a document used by one of the earliest and most numerous organised secret police forces, the Tsarist Okhrana, which took up the fiction which created 'the Elders' as the all-powerful executive committee of worldwide Jewry, administering the conspiracy in pursuit of global domination. The Protocols is the product of a mind creative enough to envisage a world of conspiracy and control, subtle enough to make it seem real and menacing. A fiction, it moved real events – as many spy fictions have.

In the first decades of organised espionage, the conflict between journalism and the services was minor, at times apparently non-existent.

The services were, self-evidently, a patriotic endeavour in and before World War I and II, when in both the UK and France spying was mainly directed against Germany. The 'coverage' was thus mythic rather than factual – since facts, anyway scarce, were potentially treacherous, the stuff which foreign agents were hired to discover. Propaganda, getting into its twentieth-century stride as the services became state-sponsored organisations, convinced the peoples of authoritarian states of the goodness of the security services: both the Soviet Cheka (later NKVD, then KGB) and the Nazi Sicherheitsdienst (SD, a section of the SS) were projected as the best men of the nation, ruthless to enemies and protective of the people.

Both tyrannies decreed a hyper patriotism from which it was unwise, at times fatal, to dissent. It called forth in patriots of all stripes a pride in the use of brutal force against enemies, and in ensuring the disciplining of society. In Vladimir Nabokov's story 'Conversation Piece 1945',[5] a former White Guard colonel, an exile in the US, anti-communist and Christian, says that, in spite of his views, he puts Stalin on a par with Ivan the Terrible (tsar 1547–84) and Peter the Great (tsar 1682–1721) as a mighty leader – 'today, in every word that comes out of Russia, I feel the power, I feel the splendour of Old Mother Russia. She is again a country of soldiers, of religion and true Slavs.'

Patriotism and belief in the goodness of one's nation was, in much less terrifying circumstances, a general sentiment in the few semi-democracies of Europe, and in North America. Military power and its projection were seen both officially and – broadly – popularly as a test of national valour. These qualities have a real and often solid base both in public and private actions; but their maintenance and support by the public depend much more on the charge of emotion than on dispassionate and neutral analysis – an approach reserved for the elite, who required it to make informed decisions.

Thus the journalism on security issues was – up to and even beyond World War II – scanty and, where it existed, depended on officially approved briefings, and on gossip. The latter was especially the case in the UK, where newspaper writing on intelligence issues was greatly influenced by the first spy fiction, often written by men who had themselves been, or still were, journalists. The tropes of these fictions entered the bloodstreams of subsequent novelists and of journalists – who depended and in some cases still depend on the support of fiction rather than research, an approach which coexists with (though sometimes trickles into) the harder edged journalism of the last half century.

The importance of fiction in the coverage of intelligence – especially in the first decades of state-organised espionage agencies when dispassionate news coverage was hard to find, officially disapproved and seen as potentially treacherous by many journalists themselves – is large. Almost all journalism operates in areas which are subject to stereotyping and mythicisation, these often created by journalism itself. Politics, foreign affairs, defence, health, the economy and many other beats are encrusted with preconceived notions of their importance, their power within societies, the activities of elites within their spheres, the trust or lack of it which citizens give them. But the business of intelligence is a special case even within areas so imaginatively perceived – since the espionage and counter-espionage trade remains in the shadows; the other beats have been, over the past century and more, the subject of much more journalistic light, much of it well focused.

The power of the early fiction, especially in the UK, was great – and it remains powerful, though the messages are less monolithically admiring. Fleming's James Bond is without challenge in the global gallery of fictional spies, substantially because of the many successful (and some unsuccessful) film adaptations; and British secret service officers will at times admit to enjoying basking in the glow he sheds, even while dismissing his antics as ridiculous. From the US, Tom Clancy's Jack Ryan and Robert Ludlum's Jason Bourne have both powered best-sellers and successful films. John Le Carré's George Smiley (in *Tinker Tailor Soldier Spy*, 1974, and again in 2011; *Smiley's People*, 1979), and his later novels as *The Constant Gardner* (2001), *Our Kind of Traitor* (2010), *A Delicate Truth* (2013) and *The Night Manager* (2013), are increasingly concerned with the corruption and oppression of US, and to a lesser extent British, politics, and of corporate power. The force of their narratives both played to and helped create the default position of cynicism and suspicion among publics throughout the democratic world of the leaders they elect, the corporations which supply them and the secret services which claim to keep them secure. In the conjuring of phantasmagorical worlds where no one is what they seem, Le Carré has no peer in spy fiction – though he is resented by many of his ex-colleagues and their successors in the intelligence world for misrepresenting work they see as straightforwardly necessary and patriotic.

* * *

Among the first in a subsequently crowded field of espionage novels are Rudyard Kipling's *Kim* (1901), set in India and using the background of the 'Great Game' of Russian and British imperial contest for control over Central Asia; Colonel F. N. Maude's *The Sack of London in the Great French War of 1901*, foreseeing a French invasion of Britain backed by the Russians (the French general staff had studied the possibility in 1900); and Erskine Childers's 1903 novel *The Riddle of the Sands. Kim*, the greater fiction, is exotic and imperial in its concerns: Childers dealt with what for the British was a more potent and much closer threat. The novel, written in Childers's imperialist phase (he later fought as an ardent Irish Republican and died in Ireland, executed by the pro-Treaty side of the Irish civil war), is a derring-do fiction in which two young English gentlemen, one a young diplomat, while on a sailing trip round the Frisian Islands off the German coast discover preparations for landing a German army in the UK. Childers described it as 'a story with a purpose' which was 'written with a patriot's natural sense of duty'.[6] It was essentially a long and fictionalised editorial, aimed at changing the establishment view by alarming the populace. Its effect was satisfyingly large, prompting a strengthening of UK naval defences. It underscored another potent theme, in politics and journalism as well as fiction: that of a warning against governmental and military insouciance in the face of a future enemy's steady preparation for war.

Britain, motherland of a huge empire, published the largest range of spy fiction before the 1950s (when the US took over). France, also the centre of a large empire, had a less developed tradition, though Gaston Leroux, best known for his 1910 novel *The Phantom of the Opera* and for the 1907 *The Mystery of the Yellow Room* (the first mystery of a murder in a room locked from the inside, with no other means of entrance or exit), dipped into the theme with novels featuring the amateur detective Rouletabille – like the author, a newspaper reporter – notably in the 1917 book, *Rouletabille chez Krupp*. The novel has Rouletabille, a reporter on the Parisian daily *L'Epoque*, serving as a corporal at the front, recalled to his paper by the editor, who then takes him to a meeting at the Ministry of the Interior. There he hears that a scientist, Fulber, has invented a rocket with the power of an atomic bomb, and has taken it to the British, who had constructed the rocket, tested it, then had the plans, design, Fulber and his assistant all captured from them by German spies while they toasted the success in champagne. The news is brought by a high British official, Cromer – who emphasises that the Germans now have the power to destroy Paris or London in one blow. Only one with the street cunning and fluent German of the reporter Rouletabille can intervene to stop a horror and certain defeat.

The most practically influential authors in their time are not always those best remembered. The hugely prolific French/British author William Le Queux was probably the master in the early years, writing more simply and graphically than the author of *The Riddle of the Sands*, playing on the common fears of Germany, his status such that he could fairly claim to be an influence on the government's creation of the first secret services. Alfred Harmsworth (later Lord Northcliffe), creator of the *Daily Mail*, had commissioned Le Queux to write a serial for one of his magazines on a French invasion in 1893, three years before founding the *Mail*. He was commissioned again by the *Mail* to write, in 1906, *The Invasion of 1910*, an attack this time by the Germans, strongly influenced by the views of Field Marshal Earl Roberts, who had tried and failed to convince the government to institute national service. The novel greatly increased the paper's circulation, and it was changed at Harmsworth's instructions to include a number of larger towns in the narrative, where the sales of the *Mail* were higher than in the villages in the original.

Le Queux occupies some 20 pages in Christopher Andrew's *Her Majesty's Secret Service* (1985). That book is subtitled 'The Making of the British Intelligence Community': Andrew underscores the central role of fiction in that construction, as Le Queux, enormously prolific, built up the fears of the (real) growing hostility of Germany, and the increasing conviction, including within the government, that Britain was infested with highly trained German spies. His and other authors' books were written in a documentary style, deliberately blurring fact and fiction, the writers claiming they had done extensive research.

The more surprising element of their work was the high level of alarm these apparently trashy novels excited. Viscount Haldane, the Secretary of State for War (1905–12), educated in the universities of Edinburgh and Gottingen with a first-class degree in philosophy, was so moved by the spy fever the novels fed that he created a high-level subcommittee of the Committee of Imperial Defence which he chaired, and which included the Home Secretary, the commissioner of the Metropolitan Police and the First Lord of the Admiralty. Major (later General) James Edmonds, head of the Military Operations Directorate, told the committee that the rapid rise in reported cases of German espionage had happened 'only since certain newspapers have directed attention to the subject' – the veracity of the newspaper reports being implicitly accepted. Andrews writes that Edmonds, who believed that the German network was so extensive that 'a German general landing a force in East Anglia would know more about the country than any British General' was wholly ignorant of the facts – which were that the German network was small, poorly paid, part-time and had largely been closed down by the time the war began.[7]

John Buchan, a Presbyterian minister's son born in Perth, was an editor of the *Spectator* in his early thirties, and a *Times* correspondent in France during the 1914–18 war. These spells alternated with longer periods as a political aide (in South Africa) and as Director of Propaganda in the latter part of World War I. In later life, he rose to become Governor General of Canada from 1935 until his death in 1940.

Buchan's fiction was popular throughout his life, particularly his (shortest) novel *The Thirty-Nine Steps* (1915) in which he introduces Richard Hannay, a Scots-born mining engineer returning to London from South Africa, who, in the course of the novel, manages to foil a German plot with the aid of a senior intelligence officer, Sir Walter Bullivant. These two are together again in *Greenmantle* (1916) where they once more foil a potentially fatal German plot. *Greenmantle*, out a year earlier than *Rouletabille chez Krupp*, Leroux's tense but less jingoistic thriller (not yet translated into English), uses the same narrative lines: like Rouletabille, Hannay – a major, not a corporal – is taken away from the front; like Rouletabille, he is given a task in which he is likely to fail, and to die failing; like Rouletabille, the stakes are the highest.

In *Greenmantle*, Bullivant tells Hannay that he may be sending him to his death. Rouletabille's editor also warns that the stakes are as high as saving Paris, and that his death is likely. Leroux's means by which the Germans will succeed in conquering France and Britain is a huge rocket; in Buchan's novel a Muslim prophet will rouse the tribes of the Middle East to support the German war effort and sweep the British forces before them.

Both authors prefigure, remarkably well, real events and developments of the twentieth and twenty-first centuries. Leroux's device is even a Multiple Independently Targetable Re-entry Vehicle (MIRV) type of ballistic missile, in which smaller warheads are encased in one vast rocket, the real MIRV only being developed in the 1960s. Buchan's prophet out of the east evokes al Qaeda's bin Laden or IS's al Baghdadi. The strongest and most influential of the themes present in the work of both the French and British thriller writers is that only one man, at times with a few trusted companions, can save the country, or even the world, from a barbarian invasion. James Bond and Jack Ryan were born then.

The uncontroversial shuffling between political service, government propaganda work, novel writing and journalism illuminates a central point in early writing on espionage: the 'natural sense of duty' which Childers invoked as an explanation for his novel writing covered, before the 1950s, journalism as well as all other fields. The security officials were defenders of the nation, sacralised by the danger of the craft and the constant need for dissimulation at the expense of their own private lives. The most a spy-thriller author would permit himself was some well-bred irony, tending towards the *de haut en bas*: as did W. Somerset Maugham, an acerbically elegant writer of novels, plays and short stories, who in his 1928 novel *Ashenden; or The British Agent* wrote loosely linked stories which had as eponymous hero a British dramatist recruited by MI6 and sent to Geneva. Ashenden, who though properly patriotic and prepared to take up the challenge of espionage work without any apparent hesitation, still retained a certain authorial reserve: as presumably Maugham himself did, when working for MI6 in 1916–17 in Switzerland and Russia. As he put it in the foreword 'In 1917 I went to Russia. I was sent to prevent the Bolshevik Revolution and to keep Russia in the war. The reader will know that my efforts did not meet with success.'[8] In the novel, Ashenden meets a colonel at a party, and is asked for 'a chat' the next day. Turning up at a shabby house, he is asked by the Colonel – apparently the head of the secret service – to join the agency, encouraging him with the thought that his experiences will make good copy on the page or the stage. The interview ends with a fine piece of stiff-upper-lippery:

> Colonel: *There's just one thing I think you ought to know before you take on this job. And don't forget it. If you do well you'll get no thanks and if you get into trouble you'll get no help. Does that suit you?*
> Ashenden: *Perfectly.*
> Colonel: *Then I'll wish you a good afternoon.*[9]

The other spy writer of note – now largely neglected – was Alexander Wilson, a restless and daring man who was an accredited MI6 officer during World War II but had begun to write successful and well regarded spy novels – such as *The Mystery of Tunnel 51* and *The Devil's Cocktail* – in the 1920s, and may have been a undercover agent for many years. The writer Tim Crook, who wrote his biography,[10] said of him in an interview that the hero of the novels, Sir Leonard Wallace, bore 'an uncanny resemblance to the first head of MI6, Sir Mansfield Smith Cumming', known as 'C.' When Crook researched his past, he was not allowed to see files on him in MI6 but was allowed to speak to agency officers, with whom, said Crook,

I always stressed the negative – that Wilson was a fantasist, his books luckily perceptive rather than the work of an insider and his post-war decline his own fault. But when I spoke to my sources, the positive was strongly pointed out – that Wilson might well have been doing a great job for his country, an unsung hero in contrast to others from the era, like Anthony Blunt or Guy Burgess.[11]

Was this the MI6 man claiming a hero to set against the embarrassing traitors whom they had clasped for so long to their unsuspecting bosom? Or was Wilson simply a clever and lucky fantasist? The fictional and the real are again intertwined, with the agencies deliberately encouraging a romantic mist to settle permanently about their activities.

The exception – the only one I know of – was the writer Sir Compton Mackenzie, best known for his comic novel *Whisky Galore* (1947). He had been an MI6 officer in World War I, engaged in counter-intelligence during the Gallipoli campaign and later founding the Aegean Intelligence Service. In retaliation for the suppression of his memoirs (not published until 2011), Mackenzie wrote a satire, *Water on the Brain* (1933), an account of the Directorate of Extraordinary Intelligence, MQ 99(E), run by a man named N. The organisation's headquarters, Pomona Lodge in north London, became a lunatic asylum, 'for the servants of bureaucracy who have been driven mad in the service of their country'.[12]

As with world domination, Britain ceded its pre-eminence in spy writing after World War II to the US. Pre-war, there was little American spy writing of any consequence, either in journalism or in fiction – for though there were spies, there were no agencies. The one book of any note which concerned itself with spying was not a novel (though a 1935 film, *Rendezvous*, was based on it), but a memoir by Herbert Yardley, an expert code breaker. In the 1920s, he headed MI-8 or the Cipher Bureau, which came to be called the Black Chamber: a forerunner of the National Security Agency (NSA) in intercepting communications and reading, in its case, the content rather than the 'metadata.' It was closed in 1929 when

Henry Stimson, the Secretary of State, judged that 'gentlemen do not read each others' letters.'[13] Like Mackenzie a few years later, Yardley reacted by writing an account of the Bureau, *The American Black Chamber*, which was popular at home and abroad – especially in its Japanese translation, since Japan's coded messages were a prime target of the bureau. Yardley was accused, it seems rightly, with prompting several states to change their codes and revealing sources and methods. He was not, however, prosecuted.

The heroes of the British spy novels, *Kim* apart, were one-dimensional characters, as were the villains: they were the more widely popular and powerful for being so. They were written in the late heroic period of the British Empire, when the establishment, Liberal and Conservative, was largely united in support of the empire, differing only on the nature of their rule over it. The later fiction, especially after World War II, could not credibly deploy 'clean-limbed' establishment products as heroes. At one, unique extreme, the hero was an ironic super-cool superman, James Bond; the mainstream became the despairing patriots of Len Deighton, and above all of John Le Carré – products of a failing post imperial state, dominated by venal politicians, corporate sharks and temporising officials, with a few decent people, like the MI5 agent Leonard Burr in *The Night Manager* (a woman, Angela Burr, in the TV dramatisation of 2016). As the popular novelists wrote within the imperial consensus, so did most journalists, since that was what their proprietors, editors and publics demanded.

* * *

World War II caused a rapid expansion – or creation – of intelligence services. In the UK, the Special Operations Executive (SOE) – 'Churchill's Secret Army' – was created, largely charged with behind-the-lines subversion and thus mainly worked in collaboration with resistance movements. It also had an intelligence function, which meant it clashed inevitably with MI6 – a clash never toxic, and settled by what Keith Jeffery, the official historian of MI6, called 'a typically effortless assumption of bureaucratic superiority … able deftly to out manouevre attempts by less practiced Whitehall warriors to change (downgrade) the status' of MI6.[14] The SOE was a genuinely dashing organisation, perilous for its agents and allies, often very effective: it had great coverage in films after the war, and two of its agents – the head of the French Section, Maurice Buckmaster and his aide, the Jewish-Romanian-born Vera Atkins, may be models for Ian Fleming's Bond and Miss Moneypenny. Novels – such as Thomas Pynchon's *Gravity Rainbow*, Ken Follet's *Jackdaw*, Elizabeth Wein's *Code Name Verity*, Sebastian Faulks's *Charlotte Gray* and Mal Peet's *Tamar*, mostly written many decades after the fact – all use the SOE to different degrees; the journalist Sarah Helm wrote a biography of Vera Atkins, *Vera Atkins and the Lost Heroes of the SOE*, in 2005.

Journalism in Britain in the post-war period had added, to the already-established rumbustiousness of its political reporting and commentary, increasing doses of scandal and sex, stimulated by the well-grounded belief on the part of the popular press proprietors and their editors that these would assist circulation. In the early 1960s, as media criticism and mockery of 'the Establishment'[15] mounted, a series of spy scandals gave the newspapers, and even the still-staid BBC and the brasher ITV, huge amounts of copy. They included the ring of spies under the direction of Gordon Lonsdale (real name Konon Molody, a KGB agent posing as a Canadian businessman) who smuggled out details of UK nuclear submarine design and weaponry; the arrest (1961) and then the escape from Wormwood Scrubs prison (1966) of George Blake, an MI6 officer, enrolled in the KGB while a prisoner in North Korea, whose revelations of a tunnel built by the British agency under the Berlin Wall within which they tapped phone lines had, together with other leaked details, caused the arrest and execution of up to 40 operatives in the Soviet bloc; and John Vassall, blackmailed by the KGB (who had photographs of his homosexual activities) into espionage, and who sent a range of classified documents, again mainly concerned with naval technology.

The crowning scandal was the Profumo affair, the bit-by-bit revelation that John Profumo, Defence Minister in the second Conservative government of Harold Macmillan (1959–63) had had an affair with Christine Keeler, a model. She also had as a lover Yevgeny Ivanov, a Soviet diplomat in London, an agent of the military intelligence agency, the GRU. The story was brought to a climax in 1963 by the persistent questioning by the leader of the Labour opposition, Harold Wilson. Profumo, who had denied the rumours in the House of Commons, was forced to recant his denial, resigned and spent the rest of his long life doing charity work in London's East End.

These stories were both made for the popular press – dominant then as now – and were in part made by them. The main actors, especially Keeler and her friend and housemate Mandy Rice-Davies, were paid large

11

sums by newspapers for their 'confessions' and 'memoirs'. In his book on the period, Richard Davenport-Hines writes that 'the Profumo affair was made in Fleet Street ... incited, publicised and exploited by journalists'.[16] This is vivid, but misleading: the main incitement, and the one the government had to take seriously, was done by the relatively young Harold Wilson, using information supplied by George Wigg, a party colleague with links to the intelligence services.

The popular press was hot on the heels of, or at times led, every rumour and allegation; at the time, it accounted for some 90 per cent of the public's news reading. This was a time when popular papers like the *News of the World*, the *Daily* and *Sunday Mirror*, the *Daily* and *Sunday Express*, were each selling over 4 and even 5 million copies, and the BBC and the more demotic ITV (launched in 1955) were increasing their grip on the free time of the population. Davenport-Hines writes that

> the Profumo affair roused a Fleet Street frenzy of ferocity. It managed to glorify what was shabby and had an enduring influence on investigative journalism ... the gutter press, with its entertaining scrapes and vicarious punishments, provided a histrionic morality for its readers and frontier markers for society. Its contents were a map of moral landscaping, showing the contours of normality, the roads to right and wrong, the boundaries that must not be crossed.[17]

It was an age where members of the elite in journalism both bemoaned the decline of manners and morals, and when asked by the popular press which they derided, provided mordant and well-rewarded commentaries on their own class, which had seen itself as initiator and guardian of these manners and morals. Malcolm Muggeridge, who when Rector of Edinburgh University (1966–8), inveighed against the students' 'pot pills and promiscuity', wrote that 'the Upper Classes have always been given to lying, fornication, corrupt practices and, doubtless as a result of the public school system, sodomy'.[18] Sodomy – homosexuality – was regarded by the popular press as a disgusting 'perversion', and was used as a major reason why the Cambridge spy ring – Guy Burgess and Donald Maclean (who was bisexual), later Anthony Blunt – were traitors.

Though the national newspaper reporters were both connoisseurs and shapers of scandals, there was little attempt at forensic investigative journalism, whether on the secret services or any other aspect of British, or foreign, life. In the case of the security services, this was because they were officially chimeras of the press's and public's imagination, and the political and civil service classes had never heard of them. Reviewing, in the *New York Times*, a 1986 book, *Her Majesty's Secret Service*, by the Cambridge historian and expert on the secret services Christopher Andrew, the Regius Professor of Modern History at Oxford Sir Michael Howard wrote that

> so far as official Government policy is concerned, the British security and intelligence services, M.I.5 and M.I.6, do not exist. Intelligence is brought by the storks, and enemy agents are found under gooseberry bushes. Government records bearing on intelligence activities are either industriously "weeded" or kept indefinitely closed. Members of Parliament who ask questions are listened to in icy silence and choked off with the most abrupt and inexplicit of replies. Serious historians, deprived of documentation, tend to accept the situation and do not ask questions to which they know they cannot provide the answers.[19]

Journalists were also in the dark – or where not, could not publish much of what they had learned, or suspected. As Davenport-Hines has shown in his *An English Affair*, journalists revelled in the clouds of obscurity round the services, which both excused and increased the sensationalist myths, intertwined with truths, which they printed.[20] The other advantage was that, since they did not exist, they would not sue.

In the 1960s, the journalism trade was colonised by a post-war generation of graduates, many from Oxford and Cambridge, who saw themselves as at least the social and intellectual equals of the political and administrative classes, unlike the previous generations of British reporters who – a US colleague, quoted by Davenport-Hines, wrote in 1965 with the condescension which Americans tend to ascribe to the British – had 'provincial accents and tea-boy educations; many of them held the old spit-and-polish, school-of-hard-knocks, learn-the-hard-way-on-the-stone and other equally soporific philosophies for journalistic success'.[21] This new breed was influential in developing the first organised efforts at investigative journalism in the *Sunday Times*, from the 1960s onwards, especially under the editorship of Harold Evans, but continuing after he had gone.

These included investigations into Kim Philby's activities (1967), Israel's possession of nuclear weapons (1986), a serialisation of *Spycatcher*, a book (banned in the UK) by the former agent Peter Wright alleging penetration of MI5; the allegations that Michael Foot, former leader of the Labour Party, was a KGB 'agent of influence' (Foot won large damages for this, when it was judged false) – and, in the early 2000s, the revelations of the renditions of suspected jihadists for interrogation and likely torture by Stephen Grey at Insight and others.

The man who, from the 1950s, did most to reveal something of their workings, was not from the elite, but proved adept at moving in elite circles. His father, formerly a major in the Indian army, kept a pub in Northumberland, and his mother had been an actor. He was not easily categorised as either a gentleman commentator or a workaday hack. He credited his upbringing above the pub for his ability to speak to all ranks, and to get them to talk – one of the greatest gifts a reporter can possess.

Chapman Pincher was educated in a grammar school and took a science degree at London's Kings College, taught physics, joined the army's technical branch during the war and was hired after it, and became Science and Defence Correspondent for the *Daily Express*. The newspaper is now a reactionary shadow of its former self: in the years he worked for it – from 1946 to 1979 when he retired to concentrate on book writing, still on the same beat but with the title of Assistant Editor – it remained a popular if slowly declining title, commanded despotically by its proprietor Lord Beaverbrook (1879–1964), slipping below 4 million daily sales in 1967 and below 3 million a few years before Pincher left.

An insult, of which Pincher was apparently proud, illuminates something of his method, and of the way in which the security world was represented by its most assiduous chronicler. The insult came from the left intellectual E. P. Thompson, who wrote in the *New Statesman* in 1978 that Pincher was 'a kind of official urinal' in which top people in the security and defence establishments 'could stand patiently leaking'.[22] Thompson had earlier written that British spies lived as if characters in a Buchan novel: an out-of-date assessment of those who, in the main, spent their lives sifting dubious data on the Soviet Union and attempting to keep up a network of agents living always on the brink of discovery.

Yet there was something in the leaking comment. Pincher's gift for making himself agreeable and interested allowed him to appeal to both establishment figures and the readership of the *Daily Express*. With a Beaverbrook-approved expense account from the paper which allowed him to host lunches for his contacts at the Ecu de France[23] and other costly St James' restaurants, he spent much of his time and his employer's money on highly placed officials, and reaped large stories from the men so irrigated.

E. P. Thompson's contempt also overlooked a large fact, central to journalism's practice. Until the internet age of journalism and even in it, details, plans, policies and debates hidden within government and state institutions were accessible largely and often only through politicians, officials and advisers, in post or recently moved or retired. They might respond to the flattery of an expensive lunch with a journalist they knew or knew of, who had some working knowledge as well as an intense professional interest in the subject with which they dealt day after day – that interest being an even more effective form of flattery. His King's College science degree and his work, both in the army and in civilian life, as a munitions expert and instructor gave Pincher a basic understanding of the technical details of the issues with which he dealt, unlike most journalists who either had no university training, nor had read classics or the arts.

Pincher wished to be 'used' – at least by some of his informants, who shared his strong anti-communism and his belief in the porousness of the intelligence services to subversion. Being 'used', for him, was taking part in a joint endeavor to secure Britain, a task more important than any demands – not then very strong – that journalism be independent of political power. When, in an interview given when the former *Express* man was 97 and 'still working every day', the journalist Ian Jack asked him if he felt used, he responded 'Absolutely! But my motto was, if the story is new, and particularly if it's exclusive, I'm open for use any day.' Noting that government expenditure on defence after the war had increased because of the state's investment in nuclear weaponry, Pincher said that 'the taxpaying public had to understand why. Governments realised I was a good medium for getting that across'.[24]

He had developed a nose for those who would yield secrets – either because they thought the secrecy excessive, or because they wished to impress a journalist with their knowledge or access, or because they wished to boost their own professional and departmental interest and/or damage that of others, or because they had received the nod from superiors to insert, non-attributably, some facts into the public arena, or because of simple gratitude, even friendship. Every reporter trawling for stories through the maze of state and corporate interests must take advantage of these motives for leaking; that some of the leaks to Pincher embarrassed governments is attested by the irritation of prime ministers and permanent secretaries when the stories were published. Like reporters everywhere, then as now, he sniffed out and played on divisions among ministries, ministers and officials.

One controversial scoop with contemporary resonance was published in the *Express* edition of 21 February 1967. In a front-page story, Pincher wrote of 'a Big Brother intrusion into privacy which ranks with telephone tapping and the opening of letters'. The substance was that all overseas cables were daily collected from the office of the company Commercial Cables and Western Union, taken to the Ministry of Defence for checking then returned after a two-day delay. Pincher, who had the story as an exclusive, checked it was fit to be published with Colonel 'Sammy' Lohan, secretary of the D-notice committee, a mechanism through which journalists could check on the sensitivity of stories with a representative of the state, invariably a high-ranking former military figure.

The conversation, in the traditional expensive restaurant, produced a misunderstanding. Pincher claimed that Lohan had said there was no problem, Lohan said he had not given permission to publish. The case was then given 'legs' by the refusal on the part of Harold Wilson, then prime minister, to let the issue drop. He appointed a committee of privy councillors to examine the issue, which sided with Pincher. Ignoring that judgment, Wilson had a White Paper published on D-notices. In the debate on the paper, he directly blamed Lohan for his 'over-close association' with journalists. He was roasted by the opposition and in the press, alienated many in his cabinet – a triumph for Pincher and the press.[25] Wilson was probably at least partly right.

The larger issue is not that reporters should not seek leaks, whether given on moral grounds or prompted by the last glass from a bottle of expensive wine; they must. It is that they are rarely the whole story. Journalists in search of a narrative, or conducting an investigation, use these confidences as parts in a jigsaw which, when completed, yields a picture coherent in its own terms. Pincher was not an investigative reporter as it is now defined (though he was later to claim he was): for much of his career Britain had no such explicit sub-category of the journalists' trade.

He needed scoops, because the *Express* needed them and he became its premier supplier. He told Ian Jack that among his most pleasant memories was 'coming out of l'Ecu after a nice lunch, walking back to Fleet Street in the sunshine and feeling great, knowing that I'd got two bloody big scoops that nobody could touch and they were bound to lead the paper. Oh, it was wonderful, quite wonderful.'[26] Few reporters of any experience haven't had that feeling when being first, or going deepest, or revealing most, whether or not after a nice lunch.

Pincher got scoops day by day – in one early success, he secured through the kind act of a friend a report on US nuclear weaponry not then published in either the UK or the US, and led the paper with excerpts from it for seven days. But he had a long-term and quite serious ideological mission too, which produced both scoops and long narratives and which he turned into books written after his Fleet Street career ended. Strongly anti-communist, he became an expert in treachery within the secret services: he focused, it seems wrongly, on Roger Hollis, whose career in and leadership of MI5 he believed concealed a loyalty to Moscow, and a servicing of its intelligence needs. His 2011 book, *Treachery, Betrayals, Blunders and Cover-Ups: Six Decades of Espionage* – was an extended enquiry into Hollis's alleged treason, strongly dependent on the bitter testimony of Peter Wright.

Wright was a former senior MI5 officer (and like Pincher, a scientist by education) who had chaired a committee while in MI5 investigating possible treachery – a job which drew him to the conclusion that Hollis, the chief, was the main 'mole'. Wright's 1987 book, *Spycatcher*, in which the charge was laid out, was banned in the UK but published in Australia, and became – because of the ban – an international best-seller, selling 2 million copies and making Wright a millionaire. The ban prompted a 1991 judgment from the European Court of Human Rights condemning the UK government for breaching the Convention on Human Rights by censoring its own press.

Pincher's book was an updating of Wright's, with further evidence: but both men were disappointed in not having their view confirmed officially. Wright's co-author on *Spycatcher* was Paul Greengrass, then a director on the Granada TV investigative documentary series *World in Action*, and later director of two of the films in the 'Bourne' series, *The Bourne Supremacy* (2004) and *The Bourne Ultimatum* (2007). The second of these featured a *Guardian* journalist who gets part of the web of stories surrounding the CIA fugitive Jason Bourne and is murdered by a CIA-appointed assassin – an example of the still-potent mutual flows between fact, fiction and paranoia in the representation of the intelligence services.

Pincher's approach to journalism was conventional, if much more active and shrewd than most of his fellows: his success was unusual, and long-lasting, driven by his own desire to 'lead the paper', his assiduous cultivation of contacts and useful friendships and his strong work ethic. That approach was designed to accord with what had emerged, post-war, as the way in which the secret services bypassed their non-existence[27] to

17

leak material sanctioned by their leaderships and by ministers, and material not sanctioned but usually useful at some level of the agencies. Pincher was more successful than most in this era because of his, and his newspaper's, strong anti-communism – naturally popular with officials whose existence depended on the view that the Soviet Union was the main threat to British security. But he also was personally able – in part because he was personable – to negotiate the shoals and currents of British officialdom, and to seek out those who would best serve his purpose as much as he served theirs.

Pincher's frank patriotism had been unexceptional when he began in journalism, and was in tune with his newspaper; by the time he retired from regular newspaper work, it was going out of fashion, replaced with a sceptical approach which shaded, in many cases, into an aggressive suspicion of authority. He was able to get the scoops he did – some were no more than what the services and the government wished to see published, but some exposed internal struggles and divisions which were certainly not welcome – because he was assiduous in discovering those who had, or took, a licence to leak. He was also an enthusiastic actor in the dramas he described: his anti-communism grew as his fame did and he learned more of the Soviet system.

The books he wrote, mostly after he had ceased daily reporting, were both well documented and pugnacious: in the introduction to a 1985 book, he wrote that 'to the Western mind, peace is the absence of war and a state of friendliness to other countries. To those few in the Kremlin and to the millions never given any option but to agree with them, peace means what Lenin proclaimed – that there can be no peace until there is Communist world control, and the struggle for that control must be ceaseless.'[28] Pincher's reporting was properly concerned with Soviet infiltration and subversion, but the hard reporting was mainly directed to the naming of Soviet moles within the services, with polemical writing aimed against those who were blind to the threat he believed they posed. Far from full and balanced, Pincher's assiduous work was still often the best available in the journalism of the time.

* * *

Spying in France is a venerable trade. Julius Caesar writes of his use of it in his Gallic Wars; the kings and princes of the medieval courts kept spies about them (or abroad). It was in the Middle Ages when tactics still used were developed – the interception of communications, codes, disinformation, the use of merchants and other travelling folk as spies and messengers. The French were the first to create a Ministry of War, in 1567 under Charles IX; and in 1589, under Henry IV, a Foreign Ministry – two centuries before the US and the UK. The conclusion of the Treaty of Westphalia gave international agreement to the sovereignty of the nation state, and therefore a multiplicity of possible enemies – thus prompting a further development in espionage organisation; the French king Louis XV created a network of agents across Europe.[29]

In the nineteenth century, the French military, one of the largest and most splendid armies in the world, created a series of institutions, some of which bordered on security – such as the statistics section in the 1820s and the department of fortifications in the late 1830s. A department dedicated to intelligence had to wait till the 1880s and it was in that department that an 'affaire', one of the most important in the modern history of the country, developed.

The case of Captain Alfred Dreyfus, sentenced to life imprisonment on Devil's Island in 1894 for an act of treachery – passing confidential information on French artillery to Germany – he did not commit, as a consequence of widespread anti-Semitism, stands at the head of the development of the French secret services and is still a potent memory in French political life. The case was a test for the French press of the time (1880/1890s): one which, by contemporary standards, it failed. Though diverse and lively, the newspapers were also tied closely to particular commercial and political interests, and made little discrimination between advertisements and editorials: indeed, the latter were often a platform for the former, as well as shills for a particular political or commercial venture. They were also, according to the German spy chief Wilhelm Stieber, 'incorrigibly talkative',[30] and aided his espionage activities greatly. (Guy de Maupassant's *Bel Ami* (1885) is a fine satire on the press of the time, as the hero, Georges Duroy, rises in society through an adroit mixture of seduction and journalism.)

In his account of the Dreyfus Affair, the novelist and historian Piers Paul Read lays stress on the sharp and animus-filled divisions in France's Third Republic – especially the anti-clericalism espoused by the republican radicals, who won the election of 1876 and embarked on a resolute programme of de-Catholicising national institutions and the power of Catholics within the state structures. Read writes that 'Catholics from families who had traditionally served in the French administration were now debarred. The higher strata of the old bourgeoisie were excluded from power in this generation, as far as it was Catholic or royalist, and on the whole it was both. The gap they left was filled with Protestants, and to a lesser degree by Jews.'[31]

'L'affaire' resounded round the world: within France, it touched on every nerve of political and social life, setting Catholic against Protestant against Jew, class against class, in a state where defeat by Germany and suppression of the Paris commune's revolt against the new national government, which had signed the armistice with Germany in February 1871, had left little space for more than formal reconciliation. Dreyfus, whose Jewishness made him a prime suspect when leakages of vital information to the military attaché in the German embassy were discovered, was rapidly tried, found guilty and sentenced to life imprisonment in the most degrading circumstances on a former leper colony named Devil's Island, one of the Salvation Islands group off the French colony of Guiana, which was used as a gulag. Popular hostility was evident and large; his family and friends and a few others convinced of or suspecting his innocence were regarded as traitors. Only when a new chief of the Deuxième Bureau's Statistical Section, Colonel Georges Picquart, took over in 1895 was there an officer conscientious enough to question and then to dismiss the flimsy evidence which had convicted Dreyfus.

The long route to release and a (limited) rehabilitation continued to divide and shock many in the country – especially the revelations that the highest officers in the army had refused to believe plain new evidence, or had been party to fabrications of the old. Dreyfus emerged, at least to liberal opinion, as an enlightenment and secular hero, not just in France but more widely. The affair itself showed divisions within the military, between it and the government, between liberals and the left who belatedly took Dreyfus's side; and conservatives who continued to regard him as in some way guilty. Of the several individuals who led the campaign against his imprisonment, the one best remembered is Emile Zola, France's most popular novelist of the time, whose impassioned article 'J'accuse'[32] was published in 1899 in a newspaper founded only in 1897, by George Clemenceau – the journalist who later became, twice (1906–9, 1917–20), Prime Minister of France. Among the targets were two of the many papers which printed lies about Dreyfus – *L'Eclair* and *L'Echo de Paris* – both of which were willing collaborators in 'an abominable campaign' run by the war department to 'mislead (public) opinion and cover up their own faults.'[33] In his naming of the guilty men at the top of the army and politics, Zola courted danger and was tried for criminal libel later the same year, and convicted – escaping from France to the UK to avoid jail, returning the following year to accept a pardon, for which he had to admit guilt. He was later completely vindicated. Both for its urgent spelling out of the truth and for the courage of the writer, it has remained a prime example of journalism engaged for justice.

With this massive political, religious and emotional freight, the divisions of the Dreyfus Affair come right up to recent times. In 1985, President Francois Mitterrand proposed to have a statue of Dreyfus erected in the Ecole Militaire – an offer refused, on the grounds that 'it was perceived as a reminder of division and humiliation'.[34] Only in 1995 did the French Army make an official declaration of the officer's innocence, through the Director of its Historical Section. The fact that the nascent intelligence service was deeply involved – first in faking forgeries which sealed Dreyfus's fate, then in an attempt by Picquart to set the record straight which was sabotaged by his colleagues and stamped on by the hierarchy – left a deep unease.

Philippe Hayez, a security scholar, previously a deputy director of the Direction Général de la Sécurité Extérieure (DGSE, the External Intelligence Agency), writes (with Jean-Claude Cousseran) that

> Admiral Pierre Lacoste, the DGSE's director general from 1982–85 (together with foreign experts) were supporting the thesis of a 'French disease' in intelligence. In their view, the French 'Intelligence culture' had been suffering, since the affaire Dreyfus, from a paradoxical history of politicisation and distance between the political authorities and the services. Intelligence policy was obviously too sensitive to be accounted for and managed as a public policy, and thus better left untouched.[35]

Where the 'Anglo-Saxons' see in the genesis of their secret services square-jawed patriots and doughty and decent men and women opposed to tyranny everywhere, the French see a much more complex picture, retrospectively shameful and presently politically manipulated.

Nigel Inkster, a former high official in MI6, now a senior analyst at the International Institute of Strategic Studies, says that 'the reason that the British are by and large supportive of the secret services is that they have no experience of being repressed or treated badly by them. You cannot say the same about the Germans, for obvious reasons: and in France, the shadow of Dreyfus is a long one – and there is really little effective oversight even now, while the press has been very complaisant' (see Conclusion). Inkster concedes that the services are now in better shape and that the press is more inquiring.

The US historian of the French Secret Services, Douglas Porch, writes that

> the Dreyfus affair had revealed an emerging character, one might even say a 'culture', of French intelligence which would become increasingly defined in the 20th century ... [it] would be poor civil – intelligence relations. Of what use was intelligence ... in the hands of men whose preconceptions or prejudices predisposed them to distort, ignore or misuse information?[36]

This distrust is not unique: indeed, it is common, if usually in milder forms than occurred in France. The US administration of George W. Bush, especially the Vice President Dick Cheney, believed the CIA to be insufficiently engaged in finding evidence of weapons of mass destruction in Saddam Hussein's Iraq, and created a parallel service more amenable to the belief. Harold Wilson, UK Labour Prime Minister in the 1960s and 1970s, believed that MI5 officers were plotting against him – a suspicion which had some foundation, though the more lurid charges were dismissed by the historian of secret services Christopher Andrew. However, Andrew's *Defence of the Realm* (2009) says that he was alone among post-war prime ministers to have had a file kept on him, by a service concerned that his pre-office contacts with East European officials in pursuit of business interests cast suspicion on him.

In France, however, both the distrust and the politicisation of the services have been a more constant element in the relationship. Eric Denécé, head of the Centre for Intelligence Research, writes (with Gerald Arboit) that 'since the Dreyfus affair, our intelligence services have been the victims of distrust from politicians' and claims that 'the common characteristic of the heads of the intelligence services and of the security of France from the time of their nomination is to be incompetent in concrete issues but to be obedient to the orders of the executive power'.[37]

The defeat and subsequent occupation in 1940 splintered the French political class among the collaborationist Vichy government, the Gaullist Free French in exile and the Communist-dominated resistance in the later years of the war. These marked the post-war efforts to build security services with pervasive feuds and (often well-founded) suspicions of Communist leaking to the Soviet Union, especially when the Party had ministers in the government and members high in the civil and military service in the years immediately after the war.

Thus while the Anglo-Saxon agencies could bask in their part in winning World War II – an effort heroic in many theatres, though at first fairly chaotic, especially on the inexperienced US side – the French agencies were caught in a series of political cul-de-sacs. The French Communist Party, which had played the leading role in resistance to the Nazi occupation once the Wehrmacht had invaded the Soviet Union in June 1941, achieved a vote in the first post-war general election of over 28 per cent. The result ensured its participation in the post-war coalition governments – until it was expelled in 1947, as anxieties mounted on the Party's loyalty and as the US insisted on its expulsion as a condition for the receipt of Marshall Aid. The Party retained up to 30 per cent of the popular vote, and mobilised much of the industrial working class – whose militancy it was its main concern to increase after expulsion from government, and with the encouragement of Moscow.

The French secret services, drawn in large numbers from the espionage network created by Charles de Gaulle while in wartime exile in London, was strongly anti-communist and regarded as the enemy within by Party members. The contrast with the UK's much more moderate left was stark: there, the post-war Labour government quickly dropped its suspicions of the secret services, especially through the agency of Ernest Bevin, post-war Foreign Secretary. Douglas Dodds-Parker, a former member of the wartime secret services, recalled that, through MI6, Bevin had 'become aware for the first time of what the USSR were doing to undermine and destroy, if possible, freedom in the still-free world … from [the SIS] he learned the full facts of the activities of the USSR in fomenting subversion, sabotage and strikes'.[38]

The withdrawing tide from imperial possession gave a louder roar in France than in Britain, both the withdrawal from Vietnam and Algeria. The intelligence services were caught up in allegations of brutal torture, especially in Algeria – where its officers ended up on both sides of the murderous argument between the 'pied noirs', or white settlers in Algeria. From 1 November 1954, when plastic explosives in Algiers and other Algerian cities announced the start of the Algerian insurrection (to the shock of Francois Mitterrand, then Interior Minister in Prime Minister Guy Mollet's socialist government, who blamed the secret services for giving him no warning), to the concession of independence in 1962, the French secret services were deeply involved in the Algerian war.

Together with the army, they used the most brutal methods, imported from the defeat in Vietnam, against the indigenous population. The cell structure adopted by the Algerian Front de Libération Nationale made gathering intelligence difficult and the resort to torture and indiscriminate murder of groups of Algerians in reprisal for FLN assassinations, though the methods did provide some information, still ensured much more hatred.

Douglas Porch writes that

> much intelligence activity actually served to weaken France's argument – directed particularly at allies and the United Nations – that she was dealing with a civil war, an internal French matter of no concern to the outside world. This was no mere diplomatic subterfuge. It was an ethnocentric vision which shaped and guided French policy and one to which the French intelligence community subscribed wholeheartedly.[39]

The services did little better on the French mainland: according to Alastair Horne, the internal security service, then called the Direction de la Surveillance du Territoire (DST), showed 'extraordinary incompetence' in allowing a network of funding, hiding terrorists and transporting French deserters out of Algeria, run by a Marxist professor, Jeb Jenson, to exist for three years.[40]

Both the military and the secret services were at least sceptical about and often directly hostile to the governments of the Fourth Republic, as short-lived prime ministers succeeded each other after a few months throughout the 1950s. De Gaulle, assuming the presidency in 1959, was left with intelligence services divided within themselves, and hostile to a government which could not trust them. Horne writes that the bitterness of the struggle, and the influx of millions of Algerians fleeing the Algerian civil war in the 1990s, had left unresolved enmities – as between the Algerian 'harkis', those loyal to France in the 1950s, whose families came to France on liberation, and the newcomers – 'in lieu of the decisive post colonial divorce that was envisaged in 1962, a messy relationship continues, with each country deeply and unpredictably involved in each others' histories. All of this is grist to the mill of Al Qaeda – and Le Pen'.[41]

As we will see in Chapter 5, the French news media have become much more alert to issues of human rights, accountability and corruption than was the case in the 1950s and 1960s – when the strong political divisions among the papers, and the state control of much of broadcasting, worked against long-form and neutral investigation – a form of journalism then thought to be, and still in some quarters considered, an American style. The more enquiring approach has been encouraged in the 2010s by Wikileaks disclosures, and most of all by the revelations of Edward Snowden's leaked NSA documents – which included the fact that the personal phone of President François Hollande had been bugged by the CIA.

* * *

US reporting during World War II was, like the British but with a greater propensity to reveal, relatively accurate within limits. Defeats were reported as defeats, and eye-witness accounts of war horrors were, in most cases, published. Unlike the British, the American system of censorship was voluntary: though in neither case were the activities of the intelligence services – MI6 and the SOE in the UK, and in the US, the new Office of Strategic Services (OSS), similar to the SOE – given any more than brief or accidental mention. President Roosevelt, citing a 1938 law, issued an executive order in May 1940 (before the US joined the war) which imposed presidential control over the classification of press communications: he was determined, however, to avoid the severe espionage laws exercised by President Wilson in World War I, and set two criteria only: that the stories must be accurate and must not aid the enemy.

The media relations programme was headed by Byron Price, the executive news editor of Associated Press: he determined that censorship should be voluntary, and issued a code, revised throughout the war. Robert Hanyok, a historian working for the NSA, writes that

> Price put the onus for censorship directly on the journalists. His methods were to nudge and talk them into compliance under his motto: 'Least said, soonest mended.' The civilian censors had no authority to excise material prior to publication or punish violators, although they could publish the names of those who stepped over the bounds ... this kept the Censorship Office out of numerous controversies. A case in point was the famous episode in which Gen. George Patton slapped a soldier suffering from battle fatigue. Newsmen filed requests to print the story; Gen. Dwight Eisenhower, the Supreme Allied Commander, gave his approval.[42]

As a generalisation, US reporting was more demotic than the British, reflecting both the culture of the journalists and that of the US military.

The major reservation was that the US military was segregated: black officers and soldiers did not relax, eat or bunk with their white comrades, though they did fight with them. In June 1944, a black NCO, Corporal Rupert Trimmingham, wrote a letter to *Yank*, the army's weekly, which described how, when travelling with others in his unit through a town in Louisiana, they saw German POWs being fed, under guard, in a restaurant, which they were barred from entering. He continued:

> Here is the question each Negro soldier is asking. What is the Negro soldier fighting for? On whose team are we playing? ... Are [the German POWs] not sworn enemies of our country? Are they not taught to hate and destroy all Democratic governments? Are we not American soldiers, sworn to fight and die if need be for this country? Then why are they treated better than we are? Why does the government allow such things to go on? Some of the boys are saying you will not print this letter. I'm saying that you will.[43]

US journalists reported on the military colour bar and much else which would have been uncomfortable to many of their readers. The hero among them was Ernie Pyle, a reporter for the Scripps Howard newspaper chain, who covered the war in Europe, then transferred to the Pacific war where, with the war nearly over, he was killed in a roadside ambush. His Pulitzer Prize-winning journalism, factual, vividly descriptive and empathetic, became a model for later reporters. In a preface to a collection of pieces by reporters on the war, Stephen Ambrose compares the literary style of Ernest Hemingway's war reporting with Pyle's direct style:

> [Hemingway's] dispatches to Colliers were about what he saw and did. 'Never can I describe to you the emotions I felt', he opened his August 1944 from liberated Paris, before going on to three columns about how he felt ... everybody already knew that Hemingway was brave, foolish and sentimental. What they wanted to know was what the GIs were doing. That was what Pyle wrote about, as did the majority of his fellow reporters.[44]

The direct, factually-based reportage became the approved default style of US journalism. While the war raged, the Hutchins Commission, formed on the suggestion of and funded by Henry Luce, the publisher of the mass circulation *Time* and *Life* magazines, began deliberating the place and responsibilities of the press in a democracy, reporting in 1947.[45] The Commission, nearly all scholars with no journalists or women among them, proposed a 'social responsibility' model (this at a time when the press was under criticism for monopolistic practices and commercial bias) – under which the press first recognised that it had large power over the population's minds, and should use that power responsibly. In a crucial passage, the Commission wrote that

> With the means of self-destruction that are now at their disposal, men must live, if they are to live at all, by self-restraint, moderation, and mutual understanding. They get their picture of one another through the press. The press can be inflammatory, sensational, and irresponsible. If it is, it and its freedom will go down in the universal catastrophe. On the other hand, the press can do its duty by the new world that is struggling to be born. It can help create a world community by giving men everywhere knowledge of the world and of one another, by promoting comprehension and appreciation of the goals of a free society that shall embrace all men.[46]

The recommendations of the Commission, coming as they did soon after a hugely destructive war and the explosion of two nuclear bombs in Japan, were influential with the generation of journalists who had fought in or reported on the war. Some of these – Pyle, Hemingway, Martha Gelhorn and the broadcasters Edward Murrow and William Shirer – had become famous through it and role models after it.

The central duty – as laid out by the Hutchins Commission – was to give 'a truthful, comprehensive and intelligent account of the day's events in a context which gives them meaning'.[47] The scholars who made up the committee put as the prime requirement

> that the media should be accurate. They should not lie. Here the first link in the chain of responsibility is the reporter at the source of the news. He must be careful and competent. He must estimate correctly which sources are most authoritative. He must prefer firsthand observation to hearsay. He must know what questions to ask, what things to observe, and which items to report. His employer has the duty of training him to do his work as it ought to be done.[48]

Post-war journalism, in the large city papers (frequently family-owned) and the newspaper chains, as well on the rapidly growing national broadcasters (especially CBS), took on board the ethical journalistic principles laid down by Hutchins: these were complemented by an increasing sense of journalism's power to ferret out information, resting on the protection of the Constitution's First Amendment – that 'Congress shall make no law respecting an establishment of religion, or prohibiting the free exercise thereof; or abridging the freedom of speech, or of the press; or the right of the people peaceably to assemble, and to petition the government for a redress of grievances.'[49] The avowed aim became to describe the politics, society, growth, economic structure and foreign policies of America – a large and exciting task. It was one in which the new generation of journalists – inspired by the social and ethical dimension of their trade and less under the thumb of powerful and ruthless mass-circulation press owners than their colleagues in the UK, or in the US in the nineteenth- and early twentieth-century high watermark of power of the press proprietors – could insist on standards of accuracy, fullness and balance in a way in which the British raucous, often abusive, tabloids bought by the majority did not.

The Americans also had a model similar to the latter: the 'muckrakers', the group of highly talented and motivated reporters such as Lincoln Steffens, Ida Tarbell and Ray Stannard Baker, who worked for *McClure's Weekly* at the beginning of the twentieth century. They saw their task – encouraged and feted by the then president, Theodore Roosevelt – to expose the underbelly of US society and economy, acting as a kind of journalistic research bureau for a reformist administration. The power of the press thus relied only partly on circulation and giving the people what they wanted: it also contained an overtly responsible stance, giving the people what the journalists believed they needed. This approach was aided by the fact that the newspapers were city-based, needing to appeal to a community with diverse views rather than concentrating on one slice of a large national pie.

The adoption of high journalistic standards coupled with the strong growth of profitability in media corporations dictated a proprietorial and editorial agreement on the need for freedom from any kind of state control, and a determination to publish at all costs, even if the material published was inconvenient to the powers that be. Investigative reporting was enshrined as the apex of the profession, ritually awarded the highest honours. It is an attitude which has been emulated elsewhere, and which is now, in the twenty-first century, seen as the highest form of journalism. This meant that, much earlier than in other journalistic cultures and even now more comprehensively and deeply, American journalists tried to get to grips with the 'secret state' – in the belief that nothing should in principle be kept from the people, especially when undertaken by their elected representatives.

An example illuminates the principle.[50] In 1961 in the early months of the John F. Kennedy presidency, a 'top secret' invasion of Cuba was planned, where the one-party rule of Fidel Castro was seen by US intelligence as leaning heavily towards the Soviet Union. The previous administration of Dwight Eisenhower had agreed with the CIA that the agency should organise an invasion force composed of anti-Castro Cuban exiles, with their mission to overthrow his government. Some 1,400 paramilitaries were trained in Mexico and then moved to Guatemala prior to an invasion which went ahead, after raids by USAF bombers on Cuban airfields, on 16 April. The project, initially successful, failed; the Castro-led counter-attack stopped the invasion in its tracks, took much of the force captive and paraded them in public.

The US press naturally covered the humiliating end to the invasion in detail: but, the intention to invade was reported even before it happened. These articles were not officially suppressed. But nor were they simply allowed to be published without interventions at the highest level aimed at stopping, or diluting, their publication, many of which were successful.

The first tip which dropped the issue into the news arena came from an academic, Ronald Hilton, director of Stanford University's Institute of Hispanic American and Luso-Brazilian Studies, who in November 1960 wrote in his *Hispanic American Report* newsletter that the Guatemalan base in which the invasion was being prepared was 'common knowledge' in the country. Carey McWilliams, the editor of *The Nation* weekly was told of the report by a Stanford colleague of Hilton's, the Marxist economist Paul Baran: McWilliams wrote an editorial – it appeared on 19 November 1960 – on the issue, sending out the proofs before publication to over 70 news organisations so that it might be more widely publicised. McWilliams made it clear in the editorial that he had 'no first-hand knowledge of the facts' – but added that 'if the reports as heard by Dr Hilton are true, then public pressure should be brought to bear upon the Administration to abandon this dangerous and hare-brained project'.[51]

After initial scepticism, newspapers began to research the facts behind *The Nation* editorial: some stories appeared which, tentatively, confirmed the original tip, especially in the Latin American press and in the *Miami Herald*, whose city contained the majority of the Cuban exiles.

President John Kennedy, and the CIA director Allen Dulles, were disturbed by the reports, and managed to persuade some papers and magazines to stop running them. The authors of the account of the coverage of the invasion in the *Columbia University Forum* write that

> Mr [Arthur] Schlesinger [a close Kennedy aide and a historian of the administration] reports in his 'A Thousand Days' that in March 1961 the New Republic *set aside a detailed expose of invasion preparations in Miami at the request of the White House. Of the magazine's acceptance that the piece be dropped, Mr Schlesinger comments that it was 'a patriotic act that left me feeling a bit uncomfortable'.*[52]

The Associated Press (AP), the national wire service which all news outlets took, did not deploy any of its hundreds of reporters on the story – because it, too, was asked not to, and agreed. The managing editor of AP, Alan J. Gould, reflected on the occasion obliquely in his retirement address, saying that 'I think the people in Government should have learned a lesson for all time on the handling of the Cuban affair. Occasionally we have withheld stories for a time in the national interest. When the President of the United States calls you in and says this is a matter of vital security, you accept the injunction.'[53]

The *New York Times* was slow to follow up on the story, either because its editors did not wholly believe it or because they did but thought it should not be published. It did, however, put some of the facts of preparation into print before the invasion. The paper's Latin American correspondent, Tad Szulc, had referred to the story in January 1961 – as did the *Los Angeles Times*, but with little detail. At Easter, visiting friends in Miami, Szulc picked up rumours that some of the invading force had been trained in that city and gathered enough of the facts to write a story on 7 April headlined 'Anti-Castro Units Trained to Fight at Florida Bases'.[54] The story had revealed that the project was under the aegis of the CIA and that the probable date for it was 18 April – but both of these details were cut out by the editor, Turner Cartledge – reportedly in deference to a call from Kennedy, a decision which caused a furious row around the news desk.

In a meeting with news executives after the Bay of Pigs fiasco, Kennedy scolded the *Times* for publishing the stories it did: when told that these had appeared in other papers before the *Times'* stories, Kennedy replied 'It was not news until it appeared in the *Times*'.[55] A year later, Kennedy reversed his view, telling the publisher, Orvil Dryfoos, that he wished the *Times* had published much more, to save him and the US from the catastrophic invasion. In May, a month after the invasion, the *Times* editorialised:

> the Cuban tragedy has raised a domestic question that is likely to come up again and again until it is solved. The cause may be something that is happening in Laos (or Vietnam?), in Central Africa or in Latin America, but the question remains the same: is a democratic government in an open society such as ours ever justified in deceiving its own people? A democracy – our democracy – cannot be lied to ... The basic principle involved is that of confidence.[56]

The 'domestic question' has not been solved: the leaks of the first two decades of the 2000s have made the question – 'is a democratic government in an open society ... ever justified in deceiving its own people?' – much more acute. In fact, American and other news media in democratic states did suppress much material during, and bearing on, the Cold War, and after.

* * *

From the early 1950s to the late 1980s, security services East and West were configured for and absorbed in the Cold War, in which they were the most active state players. Once the suspicious West had been convinced it was over, and both the turn to democracy by, and the ruinous state of, Russia had lulled them into believing that the state was no longer a threat, the intelligence services everywhere suffered from the cuts which the peace dividend brought. They feared that they would be seen by their political masters, and by the public, as unfit for any further purpose.

> A huge intelligence gathering machine had been built – men clamped with headphones in the far-flung corners of the planet, satellites scouring from space, dishes on earth picking up signals – all to try to provide a few precious moments of warning. 'We lived on their networks', was how one former British analyst described the way in which the US and the UK enmeshed themselves inside Soviet communications. But with the end of the Cold War, this vast bureaucracy seemed redundant.[57]

The decade of the 1990s was a perilous one for the agencies; their budgets were cut by up to one-third, and the Russian and other linguists pensioned off. They were saved from redundancy by the salience of another zone of danger – proving to be, over the next decades, one much more unstable than that of the Cold War. As the end of the Cold War had not yet been officially stamped, in August 1990, Iraq invaded the neighbouring and tiny state of Kuwait – an attack for which GCHQ, with a small team in Kuwait, was able to give advance warning. Though the Iraqis were routed by a largely American force later that year, the Middle East and North Africa from then on grew steadily into the major preoccupation of Western intelligence. The next year, a vicious civil war broke out in Algeria as the regime fought to prevent the jihadist Islamic Salvation Front from enjoying the fruits of an election which it had won. In the same year the break-up of Yugoslavia sparked off wars on several fronts, into which the West – with reluctance – was finally dragged. These were hot, not cold, wars, and at that point did not seem to have, for the West, the existential stakes of the nuclear standoff. But they underscored the need for continuing flows of intelligence.

The Cold War was a single focus: the post-Cold War threats included continuing attention to terrorism, such as the IRA; an increased interest in organised crime, itself growing; and North African terrorism, especially in France. At the same time, scholars recognised that the weapons and technologies developed in the late twentieth century were two-edged – both protective and a threat. The former journalist and academic Peter Hennessy quotes several authorities in this context,[58] who saw that, as Sir Michael Howard put it, the triumph of liberal capitalism was 'regarded with smouldering resentment' in areas of social upheaval caused by the collapse of the bipolar world, a resentment which would 'find expression not in traditional inter-state conflict but in horrific acts of terrorism directed against the most secure and prosperous regions of the developed world';[59] while the Czech-born philosopher and anthropologist Ernest Gellner, deeply knowledgeable about the societies of both Eastern Europe and the Middle East, wrote that millennial terrorist groups would strive for ever more destructive weapons, and use them against the Western targets and that 'the present [i.e. early 1990s] increase in international terrorism offers a small but frightening foretaste, as yet on a moderate scale, of such a situation'.[60] The legal scholar and former US presidential aide Philip Bobbitt used his book *Terror and Consent* (Allen Lane, 2008) to make a sustained argument that WMD will become increasingly easily available, and that both these weapons and communications technologies used by secret services are also mastered and used by terrorist networks, to be turned against the democratic states which are the main object of their attacks.

The agencies, which had been able to assume substantial agreement on their mission and expense when deployed against an obvious enemy like the Soviet bloc, now had to pay more attention to securing public support, and thus reached out more to the news media in the hope of impressing them with the enduring need for their existence. It was in the 1990s that the British and the French services, traditionally limiting their contacts to a handful of trusted media, began to enlarge the tent containing those granted some insight into their work – naturally, that which underscored their efficiency and indispensability.

2

Losing and Finding the Plot

We have to ask the question of the media – how hard do you want my job to be?

(John McLaughlin, former deputy
and acting director, CIA, in interview)

Dan Rather was an eminent news presenter on US television, on CBS, where his career spanned 44 years, 24 of which, from 1981 to 2005, as the main news host and producer, a longer span than any other of his trade. He had never become the avuncular figure, nor had the reputation of being 'the most trusted man in America', which his predecessor, Walter Cronkite (main news presenter 1962–81) enjoyed. The time when a news anchor could occupy such a position had gone, no matter who the anchor was. CBS news dipped at times below the ratings of the other two networks news shows, hosted by Peter Jennings (ABC) and Tom Brokaw (NBC) – the latter taking the 'most popular' slot until his retirement in 2004, just before Rather.

The CBS anchor preferred to project a sterner, more sceptical demeanour than Cronkite, emphasising the need for robust inquiry. Soon after his departure from CBS, he told a newspaper reporter before a speech he gave in Seattle in January 2006, that 'In many ways on many days, [reporters] have sort of adopted the attitude of "go along, get along" … What many of us need is a spine transplant. Whether it's City Hall, the State House, or the White House, part of our job is to speak truth to power.'[1]

It was thus a significant matter that, on *Late Night with David Letterman* six days after the attacks on the Twin Towers and the Pentagon, Rather, clearly deeply moved, had said that 'George Bush is the President, he makes the decisions and you know, as just one American, wherever he wants me to line up, just tell me where.' Some years later, in April 2007, Rather appeared on a show on the PBS network, hosted by the presenter Bill Moyers (who had worked with Rather in the early 1980s, as a media commentator on CBS news): the show was called *Buying the War*, and had a strongly critical slant. Moyers asked Rather about his statement on the Letterman show: Rather said – 'I didn't mean it in a journalistic sense. I know it may have come across that way. I meant it in a sense as an individual citizen. Mr President, if you need me, if you need me to go to hell and back for my country, I will do it.'

It was, of course, a time of high anger and emotion. On NBC, Brokaw had exclaimed, early in his commentary on the unfolding events, that 'This is war. This is a declaration and an execution of an attack on the United States' – a comment anticipating something of the line taken quickly by President Bush, when he declared 'war on terror'. ABC's Peter Jennings, appeared to be close to tears once, when he said that his children had called, were safe but shocked – and advised others to talk to their children because of the shock many of them would also feel. He was, however, later praised for remaining relatively unemotional and professional throughout a 17-hour presenting stint.

But the PBS show was years later and Moyers was hunting. He came back at Rather, 'What I was wrestling with that night listening to you is: once we let our emotions out as journalists on the air, once we say: "We'll line up with the President" can we ever really say to the country, "The President's out of line".' Rather didn't accept the point. 'No journalist should be a robot', he said, and no American journalist should pretend indifference to the slaughter of 9/11. He continued:

> By the way, Bill, this is not an excuse. I don't think there is any excuse for, you know, my performance and the performance of the press in general in the roll up to the war. There were exceptions. There were some people who, I think, did a better job than others. But overall and in the main, there's no question that we didn't do a good job.[2]

In thus spreading the criticism beyond his Letterman outburst, Rather put his 'performance' on a par with the majority of other US journalists between 11 September 2001 and the invasion of Iraq in March 2003. It was a period when Walter Isaacson (then chairman and CEO of CNN) said on the Moyers show, 'there was a patriotic fervour and the administration used it so that if you challenged anything you were made to feel that there was something wrong with that … and there was even almost a patriotism police which, you know, they'd be up there on the internet sort of picking anything a Christiane Amanpour or somebody else would say as if it were disloyal'. Isaacson said that 'there was no direct pressure from advertisers' but that 'big people in corporations were calling up and saying, "you're being anti-American here"'.

Both Rather's and Isaacson's comments speak to what is still the weightiest debate in US media circles today. That is, that journalists, after 9/11, either because of their own feelings or because of pressure from editors and owners, did not do their jobs, which Rather defined (the phrase is a well-used one) as 'speak(ing) truth to power.' Instead, they reflected back to power what power wished to hear – because power had just said it. Rather's revised view on pre-Iraq war journalism has become the dominant one, helped by an apology by the *New York Times* in May 2004 for what it characterised as careless and too-credulous pre-war reporting.

The importance of the view that this was a fundamental error by the *Times* was underscored by its leading economic commentator, Paul Krugman, when he returned to the subject more than a decade later in a column of May 2015. This was prompted by President Bush's brother, Jeb, then a candidate for the Republican presidential nomination, who said 'mistakes' had been made. Krugman argued that this was – inverting the saying attributed to the French eighteenth-/nineteenth-century diplomat Talleyrand – 'worse than a mistake, a crime', because it was

> a war the White House wanted, and all of the supposed mistakes that, as Jeb puts it, 'were made' by someone unnamed actually flowed from this underlying desire. Did the intelligence agencies wrongly conclude that Iraq had chemical weapons and a nuclear program? That's because they were under intense pressure to justify the war. Did prewar assessments vastly understate the difficulty and cost of occupation? That's because the war party didn't want to hear anything that might raise doubts about the rush to invade. Indeed, the Army's chief of staff was effectively fired for questioning claims that the occupation phase would be cheap and easy.[3]

(A CNN Fact Check later said that the claim that General Shinseki was 'effectively fired' – made at the time by the Democratic Senator John Kerry, later Secretary of State – was inaccurate, since the General retired having served his full four-year term as Chief of Staff and the Defense Secretary, Donald Rumsfeld, had decided a year earlier on his replacement at the end of the term.[4])

The story of US journalism's relationship with the intelligence services and the state over the past decade and a half has been one conditioned, as never before in the post-war period, by a discussion within and around this theme. It is clear that, especially on TV, in the many talk shows and in the commentaries and interviews, patriotic themes were stressed and the drive towards war – in both Afghanistan, where the main al Qaeda bases and training camps were, and in Iraq, where the most assiduous promoter of terrorism and producer of aggression in the Middle East, Saddam Hussein, was president – was explicitly or implicitly endorsed. But US journalism as a whole never became propaganda, or anything near it: like Rather, the news trade was shocked by 9/11 and experienced a surge of patriotic anger which diluted their professional scepticism for a short time. But columnists continued to analyse and investigative reporters to investigate, and both to find large faults with the administration's rationale for, and intelligence about, the preparations for war and the course of the war once the US, British and other forces were in place – including in the *New York Times*.

Still, the story of the past decade in the US news media has been one of many journalists seeking out the dark sides of the US war, with a fervour and even a not-quite-suppressed anger deeper and broader than that mobilised during the Vietnam war. In one of the most commended books about that war, *The Best and Brightest* (1972), David Halberstam refers to his 'depression' that the administration did not see what he had seen in years of reporting from Vietnam for the *New York Times* and then for *Harper's Magazine* – that the war was a stalemate, unwinnable by the US: that feeling was the motive force, he said, behind his writing it. Whether or not Halberstam's descendants were depressed, the most prominent among them are also moved by a powerful force – to illuminate the nature and the consequences of the continuing 'war on terror' – waged, if not any longer under that rubric, by both Presidents George W. Bush and Barack Obama. They are especially concerned with the effects on American civil liberties and the human rights of those on whom it wages the war.

The US news media are energised by a view, more strongly held than in other democratic countries, that they are an essential check on power, a view increased by the failure of the Vietnam War and the shiftiness of successive administrations about its conduct; the willingness of the leadership to intervene in foreign conflicts and the frequent failure of these interventions; the penchant for covert actions, often only uncovered by investigations by journalists, and the huge and growing size of the security (as well as the military) state all mean that there is a wide base, across the political spectrum, for proactive and full reporting.

* * *

An extended critique of the coverage of the preparations for the Iraq war came from the journalist Michael Massing, a former editor of the *Columbia Journalism Review*, a writer whose subjects have often been American journalism. In a piece in the *New York Review of Books* in March 2004,[5] for which he won the Mongerson Prize in 2005 (the prize given by the Medill School of Journalism at Northwestern University for pieces which correct inaccurate journalism), Massing concentrated on the *New York Times*, and especially on the work of Judy Miller and Michael Gordon. Miller was a Pulitzer Prize-winning specialist on the Middle East and an investigative reporter; in 1989, Gordon (with his colleague Stephen Engelberg) was a Polk Award winner, and was the paper's most experienced expert on the military – who had written many of the pre-war stories. Both had long experience on the paper, widely seen (though not on the right), as the country's most authoritative. Miller had been hired (as a 'token woman', she wrote later[6]), in 1977, and by the time of 9/11 had written several well-regarded books on the Middle East, on the Holocaust and on germ warfare. Gordon, who joined the paper in 1985, would write with General Bernard Trainor several books on the US and Iraq, including, *The Generals' War* (1995)[7] and *Cobra II* (2007) – the latter was seen by many of its reviewers as both 'a benchmark' for other accounts, and strongly critical[8] of the Bush administration's handling of the war and its aftermath.

Massing's main point was that most journalists were 'far too reliant on sources sympathetic to the administration' and that 'those with dissenting views – and there were more than a few – were shut out. Reflecting this, the coverage was highly deferential to the White House. This was especially apparent on the issue of Iraq's weapons of mass destruction – the heart of the President's case for war.'[9]

He instances stories – such as Saddam's search for material with which to develop nuclear weaponry, like aluminium tubes and the yellowcake needed for uranium enrichment, both of which were covered by Miller and Gordon, together or separately – which turned out to be at least partly false, or exaggerated (doubt still surrounds whether or not Iraqi agents were trying to buy yellowcake from the main producer, in the African state of Niger).

He laid strong stress on the reporters who dissented from the general line that Saddam had large stocks of weapons of mass destruction (WMD). Chief among these were three journalists then working for the Washington bureau Knight Ridder, now merged with McClatchy Newspapers – both being companies with strings of city and local papers throughout the US. These were the reporters Jonathan Landay and Warren Strobel, and the editor John Walcott, who early on concentrated on the divisions which had arisen between the administration and the CIA on the existence, or lack of it, of WMD. Massing wrote that

> on October 8, 2002, Landay and Strobel, joined by bureau chief Walcott, filed a sharp account of the rising discontent among national security officers. The article began: 'While President Bush marshals congressional and international support for invading Iraq, a growing number of military officers, intelligence professionals and diplomats in his own government privately have deep misgivings about the administration's double-time march toward war. These officials charge that administration hawks have exaggerated evidence of the threat that Iraqi leader Saddam Hussein poses – including distorting his links to the al-Qaida terrorist network. ... They charge that the administration squelches dissenting views and that intelligence analysts are under intense pressure to produce reports supporting the White House's argument that Saddam poses such an immediate threat to the United States that pre-emptive military action is necessary.'

Massing commented that 'As these reports show, there were many sources available to journalists interested in scrutinising the administration's statements about Iraq. Unfortunately, however, Knight Ridder has no newspaper in Washington, D.C., or New York, and its stories did not get the national attention they deserved.'[10]

Massing also singled out Barton Gellman, an investigative reporter on the *Washington Post* – ironically, the reporter later identified by Edward Snowden in 2013 as the only mainstream reporter he could trust with his NSA material. Massing wrote that

> on December 12 ... the Washington Post *ran a front-page story by Barton Gellman contending that al-Qaeda had obtained a nerve agent from Iraq. Most of the evidence came from administration officials, and it was so shaky as to draw the attention of Michael Getler, the paper's ombudsman.*

In his weekly column, Getler wrote that the article had so many qualifiers and caveats that 'the effect on the complaining readers, and on me, is to ask what, after all, is the use of this story that practically begs you not to put much credence in it? Why was it so prominently displayed, and why not wait until there was more certainty about the intelligence?'[11]

However, the *Post*'s honour was saved, Massing believed, by its reporter Walter Pincus, who – contrary to most of the press pack – developed 'strong reservations' about the speech Secretary of State Colin Powell made at the UN on 5 February 2003, in which he marshalled a series of apparently decisive proofs of Iraqi WMD's continued existence.[12] Massing wrote:

A longtime investigative reporter, Pincus went back and read the UN inspectors' reports of 1998 and 1999, and he was struck to learn from them how much weaponry had been destroyed in Iraq before 1998. He also tracked down General Anthony Zinni, the former head of the US Central Command, who described the hundreds of weapons sites the United States had destroyed in its 1998 bombing. All of this, Pincus recalled, 'made me go back and read Powell's speech closely. And you could see that it was all inferential. If you analyzed all the intercepted conversations he discussed, you could see that they really didn't prove anything.'

By mid-March, Pincus felt he had enough material for an article questioning the administration's claims on Iraq. His editors weren't interested. It was only after the intervention of his colleague Bob Woodward, who was researching a book on the war and who had developed similar doubts, that the editors agreed to run the piece – on page A17. Despite the administration's claims about Iraq's WMD, it began, 'US intelligence agencies have been unable to give Congress or the Pentagon specific information about the amounts of banned weapons or where they are hidden ...' Noting the pressure intelligence analysts were feeling from the White House and Pentagon, Pincus wrote that senior officials, in making the case for war, 'repeatedly have failed to mention the considerable amount of documented weapons destruction that took place in Iraq between 1991 and 1998.'

Two days later, Pincus, together with Dana Milbank, the Post's *White House correspondent, was back with an even more critical story. 'As the Bush administration prepares to attack Iraq this week,' it began, 'it is doing so on the basis of a number of allegations against Iraqi President*

Saddam Hussein that have been challenged – and in some cases disproved – by the United Nations, European governments and even US intelligence reports.' That story appeared on page A13.

The placement of these stories was no accident, Pincus says. 'The front pages of The New York Times, The Washington Post, *and the* Los Angeles Times *are very important in shaping what other people think,' he told me. 'They're like writing a memo to the White House.' But the* Post's *editors, he said, 'went through a whole phase in which they didn't put things on the front page that would make a difference.'*

Massing concludes with a recognition of the press's 'feistiness,' after the war was won by the US-led coalition invasion, but stressed its 'meekness' before the war – a phenomenon which

highlights one of the most entrenched and disturbing features of American journalism: its pack mentality. Editors and reporters don't like to diverge too sharply from what everyone else is writing. When a president is popular and a consensus prevails, journalists shrink from challenging him. Even now, papers like the Times *and the* Post *seem loath to give prominent play to stories that make the administration look too bad.*[13]

This is a heavy charge, against a paper (the *Post*) which had had a large part to play, through tenacious and for some time lonely reporting, in the resignation of a president, and another, the *Times*, which had printed the Pentagon Papers. Both have a bulging record of printing revelations which no other news source had and backing them up.

Massing attracted strong denials in a subsequent issue of the *New York Review* from several journalists. Miller asserted she had been seriously misquoted, but did not elaborate; James Risen, also of the *New York Times*, wrote that he, as well as and around the same time as Pincus, had identified division in administration and intelligence ranks; and most fully, Robert Kaiser, the *Post*'s associate editor, instanced several stories of doubts and reservations, many by the reporter Dana Milbank, which Massing had failed to mention. He put the core of the case made then and since by reporters, and by many others who took a close interest in the war and its coverage – that is,

on the broader question of Iraq's supposed caches of weapons of mass destruction, we know now, or seem to, that the administration's claims were 'almost all wrong,' in David Kay's memorable phrase. But literally no one outside Iraq knew that before the war. Some suspected it, but many others were sure the claims were right – including nearly every senior official of the Clinton administration involved with Iraq. From the perspective of Washington journalists, for whom accuracy and fairness are important, it was possible to report on arguments and questions about the intelligence, but there was no factual basis for reporting that everything the administration was saying was wrong or a deception. Still today, we have no smoking-gun evidence of deliberate deception.[14]

In the following issue, Michael Gordon contributed a longer response, saying that Massing 'commits the very sins for which the critics have taken the Bush administration to task: to bolster his case he has cherry-picked the evidence'. Citing the case of David Albright, a UN weapons inspector, 'on whom Mr. Massing relies for much of his critique', Gordon writes that, though Albright did not believe that the aluminium tubes – a key part of Massing's criticism of Gordon and Miller – would have been suitable for use in developing nuclear weaponry, he nevertheless believed that Saddam might be striving to reassemble a nuclear capability. In tune with Kaiser's earlier response, he continued:

I stand by my assertion to Mr. Massing that the notion that Iraq had some form of WMD was a widely shared assumption inside and outside of the government. I made that comment not to excuse any limitations on the part of the media but to paint the context in which American intelligence was prepared and discussed. Mr. Massing takes that assertion out of context, and he cites Mr. Albright's work to challenge that observation, though his work actually supports it.

He concludes with an admission that

in this instance, key officials appear to have deceived themselves. That poses special challenges for reporters but one which journalists should be prepared to meet. There is a lesson for the media in this episode. It is possible to be too accepting of the paradigm that guides the intelligence community, nongovernmental experts, and policy officials.[15]

Getting the last word in the same exchange, Massing chose not to recognise the content of the admission, saying that 'rather than … ponder what went wrong, Gordon offers excuses and rationalisations'.[16]

Though this debate was conducted in an elite corner of the publishing world – the *Review* claims sales around 135,000 copies worldwide, of which some 80,000 are in the US – it had wide resonance, especially among the 'higher' journalists, most prone to take seriously charges in a liberal journal that they had been insufficiently sceptical about the evidence presented by a right-wing Republican administration.

Bill Keller was executive editor of the *Times* from 2003 to 2011, succeeding to the post after the forced resignation of Howell Raines. As a columnist in the several years before he was appointed, he had supported – with some reluctance – the invasion of Iraq: an 8 February 2003 column, under the headline 'The-I-Can't-Believe-I'm-a-Hawk Club', had him say that he, with other liberal-minded commentators, was 'hard pressed to see an (alternative) to invasion that is not built on wishful thinking.' In a summing up of his Club's mood, he wrote that 'many of these wary warmongers are baby-boom liberals whose aversion to the deployment of American power was formed by Vietnam but who had a kind of epiphany along the way – for most of us, in the vicinity of Bosnia' (where European states stood aside and contemplated the massacres promoted by the Serbian President Slobodan Milosevic, until the intervention of the US).[17]

His relationship with Miller, by most accounts a difficult colleague, was at times supportive, at times abrasive: he had, though less enthusiastically than his predecessor, Raines, praised her work on the Middle East. But as social media became more and more freighted with criticism that her reporting was thinly disguised support of the administration's increasingly desperate search for WMD, he became worried. A blast from the influential media critic at the *Washington Post*, Howard Kurtz, arguing that Miller was ideologically engaged with the administration had appeared in May 2003 (just before Keller became editor); Massing's *New York Review* piece appeared in March 2004 and in May 2004, Miller was summoned to see Keller and Jill Abramson, then managing editor (later executive editor). They told her they would write an editor's note, to be published on a Sunday edition of the *Times* on the front page, detailing 'collective' failings. Miller argued fiercely, and succeeded in taking out mentions of her by name: but a shortened version – 'The Times and Iraq' – was published on 26 May. Though neither Miller nor any other reporter was named, many of her stories were clearly in Keller's mind when he wrote the note, as 'the problematic articles varied in authorship and subject matter, but many shared a common feature. They depended at least in part on information from a circle of Iraqi informants, defectors and exiles bent on "regime change" in Iraq, people whose credibility has come under increasing public debate in recent weeks.'[18]

Miller had been accused of relying heavily on the testimony of Ahmad Chalabi, a wealthy, western-educated Iraqi exile whose organisation, the Iraqi National Congress, brought together men who, like him, were solidly opposed to Saddam's rule. Keller, wrote that

> Some critics of our coverage during that time have focused blame on individual reporters. Our examination, however, indicates that the problem was more complicated. Editors at several levels, who should have been challenging reporters and pressing for more skepticism, were perhaps too intent on rushing scoops into the paper. Accounts of Iraqi defectors were not always weighed against their strong desire to have Saddam Hussein ousted. Articles based on dire claims about Iraq tended to get prominent display, while follow-up articles that called the original ones into question were sometimes buried. In some cases, there was no follow-up at all.[19]

Miller dismisses most of the criticism levelled, directly and indirectly, at her: she relies, in part, on the stance taken by Kaiser at the *Post* and Gordon at her own paper – that a large majority of officials, politicians and intelligence officers believed in the existence of Iraqi WMD. She also drew on earlier, pre-9/11 reporting from the Middle East and elsewhere, which exposed her to the danger from chemical, biological and nuclear weaponry, and the acute fears these possibilities had engendered in leading politicians. She wrote that these fears reached across the political divide into the Democratic Party, and to liberal Democrats, as Al Gore, and Ted Kennedy – the latter of whom did not support the war, but who admitted that 'We have known for many years that Saddam Hussein is seeking and developing weapons of mass destruction.'[20] After 9/11, 'the CIA reported an average of four hundred specific threats a month and tracked more than twenty alleged large-scale plots against American targets' – and she quoted the National Security Council official Michael Anton as saying that 'What haunted the president (Bush) was the prospect of a nuclear 9/11: WMD terrorism.'[21] Miller's defence was not just that there was a majority opinion for the existence of WMD: it was that senior politicians and security officials from most sides of politics had been thoroughly frightened by a fusion of two deadly threats: violent, nihilistic jihadism and biological, chemical and nuclear weapons.

But there were heroes who emerged from the swamp and the favourite ones were the journalists of Knight Ridder/McClatchy, in part because they were 'little guys' in contrast to the mighty engines of the *New York Times*, the *Washington Post* and the TV news networks. The Washington newsroom, though well staffed, did not have the leverage in the administration – any administration – that the mighty engines had (though given the number of titles in the group, the stories probably went to more potential readers).

The reporters in the bureau who got the stories which disagreed with the majority, and which turned out to be right, credit one man above all with the line which the bureau took. That was John Walcott, the Washington bureau chief, who in 2008 was awarded the I. F. Stone medal for 'Journalistic Independence' for his bureau's pre-war coverage. In his acceptance speech on 7 October, Walcott said that the largest reason why his reporting differed from the pack was 'that we sought out the dissidents and we listened to them, instead of serving as stenographers to high-ranking officials and Iraqi exiles … somehow, the idea has taken hold in Washington journalism that the value of a source is directly proportional to his or her rank, when in my experience the relationship is more often inverse.'[22]

Continuing on the 'tortoise wins in the end' theme, and by inference accusing his colleagues on the large papers of pandering to the administration, to advertisers and to PR companies which might in time hire them, Walcott said that

> *Being an outsider, a gadfly, a muckraker, isn't always as much fun as being an insider, a celebrity journalist on TV and the lecture circuit. Worse, in these troubled economic times for the news media, it makes enemies, sometimes powerful ones, and it can offend readers, advertisers – and, as conditions in our business continue to worsen – potential employers in public relations and other industries … very few reporters checked out their stories, and too many just ran with what they were handed. Instead, they handed bullhorns to people who already had megaphones.*[23]

The senior reporter under Walcott was Jonathan Landay, a hard-driving man who remained at McClatchy until 2015, when – as the chain began to downsize in the face of falling newspaper sales – he moved to Thomson Reuters. He told me that

> over three years of reporting on this, we totally debunked the intelligence that was being quoted. The stuff we got was from people inside the intelligence community, we found people in the secret services who were being forced out – like because they spoke Arabic! People were telling us that the policy the administration was pursuing was going to endanger the country.
>
> The stuff about Saddam being in league with al Qaeda [a large theme which the White House ran, and for which the CIA found no proof] was rubbish[24] – how could a secular leader get into bed with Islamic radicals:[25] it made no sense. But the guys at the top – Cheney and Rumsfeld and the people around them – came to the CIA to look over the shoulders of the people doing the intel. We had very senior people talking to us. Their views were not being listened to. The National Intelligence Council [an official body which functions as a think tank for the intelligence community] was charged with surveying the reasons for going to war – said there is no evidence for collaboration between Saddam and al Qaeda.
>
> So Cheney created a parallel network – called the Office for Special Plans – it criticised the CIA for ignoring the evidence it had gathered. It talked with the people who were encouraging the attack – people like [Ahmad] Chalabi [founder and head of the Iraqi National Council] and his defectors. Yet the CIA knew Chalabi. They had created him. But they put a 'burn' notice on him, which said – don't believe him, don't talk to him.

Landay's main colleague in this reporting was Warren Strobel, who had left for Thomson Reuters earlier. He said that Walcott had reminded them that, though they wrote for provincial papers, they were often at least as deeply engaged with the war

> he said: a lot of the papers we write for are in towns next to bases. We should cover this properly.
>
> We made a decision – or John made it for us – that we would do most of our reporting from the military and from the State Department. They were less bought into it than the White House and were more skeptical of the evidence, or the lack of it.

Why did the New York Times *get it wrong? It prides itself on covering the administration better than anyone else – and the people there were giving out the wrong stuff. Yet I wasn't sure: you can't be. I had been on the* Washington Times *(a daily paper of the right) so I got to know the neocons who were in the government. In fact I thought they would find WMD after the war was over.*

We did get, though, a lot of angry emails.

The polemics over the coverage of the pre-war, and of the war and its aftermath, have subsided as other issues take over. But the effect has been large, throughout the US news media. The charges and counter charges since the war, the civil wars into which Iraq sank, the rise of IS, the continued ineffectiveness of government and civil society in Iraq and the consensus that intervention was both disastrous and prompted by false intelligence (whether deliberately falsified or merely a mistake remains hotly contested) have produced, in society, a recoil from the further committing of troops to any Middle Eastern theatre, and has increased scepticism in the reporting of the mainstream press.

Certainly the reporting on the administration – the second presidential term of George W. Bush, and the first and second terms of Barack Obama – has been more aggressive – and more detailed and concerned to uncover the 'dark side', the phrase being the name of a sharply critical and revelatory book in 2008 by the *New Yorker* writer Jane Mayer. Indeed, the output of lengthy articles, series and books, the passing of the subject matter from news coverage into film, TV, and theatre, and the still live bitterness on both sides of the argument testify to the power of the issue. Much of that power derives from coverage which, in the US, was both detailed and closely engaged.

The acquiescence of which the American journalists were accused, and accused themselves, put them on their mettle in the succeeding decade. A liberal Democrat, Barack Obama, took over in the White House from 2008 – in considerable part because he had been in the minority who opposed the war. In a speech the then junior senator from Illinois said that he was no pacifist, opposed to all wars – but that

what I am opposed to is a dumb war. What I am opposed to is a rash war. What I am opposed to is the cynical attempt by Richard Perle [an influential lobbyist for war] and Paul Wolfowitz [Deputy Defense Secretary] and other armchair, weekend warriors in this administration to shove their own ideological agendas down our throats, irrespective of the costs in lives lost and in hardships borne.

What I am opposed to is the attempt by political hacks like Karl Rove [a senior adviser to George W. Bush] to distract us from a rise in the uninsured, a rise in the poverty rate, a drop in the median income – to distract us from corporate scandals and a stock market that has just gone through the worst month since the Great Depression. That's what I'm opposed to. A dumb war. A rash war. A war based not on reason but on passion, not on principle but on politics ... [I know that] Saddam poses no imminent and direct threat to the United States or to his neighbors, that the Iraqi economy is in shambles, that the Iraqi military a fraction of its former strength, and that in concert with the international community he can be contained until, in the way of all petty dictators, he falls away into the dustbin of history.[26]

This was a brave and very much a minority speech to give in October 2002 – and one which looked good in 2008. It seemed to betoken a president in the White House who would be quite different from George W. Bush and his coterie of 'armchair, weekend warriors'. Though when given, it was fairly solidly on the left, its chiming with the mood of a disillusioned electorate seven years on from 9/11 meant that he could trump not just the Vietnam War hero John McCain (no armchair warrior he) but also Senator Hillary Clinton, who had enthusiastically supported the decision to invade, arguing on 10 October 2002, the day before the Senate voted 77–23 in favour of war, that that Saddam, 'left unchecked ... will continue to increase his capacity to wage biological and chemical warfare, and will keep trying to develop nuclear weapons. Should he succeed in that endeavor, he could alter the political and security landscape of the Middle East, which as we know all too well affects American security.'[27]

But the new President, though quite different, turned out to be no pacifist. Like President Bush on acceding to the presidency, Obama promoted a policy of staying at arm's length from involvement in foreign conflicts: since he had no event approaching the importance of the 9/11 attack to force him to change course, he more or less stuck to it. Yet he came to recognise that terrorism in the Middle East and elsewhere does, as Clinton had said, affect American security – and that a US response was necessary. The main weapon in his arsenal was not 'boots on the ground,' but technology in the air: above all, drones which were commanded by centres in the US, and which, when intelligence seemed to warrant it, blew up cars and houses in which terrorists were believed to be – and often were, but sometimes were not. That policy, and much else, was carefully scrutinised by the media, anxious that the inevitable preceding adjective attached to them by the right – the *liberal* media – would not inhibit hard reporting, as patriotism had before.

The mainstream press did not ditch what most of its practitioners regard as the crowning achievement of US journalism, that is, their attempts at neutrality, or objectivity. Though the choice of subject – torture and rendition of suspects, the effect of the drones, the treatment of leakers and of journalists by a less-than-welcoming White House – were usually drawn from a liberal menu, still the reporting of (as apart from the commentary on) each issue did not, as usually in France and often the UK, come accompanied with a polemical colouring which situated the journalist at one or other point of the political spectrum. Strobel, the former McClatchy reporter, said to me that

> there's certainly a strong trait in US journalism of objectivity. I went to the University of Missouri School of Journalism [the school is the oldest department of journalism in the US, founded in 1908 by the self-taught journalist Walter Williams] – you are trained to be very aggressive, to find the facts – but never to take sides. Though that's changing a bit with the internet – see Salon, Slate, the Daily Beast, all these. Even Foreign Policy, now. But the neutral idea – that's pretty deep in most of us.

Journalists also believed of themselves that they had saved the honour of the country at crucial times. The muckrakers at the early part of the twentieth century were exposing abuse, some of it identified for them by the Republican president with whom they, for a while, worked closely, Theodore Roosevelt. They wrote what they believed was the truth, but in an overtly prosecutorial form: the abuses were to them self-evident, they knew which side they were on, and though they investigated, they did so to denounce. The later, objective journalistic style could also accuse, but by an accumulation of facts and due weight to other points of view, including those accused of malefaction. This reporting was seen by leading journalists as much more ethically based than polemical journalism of the past: in making a case, it could, because of its obvious concern for fairness, balance and neutrality, be much more trusted and thus be a more potent engine of change.

Ben Bradlee, the executive editor of the *Washington Post*, believed that 'the press won Watergate' – though it was Congress which forced Nixon's impeachment. James Reston of the *New York Times* wrote that 'the reporters and the cameras ... forced the withdrawal of American power from Vietnam'.[28] Michael Schudson, in an essay 'Trout or Hamburger: Politics or Telemythology', dissents from this view: he writes that 'we have been told repeatedly about the power television had to turn the American public against the war ... what is the evidence for this belief? There is, it turns out, almost no evidence at all'.[29] The political scientist Thomas Patterson believes that a new view that politics were deeply sleazy underlay reporting after the 1960s and 1970s and 'the rules of reporting changed with Vietnam and Watergate, when the deceptions perpetrated by the Johnson and Nixon administrations convinced reporters that they had let the nation down by taking political leaders at their word. Two presidents had lied, therefore no politician was to be trusted'.[30]

Americans who are not journalists have tended to trust the intelligence services of their country: even years after the event, and after many revelations of torture supervised or facilitated by the CIA, a Pew Poll in December 2014 showed[31] a majority of the public thought that harsh interrogation methods were justified, and that they stopped further large-scale terrorist attacks. Yet the cumulative effects of scandals have, the heads of the main agencies believe, taken their toll: both CIA chief John Brennan and FBI head James Comey told a Senate committee in September 2015 that cynicism and mistrust now surrounded their work, and in the FBI's case, meant that its push for an ability to break encryption for security reasons was greeted with 'venom'.[32] At the same time, Americans also support strong Congressional and Senatorial oversight of the agencies, oversight which has increased over the past decade.

Though the pleas of Brennan and Comey are clearly special pleading from men at the head of organisations endowed with very strong powers, they are right when speaking to the general climate of cynicism about politics and institutions in the intelligentsia/media communities. The period when, in the early decades of the twentieth century and of the Cold War, a patriotic trust in institutions and political and other leaders was the approved position for the majority, including the majority of journalists (at least in what they wrote and broadcast), has gone. Both the Republican and the Democratic parties' primaries show that patriotism and belief in the greatness of America is the automatic position of left and right – but it is no longer automatic for the news media. One sign of this is that the years when journalists were recruited in significant numbers in the US, UK and France to assist the secret services as part-time spies have (probably) gone. The Church Committee report of 1975, in the US warned that it should stop, and it largely did – though heads of the CIA have been careful to reserve the powers to call on journalists' aid in extreme circumstances. When, in 1996, the president of Associated Press Louis Boccardi and the president of CNN Tom Johnson asked John Deutch, director of the CIA (May 1995–December 1996) for a categorical assurance that journalists would never be asked to assist the security services, he responded that 'as Director of Central Intelligence, I must be in a position to assure the president and the members of his National Security Council and this country that there will never come a time when the United States cannot ask a willing citizen to assist in combating an extreme threat to the nation'.[33]

* * *

A story in the *New York Times* on 7 October 2001 – a little less than four weeks after 9/11 – was headlined 'To Fight in the Shadows, Get Better Eyes,' written by one of the paper's writers on security issues, Tim Weiner. In it, Weiner argued that the CIA, weakened by the departure of at least 1,000 experienced men and women as the Agency's paymasters reaped the 'end of the Cold War dividend,' had to relearn tradecraft and 'rebuild its own ability to engage in old-fashioned espionage.'

But it would be dirtier than that. Weiner, reflecting a consensus among intelligence services watchers in the media and in Congress, wrote that

> the C.I.A.'s spies are ill-equipped to fight a dirty war in the world's back alleys. They have been run ragged for years meeting the Pentagon's demands for short-term intelligence on every conceivable post-cold-war threat to the military. Their overseers' priorities may be reflected by their spending: well over $10 billion a year on spy satellites and electronic surveillance; little more than $10 million a year for all C.I.A. covert operations in all of East Asia.[34]

That was not all. The agency did not have the required brutality: 'it was not ready to kick down doors and kill people in Kabul'. For these skills, the CIA would have to enlist experts in the trade of forcing confessions. Weiner continued:

> For now, American intelligence may have to rely on its liaisons with the world's toughest foreign services, men who can look and think and act like terrorists. If someone is going to interrogate a man in a basement in Cairo or Quetta, it will be an Egyptian or a Pakistani officer. American intelligence will take the information without asking a lot of lawyerly questions: the House on Friday told the C.I.A. to abandon its own guidelines on working with people with blood on their hands.[35]

Weiner was among the first to grasp something of what would happen, though that early story was seeking answers rather than detailing the lineaments of a new order in which killing people in Kabul was at the top of the agenda. Weiner wrote that 'the country has not yet had its once-a-generation debate over the role of a secret agency in an open democracy. But it probably will. If American spies are assassinated or kidnapped or kill the wrong people, the question will arise: should the nation free a twenty-first-century clandestine service from old rules and laws?'[36] In fact, the nation, in the form of the president, already had.

Weiner later answered his own question. In his critical history[37] of the CIA, lauded by his peers[38] and indignantly refuted by CIA historians, he wrote that on 17 September 2001, six days after the planes hit the Twin Towers and the Pentagon, Bush had

> issued a fourteen page top secret directive to Tenet and the CIA, ordering the agency to hunt, capture, imprison and interrogate suspects around the world. It set no limits on what the agency could so. It was the foundation for a system of secret prisons where CIA officers and contractors used techniques that included torture … this was not the role of a civilian intelligence service in a democratic society. [Emphasis added.]

The immediate post-9/11 environment in the US was one in which the slogans 'anything goes' and 'whatever it takes' were largely unquestioned. The CIA was – to the disgust of the FBI – allowed to conduct espionage and raids within the US, and the NSA was instructed to collect data on US citizens' communications. That which had been unthinkable, or certainly illegal, before the attack was not only permitted, but ordered. The Counter Terrorism Center, which had languished in desuetude since the Soviets threw in the towel, became, under a flamboyant and rhetorically bloodthirsty chief Cofer Black, the most important division within the agency: in a meeting with the president and his senior colleagues at Camp David on 15 September, Black told the politicians that it would be impossible to capture Osama bin Laden, or other al Qaeda leaders, because once cornered, they blew themselves up – adding that 'when we're finished with them they will have flies walking on their eyeballs.'[39] According to Bob Woodward's account, Black's 'image of death … left a lasting impression on a number of war cabinet secretaries. Black became known in Bush's inner circle as the "flies on the eyeballs guy".'[40]

At a meeting in Washington with British secret service colleagues with experience in Northern Ireland around the same time, Black said to a colleague, the former head of CIA operations in Europe, Tyler Drumheller, that 'We'll all probably be prosecuted' for the actions they were planning to take. 'Drumheller thought that Black practically relished the possibility, casting himself as a tough but noble hero, forced to sacrifice himself for his country. He was giving his Jack Nicholson, *A Few Good Men* speech, Drumheller concluded.'[41]

At the heart of the coverage – as the war in Iraq turned sour, as more and more dissidents within the intelligence service, and the state and justice departments sought, or responded positively to queries from, news media to vent their frustrations – were allegations of something which most Americans had assumed had disappeared from officially sanctioned policing, warfare and intelligence gathering. That was torture, both performed by the newly militarised CIA and its contractors, and that which was done by others – as Weiner forecast – 'interrogat[ing] a man in a basement in Cairo or Quetta, it will be an Egyptian or a Pakistani officer'.[42] Thus 'rendition' – sending suspected jihadists to countries where they could be interrogated in basements – became a sub-division of the inquiries into torture, the more urgent because it became the largest area in which torture was used.

Both the reporters and many of their sources were concerned, above all, by what they saw as the descent into lawlessness on the part of the US intelligence services and military, overseen and encouraged by the administration. What has resulted from this collusion, between the dissenters within and around the administration and journalists, has been a wealth of reportage, in books, in print, broadcasting and on the internet, which effectively indict the Bush presidencies and which have, albeit with less fervour, continued to focus on the ways in which President

Barack Obama has continued to wage war on terror, both at home and abroad. As Scott Shane put it in his *Objective Troy*:

> *In the years after 9/11, those of us covering the American campaign against Al Qaeda repeatedly found ourselves confronting moral and legal issues of gravity and consequence: secret detention; interrogation and torture; leaks to the press and the unprecedented crackdown on them; the targeted killing of suspected terrorists. Terrorism and the fear it generated pressed on elected and unelected officials weighty questions of right and wrong, sometimes in excruciating tangles. Again and again, the United States would drop principles that had defined it on the world stage, embracing practices it had long condemned.*[43]

It has been, both in intent and in effect, a journalistic mission to save the honour of the Republic: to use the self-imposed responsibility of the news media to inform audiences about how terror was fought, and what the effects have been and continue to be, first on America and then globally. The reportage, like the bulk of that on Vietnam, has been one of failure – failure, first of all, in Iraq, as the rapid defeat of Saddam's demoralised army and the capture and execution of Saddam himself was succeeded by years of conflict, both between the coalition of invading forces and the various militia groups in the country. Then, between the groups themselves, as the split between the Sunni and Shia', the main currents in Islam, turned from coexistence into open warfare in countries where the two traditions had significant communities, this in some accounts being blamed largely on the US-led invasion.

Weiner's history of the CIA is the most comprehensive of the indictments of US intelligence and covers the agency's record from its creation by presidential order in 1952 to 2006. Its intention is to clearly show that

> *the most powerful country in the history of Western civilisation has failed to create a first-rate spy service. That failure constitutes a danger to the national security of the United States ... without a strong, smart, sharp intelligence service, presidents and generals alike can become blind and crippled. But throughout its history, the United States has not had such a service ... its mistakes ... have proved fatal for legions of American soldiers and foreign agents ... the one crime of lasting consequence has been the CIA's inability to carry out its central mission: informing the President of what is happening in the world.*[44]

All of this on the first page. The rest of the work – over 500 pages of text and 150 of notes – included accounts such as that of an agency convinced a double agent called Nosenko had been sent by the Soviets to disguise the fact that it had been responsible for the assassination of President Kennedy, finally determining after years of harsh interrogation they were wrong and releasing him with a large payoff and a salary. In nearly every large issue in which the CIA had a role to play, Weiner wrote, their achievements were average at best, often disastrously misjudged.

Like most journalists who wrote on the post-9/11 period in intelligence, Weiner catalogued the huge powers the CIA and the NSA were given within weeks of the attack, powers which gave the CIA the formal power to spy inside the borders of the United States for the first time. He credits George Tenet with warning consistently both Bill Clinton and Bush that al Qaeda was a growing threat and that an attack was likely, and imminent: but he quotes Tenet's predecessor, Richard Helms (1973–7) as saying that 'it's not good enough to ring the bell. You've got to make sure the other guy hears it' and neither late Clinton nor early Bush did. But come 9/11, Weiner delivered the judgement that the failure – of many institutions – was 'a failure to know the enemy. [9/11] was the Pearl Harbour that that CIA had been created to prevent.'[45]

Weiner's book's reception is the clearest evidence of the sharply different ways in which reporters on the one hand and intelligence experts and CIA insiders on the other see the agency, and intelligence in general, in the contemporary era. It was widely praised by Weiner's peers: in his own paper, the *New York Times*, Evan Thomas wrote that it was 'comprehensive, engrossing' and 'paints what may be the most disturbing picture yet of CIA ineptitude'. In the only domestic paper the *Times* would admit as a competitor, the *Washington Post*, David Wise, himself a writer on security issues, made a few caveats – that Weiner had not given due credit to the early leaders, and that 'he is unwilling to concede that the CIA … ever did anything right' – but concluded that the book 'succeeds as both journalism and history'.[46] Other major papers, such as the *Wall Street Journal* and the *Los Angeles Times*, were similarly enthusiastic.

But Jeffrey T. Richelson, a fellow of Washington's National Security Archive and an author of several close studies of the agency, was not only dismissive, but, in his review – in the *Washington Decoded* web journal – annoyed. The book 'cannot be even remotely characterised as a history of the CIA'.[47] He continued: 'Weiner is quick to quote any former intelligence officer who now has something negative to say about any of the agency's activities, but never asks whether these views are reasonable, or whether other officials have different views in hindsight … [he has a] propensity to make extravagant judgments without hard evidence or serious thought.' He goes further, arguing that the 'kudos lavished on Weiner's book in prestigious newspapers are just as disturbing as the book's shortcomings': the mass of reviews, mainly written by journalists with long experience of covering the security beat, 'leaves one with a sinking feeling' because they were 'the kind one might expect from gullible writers who lack independent knowledge of the agency'.

He was not alone in his view. Nicholas Dujmovic, a member of the history staff at the CIA's Center for the Study of Intelligence, wrote of it on the CIA's site in similar terms – as a '600-page op-ed piece masquerading as serious history: it is the advocacy of a particular point of view under the guise of scholarship. Weiner has allowed his agenda to drive his research which is, of course, exactly backwards.' He writes that the quote from President Eisenhower about 'a legacy of ashes' which forms the title was applied not to the CIA, but to military intelligence – specifically, the president's failure to stop the services developing their own intelligence operations.[48] The opening sentence 'All Harry Truman wanted was a newspaper' seems to suggest that the president wanted only a daily digest of the world's trouble spots which might bear on the security of the US. In fact, writes Dujmovic, Truman signed off on many covert actions, including guerrilla warfare. Weiner, 'a Pulitzer Prize winning journalist, has distorted what was said, why it was said, when it was said and the circumstances under which it was said – all to support his thesis that it was a continuous failure from 1947 up to the present'.

There are usually sour grapes as well as mutual reliance in the relations between journalists and experts/academics: in the stress put on the fact that Weiner had won the Pulitzer is the suggestion that these prizes are at least sometimes based on work which is less than fully credible. Both Richelson and Dujmovic give Weiner some credit, but not much: and in their assertions on quality and trustworthiness, they both indirectly criticise the approach of the journalistic profession itself – too prone to start from a 'thesis' which, 'advanced under the guise of scholarship', is open to distortion, misquoting and tendentious argument.

These arguments would go deep into the nature of contemporary journalism. Richelson and Dujmovic were writing from within the CIA system, and thus are open to charges of an institutional bias – indeed, could only with difficulty avoid it. But journalists have institutional biases too. A dominant trope of mid-late 2000s and early 2010s US journalism has been claims to 'name the guilty men' and to act as an alarm for the good name and moral practice of politics in the republic. The temptation to do some of what Dujmovic and Richelson accuse Weiner would be strong.

Yet on the central issue of much US journalism in the 2000s, there now seems no reason to doubt that the freeing of the intelligence agencies to 'do what it takes' to keep the US safe did result in extensive brutalising of prisoners suspected of terrorism, and thus a serious, sometimes horrifying, degradation of the standards of, especially, the CIA. An imprimatur was put on that conclusion, years after journalistic coverage had reached it, by the Senate Intelligence Committee in December 2014. The report, which had endured a tortuous process from evidence to publication, was itself comprehensive.[49]

It found that the 'enhanced interrogation techniques' were largely ineffective in extracting reliable information; rested on inaccurate claims as to their effectiveness, involved techniques and imprisonment conditions 'far worse' than was represented to policy-makers and legislators, that the CIA impeded investigations of the office of the Inspector General, and others, and lied to the Justice Department. It found that the CIA held people not liable for detention under the rules, had little accurate information about who and where suspects were detained, took no action against officers who flouted guidelines and indulged in activity which 'caused immeasurable damage to the US' public standing as well as to its longstanding global leadership on human rights in general and the prevention of torture in particular'.[50] The chairwoman of the committee, the California senator Diane Feinstein, wrote in the report that 'it is my personal conclusion that, under any common meaning of the term, CIA detainees were tortured'. The report itself says that 'the US intelligence services' actions must always reflect who we are and adhere to our laws and standards'.[51]

The most powerful comment on the report as it was issued came from John McCain, the senator from Arizona, who had himself been tortured in captivity by the north Vietnamese. Calling waterboarding 'an exquisite form of torture' and 'shameful', he used the authority of his experience to say that

> *I know from personal experience that the abuse of prisoners will produce*
> *more bad than good intelligence. I know that victims of torture will offer*

intentionally misleading information if they think their captors will believe it. I know they will say whatever they think their torturers want them to say if they believe it will stop their suffering ... We need only remember in the worst of times, through the chaos and terror of war, when facing cruelty, suffering and loss, that we are always Americans, and different, stronger, and better than those who would destroy us.[52]

One of the first reports on torture had come from Dana Priest, on the *Washington Post*. The story, written with Barton Gellman, ran the day after Christmas 2002 (perhaps a sign that the editors did not want too many readers to happen upon it). Headlined 'US Decries Abuse But Defends Interrogations', the story described a cluster of metal containers, surrounded by barbed wire, in a corner of the Bagram air base outside Kabul, in Afghanistan.

The containers hold the most valuable prizes in the war on terrorism – captured al Qaeda operatives and Taliban commanders. Those who refuse to cooperate inside this secret CIA interrogation center are sometimes kept standing or kneeling for hours, in black hoods or spray-painted goggles, according to intelligence specialists familiar with CIA interrogation methods. At times they are held in awkward, painful positions and deprived of sleep with a 24-hour bombardment of lights – subject to what are known as 'stress and duress' techniques. Some who do not cooperate are turned over – 'rendered,' in official parlance – to foreign intelligence services whose practice of torture has been documented by the U.S. government and human rights organizations.[53]

It is an important landmark of a story, for it is cautious of making strong allegations of torture, and includes a rationale for 'stress and duress' treatment – 'While the U.S. government publicly denounces the use of torture, each of the current national security officials interviewed for this article defended the use of violence against captives as just and necessary. They expressed confidence that the American public would back their view' (as, later, it did).[54] It does, however, begin to describe the emerging system, which would be extended in the following year to Iraq, after the invasion: that suspects could expect a rough time, if not at American hands, then at those of their allies more experienced in stress and duress. 'In other cases, usually involving lower-level captives, the CIA hands them to foreign intelligence services – notably those of Jordan, Egypt and Morocco – with a list of questions the agency wants answered. These "extraordinary renditions" are done without resort to legal process and usually involve countries with security services known for using brutal means.'[55]

Dana Priest told me that, though she was among the pioneers in this field, she and her colleagues got off to a slow start.

> I began writing about what was involved in this after around six months from 9/11. I wanted to ask critical questions, but that was then seen as unpatriotic. We got sources slowly: it was very painful reporting. People were uncomfortable to be part of this. But there was never a time when we were told [by Post editors] that we shouldn't be doing these stories. We were always quoting unnamed sources, because they wouldn't go on the record. My position is that you want to give the readers as many details as possible, so the story is credible without named sources, it shows you've spoken to people who know.

A summary of stories written on Iraq shows that Priest, with Gellman and others, was prominent and early in divulging the techniques used,[56] but that the revelatory stories by her and many others only started to come out with any frequency from the latter half of 2002.

> I thought it important that we weren't helping the enemy. My way of working was to do a first draft of the story and then go over it with sources – to ask them if this or that was right (not of course showing them the story), and ask them if they had any concerns. From the DIA [Defence Intelligence Agency], the CIA, the NSA, they would usually come back – they would ask us to take X or Y out, would say: 'we'd rather you didn't write that.' It would go right to the top of the paper to get a yes or no.

In November 2005, nearly three years since the first story on the Afghanistan containers, Priest wrote a story on secret prisons, which had not then been publicised in the US. Headlined 'CIA Holds Terror Suspects in Secret Prisons', it was uncompromising in presenting the facts.[57]

> The CIA has been hiding and interrogating some of its most important al Qaeda captives at a Soviet-era compound in Eastern Europe, according to U.S. and foreign officials familiar with the arrangement.
>
> The secret facility is part of a covert prison system set up by the CIA nearly four years ago that at various times has included sites in eight countries,

including Thailand, Afghanistan and several democracies in Eastern Europe, as well as a small center at the Guantanamo Bay prison in Cuba, according to current and former intelligence officials and diplomats from three continents.

The hidden global internment network is a central element in the CIA's unconventional war on terrorism. It depends on the cooperation of foreign intelligence services, and on keeping even basic information about the system secret from the public, foreign officials and nearly all members of Congress charged with overseeing the CIA's covert actions.

Priest said

we decided it did reveal too much so we consulted heavily on it – we brought in the head of operations and the head of the CIA, and right up to the President. It took a month of going back and forth. It wasn't comfortable, to be faced with the government saying this will harm people. At first [Len] Downie [editor of the Post *from 1991 to 2008] said, don't run it. Then Human Rights Watch got bits of it so we ran it.*

Priest won the Pulitzer for that and other stories on 'black site' prisons: there were calls from the Senate and Congress for her to reveal her sources, and to assess if she had broken laws in her reporting. The *Post*'s reliance on the Human Rights Watch's research highlights a sub-theme in much contemporary journalism on conflict and human rights globally: the many informal connections between the reporters for news organisations and researchers for human rights NGOs. Like the intelligence services, journalistic and the NGO reports depend on discovering usually hidden facts; unlike intelligence, both journalism and human rights advocacy seek the widest possible publication, and the largest possible public reaction: they are thus often comrades-in-arms, subject to the same temptations to inflate and the same criticisms for doing so.

In a well-received book published in 2003, Priest wrote she 'begged to differ' with President Bush's declaration after 9/11 – that this was a struggle between good and evil. She wrote that

Although the war against Al Qaeda in Afghanistan was clear in purpose, we are now seeing that the hardest, longest and most important work comes after the bombing stops, when rebuilding replaces destroying and consensus-building replaces precision strikes. As the US army's experience

in Kosovo shows, the mind-set, decision making and training of infantry
soldiers rarely mixes well with the disorder inherent in civil society. The
mismatch of culture and mission can distort the role of rebuilding a country.
In the hands of poorly formed, misguided troops, it can create disaster.[58]

In 2010 Priest, with a *Post* colleague William Arkin, wrote a long investigation into 'Top Secret America' – which in a preface argued that 'The government has built a national security and intelligence system so big, so complex and hard to manage that no-one really knows if it's fulfilling its most important purpose: keeping its citizens safe.'[59] Summarising the main findings of their two-year project, Priest and Arkin wrote that they had 'discovered what amounts to an alternative geography of the United States, a Top Secret America hidden from public view and lacking in thorough oversight. After nine years of unprecedented spending and growth, the result is that the system put in place to keep the United States safe is so massive that its effectiveness is impossible to determine.'

The investigation's other findings include:

- Some 1,271 government organisations and 1,931 private companies work on programmes related to counter-terrorism, homeland security and intelligence in about 10,000 locations across the United States.
- An estimated 854,000 people, nearly 1.5 times as many people as live in Washington, DC, hold top-secret security clearances.
- In Washington and the surrounding area, 33 building complexes for top-secret intelligence work are under construction or have been built since September 2001. Together they occupy the equivalent of almost three Pentagons or 22 US Capitol buildings – about 17 million square feet of space.
- Many security and intelligence agencies do the same work, creating redundancy and waste. For example, 51 federal organisations and military commands, operating in 15 US cities, track the flow of money to and from terrorist networks.
- Analysts who make sense of documents and conversations obtained by foreign and domestic spying share their judgement by publishing 50,000 intelligence reports each year – 'a volume so large that many are routinely ignored'.

The 'lack of focus' in the overloaded system meant it was very largely ineffective. One of the main, named, sources on which Priest and Arkin based this view was a retired Lieutenant General, John Vines, a former commander in Iraq, tasked in 2009 with reviewing the intelligence system, who told them that 'The complexity of this system defies description ... because it lacks a synchronizing process, it inevitably results in message dissonance, reduced effectiveness and waste. We consequently can't effectively assess whether it is making us more safe.'[60]

Priest and Arkin then shaped their investigation into a book, published in 2011.[61] It began, as longer form journalism usually does, with a human example – in this case 76-year-old Joy Whiteman, described passing through security at the airport near Boise, the capital of Idaho state, standing in the body scanner with the aid of the security personnel while the wheelchair on which she depended was put through a separate scan. For all the inconvenience, Joy and her husband Bill were strong supporters of the security provisions: "'I don't mind at all" she told the *Post* reporters. "I don't want to blow up". "These people [security guards] are always one step ahead", said Bill'.

Painting a large canvas from the cameo, they continued:

> the scene of Joy Whiteman holding herself up on the walls of the body scanner while a crew of security guards, paid by taxpayers, made sure she didn't fall, seemed a perfect metaphor for what has transpired in the US over the past ten years. Having been given a steady stream of vague but terrifying information from national security officials about the possibility of dirty bombs, chemical weapons, bio toxins, exploding airliners and suicide bombers, a nation of men and women like the Whitemans have shelled out hundreds of millions of dollars to turn the machinery of government over to defeating terrorism without really questioning what they were getting for their money.

Like much of the reporting since the mid-2000s, Priest and Arkin's journalism directly challenged the priorities and provisions of the – by 2010, Obama – administration and the vast security state. The cameo of the Whiteman couple at Boise airport and the commentary on their passage through the scanner used a trope common to both politicians and journalists: a synecdoche which usually implicitly puts both trades on the side of the person(s) portrayed in the cameo. In the Priest and Arkin example, the Whiteman couple are the victims of a vast apparatus costing hundreds of millions of taxpayers' dollars, justified by 'vague but terrifying' information, accepted as true without questioning. The clear message is that they are victims of a false belief: that this is producing a state of national anxiety which is unwarranted, even absurd. Priest is particularly alive to this danger: in our talk, she mentioned that she is on the board of her daughter's school rowing club: a military officer, also on the board, had been obliged to report the fact to his superiors, and had been told not to talk to Priest.

Still more directly critical reportage drove Jane Mayer's *The Dark Side*,[62] the name picking up on a comment made by Dick Cheney a few days after 9/11, on the venerable (since 1947) NBC programme *Meet the Press*. Cheney said that 'We'll have to work sort of the dark side, if you will … a lot of what needs to be done here will have to be done quietly, without any discussion, using sources and methods that are available to our intelligence agencies – if we are going to be successful … it's going to be vital for us to use any means at our disposal, basically, to achieve our objectives.' It was a well-chosen remark – for in retrospect, Cheney was laying out, with some candour and accuracy, what would be the posture of the administration and the intelligence services for the rest of Bush's two presidential terms.

Though Cheney was giving the rationalisation for policies that would later include torture, rendition of suspects, imprisonment in Guantanamo for long periods, surveillance of US citizens without the public being informed, and doing so in fairly unambiguous terms, this was not, then, controversial. The programme presenter, Tim Russert, normally a sharp and sometimes aggressive interviewer, did ask Cheney if 'restrictions' would be lifted on secret service use and employment of 'unsavoury characters', to which the Vice President responded 'I think so' – adding that dealing only with 'officially recognised good guys' was not adequate. The conflict to come, he said, would be 'a mean, nasty, dirty business' and it was important not to tie the hands of the intelligence services when they descended into it. Russert also asked if Saddam Hussein was in the frame for links with the terrorists, supplying Cheney with the line that 'there's a track record there': Cheney did not deny he might be a future target, but said the 'focus now is on Al Qaeda'. Asked if any evidence linked Saddam to the 9/11 attack, Cheney gave an unqualified 'No' – a posture that was not to last.

Mayer's book is a more direct indictment of the Bush presidency, more frontally polemical. Early in her book she wrote that

> confronted with a new enemy and their own intelligence failure, [Bush]
> and Cheney turned to some familiar conservative nostrums that had

preoccupied the far right wing of the Republican Party since the Watergate era [late 1960s]. There was too much international law, too many civil liberties, too many constraints on the President's war powers, too many rights for defendants and too many rules against lethal covert actions. There was also too much openness and too much meddling by Congress and the press.[63]

Her book is itself dark – in the details of torture and captivity, in some cases of people likely innocent – but also in the roll call of the many officials and soldiers prepared to turn away from, or at times approve of, even enjoy, the torture and humiliation visited on suspects. She wrote that the amount of information of value extracted from 'stressful' sessions was 'meagre' – in part, as one expert fluent in Arabic tasked with finding out why so little information was forthcoming discovered, because at least a third of the 600 detainees in Guantanamo knew nothing. The Bush legal team, whose most proactive member was John Yoo, a Professor of Law and Deputy Assistant Attorney General, advised that 'the president could argue that torture was legal because he authorized it ... by this logic, the President was literally above the law'. Yoo, with Jay Bybee, his immediate boss as Assistant Attorney General, issued a memorandum which allowed CIA investigators to 'walk up to the edge of torture' – though few intervened to ensure they did not go over it.

In her telling, there were only a few who dissented. Alberto Mora, head of criminal investigations for the US Navy, was a political conservative who had strongly supported the Iraq invasion, but who also strongly believed that the military had to have a firm attachment to the Constitution, or the exercise of power could become illegitimate. Mora tried to oppose the instances of torture he knew about, and brought them to the attention of his opposite number Steven Morello, general counsel of the Army. Morello told him he knew of the instances, had tried to object, but 'was told to shut up'.[64]

Air Force Reserve Colonel Steve Kleinman, sent to Iraq to advise on interrogation, realised that the harsh techniques were being used, and objected: also to no purpose. He told Mayer that 'I got into serious argument with many people. They *wanted* to do these things. They were itching to. It was about revenge, not interrogation.'[65] Jack Goldsmith, another conservative lawyer, was appointed head of the Justice Department's Office of the Legal Counsel, where he reviewed Yoo's assertion – backed by academic reasoning – of absolute power to the presidency, and found it without foundation. He succeeded in moderating some of the effects of the Yoo–Bybee memo on torture, but found they were then reasserted by John Ashcroft, the Attorney General, prompting Goldsmith's resignation. In a later book Goldsmith wrote that Bush, unlike his predecessor Lincoln and (Franklin) Roosevelt, did not use emergency powers with restraint, as a means to secure constitutional freedoms, but 'has been almost entirely inattentive to the soft powers of legitimation – consultation, deliberation, the appearance of deference and credible expressions of concerns for constitutional and international values – but … instead relied on the hard power of prerogative'.[66]

Mayer found it 'humbling and reassuring' that such people were prepared to put their careers on the line in defence of what they saw as constitutional values. She admitted that, 'by the measure that matters most', the Bush measures were successful – that is, 'there have been no additional terrorist attacks since September 2001'.[67] Still, she added, 'the public has been asked to simply take the President's word on faith that inhumane treatment has been necessary to stop attacks and save lives'.

The CIA, according to the *New York Times* security reporter (and another Pulitzer winner) Mark Mazzetti, became 'a killing machine consumed with man hunting', as counter-terrorism became the central part of the agency and George Tenet became 'a military commander running a clandestine, global war with a skeleton staff and very little oversight … [he] sold the White House on a programme to capture terrorists, hide them in secret jails and subject them to an Orwellian regimen of brutal interrogation methods'.[68] Like Priest and Arkin, he saw a vast 'military intelligence complex' develop; his book reminded its readers that the CIA had been in the man-hunting business before, developing assassination plots against Cuba's President Fidel Castro and Congo's prime minister Patrice Lumumba; while under the Reagan presidency, CIA officers oversaw wars in Nicaragua and in Afghanistan.

One of the main characters in Mazzetti's narrative, a CIA official named Duane ('Dewey') Claridge who had been a leading player in the Iran Contra scandal (which saw him organise Contra forces to mount a coup against Nicaragua's Sandinista government) and served a few weeks in prison, reflects in old age to Mazzetti, in the restaurant of a retirement home, that 'the treaty of Westphalia [in 1648, which saw the underpinning of the status of nations] is over. Nation states no longer have a monopoly on military force. Just look at our own system. The only thing that isn't outsourced is the guy shooting the gun'. Mazzetti then reflects, in turn, that Claridge was understating the case: the war against terror 'had seen the USA willing to farm out government's most elemental function: protecting the state'.

Mazzetti's description of how the war is increasingly outsourced to defence contractors – as he described their new office towers in northern Virginia, 'form[ing] a ring around the capital like an army laying siege to a mediaeval town' – is something of a backhanded compliment to the power of journalism: outsourcing relieves the pressure on central government, allows deniability or at least ignorance and moves the public relations interface with the news media into companies which do not have the duty to respond to questioning which administrations do. 'The more you outsource an operation, the more deniable it becomes', a CIA officer tells him. At the same time, as he describes, the weapon of choice has increasingly become the drone, first tested in 2000 as a weapon rather than merely a surveillance tool. Hank Crumpton, a retired CIA counter-intelligence officer, told Mazzetti that he thinks it 'puzzling' that a killing of a suspected jihadist by drone is not seen as a large issue – 'there seems to be no problem with a Hellfire shot against a designated enemy in a place like Afghanistan, the tribal areas of Pakistan, Somalia or Yemen' – while if a CIA officer shoots a suspected terrorist in the back of the head in Paris or Hamburg, 'it's viewed as an assassination'.

Drones, relatively uncontentious and popular with the public, have many ethical issues only partially explored. One is, should they be used to kill Americans? Mazzetti, with Eric Schmitt, filed a story to the *New York Times* in April 2015 on the trial of the Texan-born Mohamed Mahmoud al Farekh, suspected of terrorism, captured by Pakistani security officers in 2014 and sent to the US for trial. Both the Pentagon and the CIA argued he should be killed by drone: the attorney general Eric Holder, however, doubted the case made against him and argued he could be captured and brought to trial – as he was.[69] These and other issues were brought out in Scott Shane's *Objective Troy*, an exploration of the mechanisms and moralities of drone warfare, told in parallel with the life and fate of Anwar al Awlaki, another American, born of Yemeni parents in the US.[70]

Al Awlaki was a popular imam who at first stressed his loyalty to the US, became a go-to cleric for news media seeking a moderate Muslim spokesman, then moved steadily to a jihadist position, transformed himself through his ability to preach both in person and online, into an inspiration and guide for young jihadists. Increasingly under investigation from 2000 on, al Awlaki spent two years in the UK, preaching an increasingly radical message in mosques and to gatherings of young Muslims; then on to Yemen, his parents' birthplace, where he settled with his wife and five children and put out radical exhortations on an increasingly popular blog. These messages of hatred for the 'kuffar', or non-Muslims, had passed from the ambiguous while still in the US, to the unambiguous. Where he had condemned violence after 9/11, when featuring constantly on US media, he now wrote that to eschew it was 'compromising your religion'. To stop jihad was to give the enemy what they wished for. 'Any Muslim today who is not fighting *jihad fe sabillah* [Jihad for the sake of Allah] is supporting the enemy by giving him this victory for free'.[71]

Shane, who had written a book on the corrosive effects of Western media on the Soviet Union,[72] saw in al Awlaki's effect on the impressionable young Muslims as a textbook case of the power of the internet:

> *as the Internet matured, he was quick to exploit its possibilities. He mastered the voice and video messaging service Paltalk to lecture to big virtual audiences, with his lectures announced in advance on Islamic websites. His lectures began to spread effortlessly round the web and around the world, fans passing them to their friends and posting them on site after site.*
>
> *In 2005, the year he recorded one of his greatest hits, 'Constants on the path of Jihad', three young PayPal employees were developing YouTube, which would soon become the platform that would give Awlaki's message its greatest reach ... in the privacy of their homes, young Muslims in the US, Canada and Britain were increasingly taking to their computers to satisfy their curiosity about the radical strains of Islam that seemed to terrify their governments.*[73]

The army psychiatrist Major Nidal Hasan, who killed 13 of his fellow soldiers at Fort Hood in November 2009, was an avid follower, who corresponded with al Awlaki, and al Awlaki also inspired the 'underwear bomber', Umar Farouk Abdulmutallab, a young Nigerian student at London's University College, who tried to detonate a bomb on a transatlantic flight in December 2009, but failed.

Al Awlaki had, instinctively or through observation and empathy, tapped into the motivating power of a religion which strove for complete hegemony (as Christianity once had), and into the need for 'identity, companionship and adventure in pursuit of a cause' which the young often displayed. Shane quoted a comment from the Catholic priest Monsignor Lorenzo Albacete, asked on the US PBS channel, sometime after the event, for his reaction to 9/11:

> *I recognised an old companion. I recognised religion ... that the same force, energy, sense, instinct, whatever, passion – the same passion that motivates people to do great things is the same one that that day brought all that destruction. When they said that the people that did it, did it in the name of God, I wasn't the slightest bit surprised. It only confirmed what I knew.*[74]

The Muslim cleric, moved to near the top of the mortal enemies list as it became clear he was energising a few of his followers to pass from verbal to real aggression against the 'kuffar', was killed by a drone in September 2011, while in hiding in a mountainous area of Yemen. The Yemeni authorities, who had been wooed and supported by the US, had imprisoned him, released him, then called for his capture 'dead or alive'. Two weeks later, another drone killed his son, Abdulrahman al Awlaki, who was searching for his father together with a teenage cousin. Abdulrahman was also a US citizen.

The parallel narrative to that of al Awlaki in *Operation Troy* is the use of drones. Deployed under Bush, their use was greatly expanded under Obama. Entering the presidency determined to draw a thick line between his and Bush's administrations – 'America must demonstrate that our values and our institutions are more resilient than a hateful ideology'[75] – he came to realise that drones represented the closest thing to the perfect weapon he was likely to have in his hands. It called for no American 'boots on the ground': indeed, the soldiers who fired the missiles after receiving an order to do so could have their boots resting on a desk in a base in the US. They killed 'bad guys' – though they also missed them, and killed innocents, at times women and children. The Bureau of Investigative Journalism in London took a close interest in the use of drones and their effect, dedicating a large part of its efforts and its website to adding up the victims and assessing the number of non-combatants killed: its monthly update for August 2015 shows a total of around 550 drone strikes since the inception of the programme (in 2002, in Yemen), with by far the largest number (420) fired at targets in Pakistan.[76] Between 3,500 and 5,500 people are estimated to have been killed, of which between 500 and 1,000 were civilians, including between 180 and 230 children.

In a story he wrote on drones in the *New York Times*, Shane quoted unnamed presidential aides as saying that Obama 'liked the idea of picking off dangerous terrorists a few at a time, without endangering American lives or risking the years-long bloodshed of conventional war', but Shane continued:

> *hundreds of dangerous militants have, indeed, been killed by drones, including some high-ranking Qaeda figures. But for six years, when the heavy cloak of secrecy has occasionally been breached, the results of some strikes have often turned out to be deeply troubling.*
>
> *Every independent investigation of the strikes has found far more civilian casualties than administration officials admit. Gradually, it has become clear that when operators in Nevada fire missiles into remote tribal territories on the other side of the world, they often do not know who they are killing, but are making an imperfect best guess.*[77]

Reporting the drone strikes and their effect had been difficult: 'over the Obama presidency, it has become harder for journalists to obtain information from the government on the results of particular strikes. And Mr Obama's Justice Department has fought in court for years to keep secret the legal opinions justifying strikes.'[78] Shane told me that 'the president has talked about drones, including on TV, several times. And yet everything to do with the programme is classified. Michael Hayden (director of the NSA, 1999–2005; of the CIA, 2006–9) said that he didn't know what he could legally say about drones.' The exception was when American citizens were killed: presidential aides will, 'eventually' admit to the deaths, though often off the record. In a later feature in the *Times* magazine which showcased his book, Shane wrote that a further problem with drone strikes was that they fuelled 'the central narrative of Al Qaeda and the Islamic State: that the US is at war with Islam, that it is killing Muslims and that the obligatory response is armed Jihad'.[79]

Obama, and liberal opinion the world over, has been struggling with his image as an anti-Bush progressive and his real-world actions since soon after his inauguration. Shane dramatises the dissonance by reference to the choice of the Nobel Prize committee to give him the Peace Prize in 2009, an award which embarrassed him, but which gave him the opportunity to remind the listeners to and readers of his acceptance speech that he was no pacifist: 'I face the world as it is, and cannot stand idle in the face of threats to the American people. For make no mistake: evil does exist in the world ... negotiations cannot convince al Qaeda's leaders to lay down their arms.'[80] The President was not standing idle: the drone programme was ramping up as he gave the speech in December 2009.

* * *

Nearly all reporters thought that the Obama administration would be more open than that of Bush – in part because he said it would, pledging an 'unprecedented level of openness' on the part of his presidency. For those covering the security world, 'openness' was nearly always something which had to be prised, not prized. Agencies, especially the NSA, simply did not want to say anything to anyone outside of the institution's perimeter, and especially not the press. Thus a president who came in on such a promise, and who had opposed the war on terror which had caused the huge increase in intelligence agencies and the touchiness about secrets being disclosed, was much to be welcomed.

Some of that has been delivered. In a *Washington Post* commentary in March 2015, Jason Ross Arnold, a political scientist at Virginia Commonwealth University and an expert on open government, wrote that Obama had pushed departments to respond as fully and swiftly as possible to Freedom of Information requests, and had ordered the declassification of many more documents than his predecessor. But he faulted him on much more: he had continued the practice of 'secret law', by sending memos allowing specific actions – such as permitting CIA agents to kill US citizens clearly linked to terrorist groups. And, Arnold wrote, 'the Obama administration also has prosecuted more leakers under the Espionage Act than all other administrations combined. Although the increase may have resulted partly from the discrete decisions of prosecutors as well as improved detection technologies, it also results from the choices of senior officials to prosecute leakers under a law targeting spies.'[81]

Leaking is essential to journalism. It is an ethical problem at the heart of the trade – since much leaking depends on the leaker breaking a formal or informal promise on the part of the leaker not to leak. The conundrum is 'solved' by appealing, usually implicitly, to the higher cause of holding power to account, and knowing what is happening in important institutions and meetings – even families – which wield significant power. On the leaker's side, the reasons for leaking can vary from having great moral force (at least in his or her eyes), through being an excuse for carrying on a feud under the guise of journalism, to publishing details, usually sexual, of the private life of well-known people. In the coverage of the intelligence services, and of the way in which security in the face of militant jihadism is administered, leaking at some level is necessary to get beyond bland statements and partial briefings.

The Bush administration was as angered as any before it by the leaking which surrounded its actions, especially in the second half of the 2000s: but, as Warren Strobel observed, the wars within it, in the key departments and in the security services, meant that leakers had a large interest in getting their objections out, and in weakening opponents whom they thought wrong, or dangerous. But under Obama, whose administration is more disciplined and less split over fundamental issues, and which has been directed to go hard on leakers, the pickings – say reporters – are thinner, the penalties (for the leakers) harsher.

Stephen Kim was an American, born of a South Korean immigrant family, fluent in both Korean and English, a bright student at school in New York's Bronx who went on to take a history PhD at Yale. He became a defence analyst, with an early period at the Center for Naval Analyses and the Livermore National Lab, which designs and analyses nuclear weapons, moving on to the Pentagon and then to the State Department. He was a strong proponent of a more aggressive posture to North Korea, believing that the credible threat of force was largely absent on the US side, and was deeply disappointed with the policy of negotiations and sanctions pursued by both the Bush and Obama administrations. In a lengthy piece on Kim's transition from high flier to jailbird, Peter Maass writes that

> there is a time-honored way in government for mid-level experts to convey their worries that high-level officials are misguided – they talk to reporters to raise an alarm outside the walls of whichever department they work for. This is why confidential conversations in Washington seem to take place in parks and restaurants and store aisles as much as they do in actual offices. These conversations can serve as a check on the official statements that portray prevailing policies as wise and successful, even when they are not.[82]

In Kim's case, a meeting was arranged by one of the public affairs officers for the State Department, John Hertzberg, who was – unusually for a State Department employee – himself strongly conservative-interventionist, and who approved of what he must have known would lead to a leak of information.

The reporter Kim spoke to, James Rosen from Fox News, sympathetic to the views of both Hertzberg and Kim, quickly formed the apparently close relationship which hungry reporters often develop with willing sources. In friendly but insistent emails, Rosen badgered Kim to give him details about the US–North Korea negotiations, as the UN discussed a formal condemnation of its latest nuclear test. Kim obliged up to a point, but in the end Rosen's story said that – as the headline on the Fox website put it – 'North Korea Intends to Match UN Resolution with New Nuclear Test'. It was not an earth-shaker. That the North Korean leadership would do so was no surprise, and the story was described as 'a nothing burger' by a state department official. But the story broke 'just as the Obama administration was intensifying its effort to crack down on leakers and whistleblowers':[83] Kim had done nothing unusual within the Washington battleground, and much less than many more senior warriors on that field. But he was to be an example.

At the same time as the story broke, Dennis Blair, the Director of National Intelligence, had looked at a list of officials who had been prosecuted for leaking and found, to his disgust, that of the 153 reported to the Justice Department, none had been charged. In an interview with the *New York Times*, he was robust: he wanted more leakers indicted, and found guilty. 'My background is in the Navy, and it is good to hang an admiral once in a while as an example to others.'[84] (Blair was soon 'hanged' himself, being asked to resign by President Obama after a series of turf battles and disagreements, after only 14 months in office from the end of January 2009 to the end of May 2010.) Some months later in April 2010, as Kim's case was still coming to judgment, the first leak harmful to US interests was released from Wikileaks, forerunner of a trove which Private Bradley Manning would later unload. It showed the mowing down of Iraqis, and two Reuters employees, in Baghdad by a US helicopter gunship. The administration already alerted by Dennis Blair to hang an admiral or two, now faced 'what it feared might become a hemorrhage of secrets by anyone with access to a government database' – fears well founded, three years before the Snowden 'hemorrhage'.[85]

When Kim was finally tried, the charges against him, which had been said by the FBI agents who investigated him to merit 30 years, were reduced to one, a charge under the 1917 Espionage Act for unauthorised disclosure of defence information, for which, in February 2014 he got 13 months at an open prison. While he was still in jail (he was released after 10 months), Maass was interviewed, in March 2015, by National Public

Radio's *On the Media* show.[86] He ended the interview by saying that 'you know, there's all kinds of muddying context that really brings some light to this case. There's kind of a hypocrisy where one arm of the government encourages one form of behavior, and another part of the government prosecutes that kind of behavior. It's a very confusing kind of situation.'

The confusion is in part due to the large increase in the hanging of admirals, which must coexist with a culture of leaking which is approved, even ordered. Indeed, as his defence argued, Kim's contact with Rosen was set up by a State Department public affairs official, Hertzberg, who was not charged. Admiral executions must also coexist, still more uneasily, with a defence of press freedom and free speech which is arguably the most proactive of any major country in the world: journalists' complaints that they are being prevented from getting the true story have more resonance in the US than in most other states – especially when the support for press freedom is buttressed by a stronger distrust of the state.

Of the 11 prosecutions under the Espionage Act for passing classified information to the news media, eight happened (up to the end of 2015) under Obama administrations: the president has defended the proactive policy by appealing to the dangers they could cause to military personnel – 'leaks related to national security can put people at risk. They can put men and women in uniform that I've sent into the battlefield at risk. And so I make no apologies, and I don't think the American people would expect me, as commander in chief, not to be concerned about information that might compromise their missions or might get them killed.'[87] Those charged include the CIA officer Jeffrey Sterling in 2011, who received 42 months in jail for disclosing classified information to the *New York Times'* reporter James Risen for his 2003 book, *State of War*, which first revealed the NSA's bulk collection programmes; Thomas Drake, an NSA official, indicted for retaining classified information; Bradley (Chelsea) Manning, charged under an article in the Army Justice Code which incorporates parts of the Espionage Act and sentenced to 35 years in prison; and James Kiriakou.

Kiriakou, who had resigned from the CIA in 2004 after 14 years' service including a tour in Pakistan as chief of counter-terrorist operations in the country, was found guilty of having supplied information to journalists on the names and missions of two CIA colleagues. One of the journalists was Scott Shane of the *New York Times*, who wrote in a story on Kiriakou's release after 30 months in an open prison in Pennsylvania, that General David Petraeus, Director of the CIA when Kiriakou was convicted, had said that 'oaths do matter and there are indeed consequences for those who believe they are above the laws that protect our fellow officers'.[88] He continued: 'Since then, Mr. Petraeus, who resigned after admitting to an extramarital affair, has himself come under criminal investigation over accusations that he disclosed classified information to the woman with whom he was having an affair, Paula Broadwell.' Petraeus, who was found guilty in April 2015 for having disclosed secrets to his then lover and biographer, was sentenced to two years' probation and a $100,000 fine.

A few years after his resignation from the CIA, in 2007, Kiriakou spoke publicly about waterboarding. He claimed that Abu Zubaydah, suspected of being number three or four in the al Qaeda hierarchy, had been briefly waterboarded (though it later emerged he had been waterboarded 83 times by officers convinced he was hiding a wealth of information). Shane quoted the former CIA official as saying after his release that 'my case was about torture. The CIA never forgave me for talking about torture ... and I would do it all over again.'

The worries that reporters now have about leaking focus on the Insider Threat Program and on enhanced technology. The Program, set out in detail in an October 2011 Presidential Executive Order, creates an interagency task force, headed jointly by the Attorney General and the Director of National Intelligence, tasked with

> deterring, detecting, and mitigating insider threats, including the safeguarding of classified information from exploitation, compromise, or other unauthorised disclosure, taking into account risk levels, as well as the distinct needs, missions, and systems of individual agencies. This program shall include development of policies, objectives, and priorities for establishing and integrating security, counterintelligence, user audits and monitoring, and other safeguarding capabilities and practices within agencies.[89]

A later Intelligence Community Media Directive issued by the Director of National Intelligence James Clapper, spells out the issue for officials, and the news media, more clearly. It says that the government and the intelligence community (IC – comprising all the agencies working on intelligence and counter-terrorism) are committed to transparency, and to responsible sharing of security issues, while whistle-blowing protection on issues as fraud, waste and abuse can be undertaken 'without fear of retaliation'. But

> the IC is also committed to protecting intelligence information from unauthorized disclosure. It is the responsibility of each individual IC employee not to disclose covered matters ... IC employees who are found to be in violation of this IC policy may be subject to administrative action ... if failure to comply with this policy results in unauthorized disclosure of classified information, referral to the Department of Justice for prosecution may occur.[90]

Jonathan Landay at McClatchy, with a colleague Melissa Taylor, did an investigation into the programme: Landay says that

> We got a document from the Pentagon which says that 'leaking classified information is akin to spying'. The idea is to predict who might be a security threat – and it encourages people to spy on their fellow employees. This is the way the programme is designed. They have contractors put in software to detect keystroke patterns, so they can get the people who leak.
>
> There's a new atmosphere of fear now in the bureaucracy. People won't talk to you, even if they were sources before. I called a senior ambassador for background – not for classified stuff, just to get context – and he said: I can't talk to you. They'll kill me.

Landay's colleague Melissa Taylor recalled that, at the beginning of her career before 9/11, she had done a story critical of a federal agency in Washington. There was a leak inquiry.

> I was called by someone in the agency, who said, 'We're concerned about leaks. We'd like to know your sources'. I said I couldn't give them names. The person said, 'OK, thanks', and hung up. I expected to hear more – it seemed such a feeble attempt. But that was it. They had gone through the motions, and could say, 'We asked her, she refused, and after all, this is a free press'. And nothing else happened.

Taylor illuminates another concern – this time of the administration and the agencies. 'Everything changed with Wikileaks. I spoke to someone in the administration, and they said – this is the worst nightmare. People like Wikileaks, these people – *they won't come to us*' (emphasis added). It is an important statement. Taylor's source was reflecting a worry particular to the protocol which has been in use for some decades, in relations between the administration and the agencies on one side, journalists on the other. As Dana Priest said, once a sensitive story is written, journalists who are concerned not to divulge information which might put US military or officials in danger contact the appropriate people in the administration – sometimes, as in her case, at the highest level – and a negotiation then goes on. Often, the officials will deploy the point that publication will put lives at risk, though they will rarely give details either before or after a threat to or an attack on an agent or informant as a result of a leak (in part, say agency officials, because the cause and effect is rarely clear).

In one case, during the Reagan presidency, administration officials said that at least one CIA informant in Ghana had been killed after an agency employee, Sharon Scranage, gave confidential information, including the names of Ghanaian dissidents, to Michael Soussoudis, said to be her lover, and a relative of the then Ghanaian President, Jerry Rawling. More routinely, they say that current investigations will be compromised or even ruined by disclosure of details, and that hostile intelligence agencies and terrorists will profit from the information and adjust their activities to avoid detection. Sometimes editors will take the point and delay or even excise: sometimes they will deem the objections not serious enough to warrant withholding publication or broadcast.

The second concern is the power the authorities have to find out, quickly, who talked to whom. When Rosen and Kim talked to each other, data viewed by the CIA recorded their phone calls, when they left and re-entered the building (Rosen was accredited to the State Department and had a work station in the press room) and how long they spoke. Scott Shane was quickly identified as one of the reporters to whom Kiriakou spoke – though the *Times* man was not charged. Adam Liptak wrote in February 2012 that

> it used to be that journalists had a sporting chance of protecting their sources. The best and sometimes the only way to identify a leaker was to pressure the reporter of the news organization that received the leak, but even subpoenas tended to be resisted. Today advances in surveillance allow the government to keep a perpetual eye on those with security clearances, and give prosecutors the ability to punish officials for disclosing secrets, without provoking clash with the press.[91]

Liptak quoted Lucy Daglish, director of the Reporters Committee for Freedom of the Press, as saying that she had been told by a national security representative at a conference that the agencies no longer needed to subpoena reporters – 'We don't need to ask who you're talking to,' the official had said. 'We know'. Daglish continued – 'For God's sake get off e-mail. Get off your cellphone. Watch your credit cards. Watch your plane tickets. *These guys in the NSA know everything*' (emphasis added).

One of the most often quoted sources on issues of disclosure, secrecy and reporter-agency relationships is Steven Aftergood, who directs the Project on Government Secrecy at the Washington-based Federation of American Scientists. The Federation grew out of the Manhattan Project which developed nuclear weapons and was from its initiation concerned with issues of transparency, public information and nuclear disarmament. Aftergood has been an activist on nuclear safety issues, and has successfully campaigned to have the CIA reveal previously secret details on its budget – and did the same for the National Reconnaissance Office, an institution created in 1960 and officially admitted to exist in 1992, which designs and builds government reconnaissance satellites, with an annual budget which takes nearly 20 per cent of total spending on intelligence, that is estimated to be between $80 and 90bn annually. The CIA strongly opposed the push to reveal its budget (it now does so, routinely): George Tenet, then CIA director, argued that 'disclosure of the budget request reasonably could be expected to provide foreign governments with the US' own assessment of its intelligence capabilities and weaknesses'.[92]

Tall, serious and well informed, Aftergood is in neither 'camp', though he leans towards the press in his desire for more disclosure. But he is concerned to be as objective as possible: in an article in the *Harvard Law Review*, he argued that 'to some extent, critics and defenders of Administration openness are talking past each other, and to some extent each side has a case to make'.[93]

Aftergood told me that the question of whether or not it is more difficult to do investigative journalism, as most journalists claim,

> *is itself difficult: there's not one story here. The IC Media Directive doesn't want to sever unofficial contacts between official and journalists: but they only want there to be a formally authorised control. I think this is a mistake because it makes it harder for reporters to get to the truth of any event or project – it can have a chilling effect.*

> *Intelligence agencies have to sharpen their act. The press and the national security establishment have to sharpen their act. Both it and the press have an interest in acquiring and channeling accurate information to the public. They can try to do it through press releases but that's seen as self-serving. The only credible way is to admit to wrong doing when it happens.*
>
> *I think the Insider Threat Program has the potential to be draconian, but it's still being implemented. It's an attempt to establish certain rules. There is a certain point at which it will get too authoritarian – and then people won't take the jobs. At the same time, you have to recognise – the press focuses on the points of friction and that causes some bias in the coverage. And you have to note too: we can see so much more. We can now see Russian bases from satellite pictures: 20 years ago you would have to have been a superpower to do that. The domain of secrecy has become more tightly circumscribed.*

* * *

The CIA has, in the main, staunchly defended its record during the Bush presidency, in the aftermath of 9/11. George Tenet, who had a long, eight-year stint at the top of the agency, skirted the issue of torture and rendition in his memoir, giving few details but assuring his readers that 'CIA officers came up with a series of interrogation techniques that would be carefully monitored at all times to ensure the safety of the prisoner'.[94] He said that 'no objections were raised' by the chairmen and ranking members of the oversight committees; and that 'the most aggressive interrogation techniques conducted by CIA personnel were applied to only a handful of the worst terrorists on the planet'. Abu Zubaydah, captured in Pakistan in 2002, was – contrary to press comment – a highly important member of al Qaeda and, again contrary to the press, gave 'a mother lode of information'. He 'had been at the crossroads of many al-Qaeda operations and was in position to – and did – share critical information with his interrogators'.[95]

A colleague of Tenet's, the man he appointed to head up the counter-terrorism centre, Jose Rodriguez, is much more explicit in his memoir.[96] He described a calibrated series of 'hard measures', from sleep deprivation, enforced nudity, 'dietary manipulation', slapping, being confined in a large box, wall standing (standing 4–5 feet from a wall, with arms extended and fingertips touching the wall); and finally, if all that failed, waterboarding.

The CIA claims only three prisoners were subjected to waterboarding: Abu Zubaydah; Khaled Sheikh Mohammed, the 9/11 mastermind; and Abd al Rahim al Nashiri, thought to be behind the bombing of the USS *Cole* in 2000, in the harbour of Aden, in Yemen. Waterboarding, about which most people learned only in the context of the treatment of US jihadi suspects, dates back, in different forms (but always water poured over the face to give the sensation of drowning) to medieval times and was used in combat training in both the US Navy and Air Force – perhaps giving Americans a false sense of the mildness of the operation.

Rodriguez, too, concentrates on the treatment of Abu Zubaydah, saying that while he was defiant through many of the measures he finally broke, saying that Allah would forgive him for cooperating and that al Qaeda was 'infinitely harsher' on any suspects. He said that 'the information AZ willingly provided us was by any reasonable measure some of the most important intelligence collected since 9/11. Those who say otherwise are simply ill-informed or misleading the public.'[97] Rodriguez had negotiated with Dana Priest on her 2005 story on secret prisons, begging her not to publish what he recognised as a partially accurate and thus dangerous story: she refused.

Rodriguez's memoir is bitter in many respects: he believes that leading members of Congress and the Senate, informed about much of what the agency were doing, lied about being ignorant of the secret prisons and waterboarding. Focusing in particular on Nancy Pelosi, ranking member of the House Intelligence Committee, he wrote that 'years later Pelosi said that we only briefly mentioned waterboarding but had left the impression that it had not been used. That is untrue ... I *know* she got it. There is no doubt in my mind that she, like almost all Americans less than a year after 9/11, wanted us to be aggressive to make sure that al-Qa'ida wasn't able to replicate their attack.'[97]

Michael Hayden, a four-star Air Force general whose successful career was largely spent in military intelligence, was appointed Director of the NSA in 1999, for a year Deputy Director of National Intelligence, then was appointed Director of the CIA in 2006, a post he held until early 2009 when President Obama appointed Leon Panetta as his successor. He published his memoir – '*Playing to the Edge: American Intelligence in the Age of Terror*' – in 2016, and used it both to justify torture (some of which had ended before he took the post), as Tenet and Rodriguez had done before him, but also to make a plea for more openness of the secret services, and appears at least somewhat conflicted about 'Stellarwind', the programme name for bulk collection of data, writing that it 'did indeed raise important questions about the right balance between security and liberty, and Snowden's disclosures no doubt accelerated and intensified that discussion' – close to saying that Snowden's disclosures might have done some good. In general, however, he is dismissive of or angry with investigative journalists, crediting them with – as George Packer writes – 'low motives and unfair agendas.'[98]

The valuable passages in his book, as Packer highlights, are when he writes that 'If we are going to conduct espionage in the future, we are going to have to make some changes in the relationship between the intelligence community and the public it serves ... we also need to explain to those with whom we intend to be more open that with that will come some increased risk. It can be no other way.' His defence of Stellarwind also has sense: referring to criticism from the Congress that the agencies failed to flag up the attacks on the Twin Towers, he says

> *I mention [the criticism] here only to point out that what then followed, NSA's Stellarwind program, was a logical response to an agreed issue and not the product of demented cryptologic minds, as some would later suggest ... far easier to criticize intelligence agencies for not doing enough when [political elites] feel in danger, while reserving the right to criticize those agencies for doing too much when they feel safe.*[99]

That can be reasonable criticism: but it can also be quite reasonable on the part of politicians to be critical of laxity in intelligence, then to criticise over-zealous response from the agencies. Both critiques can be right.

The stream of critical books has been journalistic, in the main: the book format allows the journalist to expand, free from the stricter constraints of a newspaper. Many of the journalists most involved in covering the 'war on terror', tasked with following strands of the story by their news organisation, used their research and contacts to expand their coverage into a narrative. As a generalisation, but not a very inaccurate one, the critical accounts were written by journalists, the defences by the main protagonists: George W. Bush, *Decision Points* (2011); Dick Cheney, *In My Time* (2011, with Elizabeth Cheney); Donald Rumsfeld, *Known and Unknown*, (2011); George Tenet, *At the Center of the Storm* (2007); Condoleezza Rice, *No Higher Honor* (2012). Colin Powell, Secretary of State from 2001 to 2005, published *It Worked for Me* (2012) in which he included a section on the 2003 speech he gave in the UN presenting apparent proofs of Saddam's possession of WMD – proofs which both he and the intelligence services believed to be solid, but which later proved, for the most part, wrong or shaky. Powell strongly criticised Cheney's memoirs for alleging that he had operated against Bush behind his back, and returned the criticism, saying that former Vice President's book was 'full of cheap shots' and that 'Mr. Cheney and many of his colleagues did not prepare for what happened after the fall of Baghdad'.[100]

* * *

The agency now has a sophisticated press service. One of its leading officials, Dean Boyd, even has a background as an investigative reporter, working with the well-known muckraker Jack Anderson, who revealed, among much else, a CIA plot to assassinate Fidel Castro – and who had been the subject of apparently serious conversations within the Nixon White House about the feasibility of murdering him – with the aid of the CIA. Boyd, amiable and balanced, says that a 'healthy tension' exists, and that much of his work is giving context – as on Syria, or Libya, usually on the phone, sometimes in briefings.

> When journalists come on classified information and we believe it might harm national security, we say so. In doing so we realise we need the support of the American people, and that the free press is important. Where it's difficult is where we believe that lives might be endangered – and there can be serious argument on this. There's a great deal of skepticism in the press about such a claim. A typical response: I don't believe you. And I can't be more specific to make the case because that would betray operational details. We do our best to convince them that we're not making this up.
>
> But increasingly journalists who have something and hold back are skewered by their colleagues. I've witnessed that: they get enormous criticism. And yet I know that there are people in the Agency who have been outed and have faced death threats – their houses and their children have been identified and they are threatened.

One of the leaders of the CIA over the past 40 years has been John McLaughlin, a long-time deputy and briefly (July–September 2004) director of the agency. He is now a professor at the School of Advanced International Studies at Johns Hopkins University in Washington, where he teaches a course on intelligence. Tenet thought him 'the smartest man in America';[101] he had been professorial – well informed and reasoned – long before he was a professor. He does, however, despair of the press: among leading papers, he thinks the *Wall Street Journal* and the *Financial Times* are 'OK', but thinks both the *Times* and the *Post* 'are biased against the secret services now'. He says that 'We do need public support: but the approach of the media is to go immediately to the dark corner of the room and to concentrate on that. It means dealing with the press is always tense.'

Still, McLaughlin is, in his academic guise, dabbling a little in journalism: he writes regularly for OZY, an online magazine founded in 2013 by the former political aide and TV presenter Carlos Watson. In March 2016, McLaughlin did a column in the form of question and answer with OZY – the subject being Donald Trump, and what he would advise him on security.[102] McLaughlin maintained a dignified neutrality, slipping only slightly when he said that President Trump would have to tackle the issue of IS's safe haven, allowing them to plan and launch attacks. He continued, with a veiled inference that the Republican candidate might be merely grand-standing: 'I don't know whether Trump really meant it when he said we should just let the Islamic State take out the Assad regime, but you would have to caution him that this would enlarge their safe haven.'

Asked about likely advice on immigration, he said that 'you would probably have the unpleasant job of reporting Mexico's refusal to pay for that wall he pledges to build. Maybe he has some secret plan to get them to pay. But I remember Nixon saying in the 1968 campaign that he had a secret plan to end the Vietnam War. Voters bought it. The war ended in 1975.' He concluded:

> to run for president requires a great deal of hubris or confidence from anyone, and almost inevitably, even when they know in their hearts and minds that these are tough, complicated problems, they find out it's harder than it seemed from a distance. I've seen it in administration after administration: They come to office and think the previous guys didn't know what they were doing. And actually, they discover that these are difficult problems.

In a conversation, McLaughlin outlined his largely critical view of the news media. He's exercised, particularly, by the excuses the media give themselves when asked not to publish, or blamed for doing so:

> The excuse the media give – why be so worried about disclosure because the terrorists know what you're doing and are already taking protective measures? It's self-serving. Yes, the terrorists are not stupid. They of course try to protect themselves. But if you are a little bit ahead and they don't know it than you have an edge. If that edge is blown then it's easier for them.

McLaughlin said that the intelligence services have a basic dilemma, which should be at least recognised.

> The dilemma felt acutely in intelligence is that you want the world to know you're doing a job to protect citizens, and want them to be able to judge what you do to prove that. That's on the one hand. On the other – you can't tell them much. You can only tell them enough to underpin the rightness of the task [emphasis added]. Journalists are sceptical of the claim that their story will cause the death of an agent or source, or the need for them to be lifted out.
>
> I've said it at times. And it's true that at times you get something from a source who would be one of a very few people who knew – and so s/he would be under suspicion. But it's fair enough for the reporter to press on this.
>
> So how do secrecy and democracy coexist? There are a number of aspects of the intelligence services that make it difficult for them to integrate into a free society. First, a free society is based on an open and free exchange of information so that citizens are well-informed – because they make the decisions in a democracy. But intelligence tends to husband information and restrict secret information, by necessity, with classification, compartmentation and such. A free society is based on law. US intelligence services follow the law but do things overseas that are sanctioned under US law but that host countries would find illegal. You can't do them in the US. If the FBI enters a suspect's house clandestinely it needs a warrant. And within their own organisations – agents have no real privacy. You can be investigated any time – you are certainly investigated every five–six years and your finances checked.

McLaughlin believes that the US is by a long way the most transparent in the world about its intelligence agencies and their activities. Although he is proud of the oversight and the openness, he said, almost in a throwaway comment, that 'our world is more dangerous now – and we show all our cards'. In a piece for *Foreign Policy* magazine soon after the Snowden revelations, McLaughlin wrote that

> *any adversary studying the frequent open congressional testimonies by intelligence officials, our daily press stories, our declassified intelligence publications, and our endless stream of leaks, would have to be hopelessly dim to not understand our priorities and deduce many of our methods. For example, the annual threat assessment that the director of national intelligence must present publicly to Congress – I have presented it myself – is a serious and detailed document that gives away no actual secrets but is certainly a reliable guide to our intelligence priorities and the main lines of our analytic thinking, as are annual unclassified reports to Congress on subjects like the foreign ballistic missile threat. Foreign intelligence officials, who do not have such requirements, endlessly ask me: Why, in heavens name, do you Americans do this?*[103]

He wrote that the US was a young intelligence nation, and contrasted it with older states

> *the French had had a 'cabinet noir' as far back as the 16th century – an organization within the post office tasked by the king specifically with reading other people's mail. The Chinese have thought systematically about intelligence since strategist Sun Tzu's historic writing in the 6th century BC; the British had an organized spy service under Elizabeth I in the 16th century; the Russians have embraced the profession for centuries, as have most of our European partners. But it was not until 1947 that intelligence really entered the U.S. national conversation with the creation of the Central Intelligence Agency.*

These older 'intelligence nations' have been able to enfold the services more comfortably into their societies. They present less of a constant challenge, and are less pursued by the press.

He does not believe relations will improve. He thinks we citizens 'don't have much privacy anyway' – and that will become much more the case when 'the Internet of Things' – machines of all kinds linked to and controlled by computers and mobile phones, generating huge amounts more data on movements, tastes and habits of almost everyone – further decreases what we have.

He ended the conversation on a slightly despairing note. 'If something is revealed that shouldn't be, things have to be changed and reconfigured, people moved, contacts lost, we can find other ways of doing something. But it will be always tougher and more expensive. We have to ask the question of the media – How hard do you want my job to be?'

* * *

Many US journalists who cover foreign affairs, the security services, defence and national politics would respond to McLaughlin's last question by saying 'harder'. The coverage of the preparations for war on Iraq and the statements and briefings of the administration and the CIA, to the effect that WMD existed in Iraq in large quantities, are seen as a grievous fault on the part of much journalism. At least as much of the blame, however, is laid at the door of the main protagonists in government – President George W. Bush, Vice President Dick Cheney and Defense Secretary Donald Rumsfeld, as well as the agencies. The evidence which has been uncovered since 9/11 of arbitrary arrests, torture and official obfuscation and worse, underscores in many journalists' minds (and not, of course, only journalists' minds), the need for much more gritty investigation now, both of the past decade and a half and of the current policies and actions – such as the use of drones.

This book's conclusion suggests ways in which a better relationship might exist between the intelligence agencies and the news media. Yet the US media (and others) have further questions to consider. The criticism and self-criticism, in its seriousness and depth, has been impressive and unprecedented: in no other journalistic culture has there been such an extensive and an unforced critical reflection on the defects of coverage.

But that criticism, sharply put by John Walcott at McClatchy, by the *New York Times* of itself, and by Michael Massing in the *New York Review of Books* of (mainly) the *Times*, still has some difficult aspects not solved by the implicit injunction to speak to more, and more diverse, sources. First, how do reporters deal with reporting a consensus within the US agencies, which was replicated in all other major intelligence services, that a certain state of affairs exists: in this case, possession by the Iraqi regime of WMD? Both the reporting of the Knight Ridder/McClatchy journalists and some of that of Walter Pincus in the *Washington Post* were based in substantial part on hunches. These were that the dissidents within the CIA and other agencies, who pointed to a lack of hard evidence of WMD and thus underscored doubts about the reasons for an invasion, could be right while the majority was wrong or – as has been frequently alleged – pressured into acquiescence to the line being peddled energetically by Bush, Cheney and Rumsfeld. McClatchy reporters will themselves say that they worried that the direction they took would turn out to be wrong: as Warren Strobel said, 'no-one knew for sure'. Journalistic insight – 'it doesn't smell right' – is a valuable commodity, even in an age of data journalism: but for most experienced reporters, that Saddam had WMD *did* smell right, even as they (most of them) were not fans of the Bush White House.

Intelligence is rarely decisive. To take a successful example: the attack, in May 2011, on the compound in Pakistan where Osama bin Laden was hidden was undertaken without certainty that this was where bin Laden lived, or was then present. The evidence was circumstantial – as it was of the Iraqi WMD. Had he not been there, an attack would have been mounted which killed a number of people to no purpose, on information which had seemed to point in one obvious direction, but had not. Intelligence, especially that gathered on a target who is well-versed in the likely surveillance deployed against him, will nearly always be fragmentary, depending in the end on inference. Journalists, at least one remove from the intelligence, cannot interpret any better than the intelligence analysts – though they may get luckier in their judgements.

The largest lesson from the reporting in the aftermath of 9/11 and of Iraqi WMD is not so much the need for scepticism – it does not appear to have suffered long-term damage – as the desirability for more focus on plans for intervention themselves, including the long-term preparations for the effects of regime change – if that is the outcome. The Iraqi debacle convinced President Obama that intervention through 'boots on the ground' would not be again attempted: Syria, and to a lesser extent Libya, underscore the cost of not intervening. It is this issue, one of the largest facing the world's major states, both democratic and authoritarian, which defines a large area of foreign relations and policy, and thus of engaged journalism.

* * *

Intervention remained at the core of Western governments' debates after the failure to step in and prevent the genocide in Rwanda from April to July 1994 and the slow response to the massacres in Kosovo and Bosnia after the disintegration of Yugoslavia, mainly ordered or assented to by Serbian President Slobodan Milosevic. The 'Blair Doctrine' was influential then: it derived from the UK prime minister Tony Blair's speech in Chicago in 1999 calling for military intervention where a state was engaged in massive oppression of its own people, and by its actions promoting a humanitarian catastrophe in the state and increasing flows of refugees. Where that happened, he said,

> the principle of non-interference must be qualified in important respects. Acts of genocide can never be a purely internal matter. When oppression produces massive flows of refugees which unsettle neighbouring countries, then they can properly be described as 'threats to international peace and security'. When regimes are based on minority rule they lose legitimacy – look at South Africa[104]

Powerful advocates like Samantha Power[105] influenced the policy mindsets of politicians and leaders, arguing passionately against 'America's toleration of unspeakable authorities, often committed in clear view'.

The case for intervention suffered – for some, finally – on the killing deserts of Iraq: Power herself, taken into the Obama administration and made UN Ambassador in 2012, was constrained to serve as best she could a president whose opposition to the Iraq invasion developed into a strong disinclination to intervene other than with air attacks (planes or drones). Evan Osnos, in an extended portrait of Power in her UN ambassadorial role, concluded that she is confined to pushing for policies – such as intervention in Syria – from which Obama recoils:

> After nearly six years, Power still believes that America retains the capacity for brute or moral force to shape the course of global events – to bend the curve – but Obama, by his own account, does not. To some degree, there has always been a contradiction between the Administration's determination to retrench from the costly adventures in Iraq and Afghanistan and the expectation of restoring American credibility through moral leadership and actions.[106]

Some of that recoil is based on the experience of faulty intelligence guiding the reasons for intervention. It is clear that the Bush presidency, especially Vice President Dick Cheney and Defense Secretary Donald Rumsfeld, though they did not order the intelligence to be falsified, did shape the intelligence as far as possible in the image of their determination to attack

Saddam Hussein's Iraq. It is also clear that the burden of intelligence pointed to Saddam's retention of WMD. Intervention must have the best possible intelligence, and in the Iraq case, McLaughlin stressed to me, 'they just got it wrong'. In that judgement, McLaughlin repeated more succinctly the conclusion of the bipartisan commission which, in 2005, reported on the 'Intelligence Capabilities of the United States regarding Weapons of Mass Destruction'. It concluded that

> the Intelligence Community was dead wrong in almost all of its pre-war judgments about Iraq's weapons of mass destruction. This was a major intelligence failure. Its principal causes were the Intelligence Community's inability to collect good information about Iraq's WMD programs, serious errors in analysing what information it could gather, and a failure to make clear just how much of its analysis was based on assumptions, rather than good evidence. On a matter of this importance, we simply cannot afford failures of this magnitude'.[107]

The Commission, however, found no indication 'that the Intelligence Community distorted the evidence regarding Iraq's weapons of mass destruction. What the intelligence professionals told you about Saddam Hussein's programs was what they believed. They were simply wrong.' The same conclusions were reached by the UK's 'Review of Intelligence on Weapons of Mass Destruction' of 2004, chaired by the former Cabinet Secretary Robin Butler, which recommended, as the US Commission report was to do, the need for the services to more carefully underscore how far intelligence was doubtful or weakly sourced.[108]

A suspicion remains that both the Bush and the Blair governments pressured the agencies into producing, not so much dispassionate intelligence, but rationales for their determination to invade. Some assert that both president and prime minister lied. Those who believe so were heartened by the publication, in July 2016, of the Chilcot Inquiry report, which criticised Prime Minister Blair, with President George W. Bush, stating that he had 'used flawed intelligence to justify the invasion, that Iraq posed no immediate national security threat, that the allies acted militarily before all diplomatic options had been exhausted'.[109] Those who believed he lied, however, were disappointed that Chilcot found no evidence that he had: he thought that the secret service advice, that Saddam had weapons of mass destruction, was correct.

* * *

How could the US agencies open up more?

The size and complexity of the US security agencies put them in a different league from all other agencies in the Western hemisphere. I have noted before that the culture of the US is more open to journalistic inquiry and investigation than most others, and thus recommendations for briefings and press conferences, which are good ideas for the British and the French, are less relevant here.

But the scale of the secret state demands that more be done. The work of Dana Priest and William Arkin at the *Washington Post* on 'Top Secret America', highlighted above, is said by them to be 'an alternative geography of the United States ... so massive that its effectiveness is impossible to determine'. If this is even partly true, the hundreds of thousands of security-cleared workers, the proliferation of private contractors (1,931 when they wrote in 2010) and government agencies concerned with security and counter-terrorism (1,271) represent an archipelago mostly beyond the ken of those who pay for it through their taxes.[110]

That Priest and Arkin, without security clearance, could by diligent reporting find out so much speaks very well for the journalistic trade. But there are limits to reporting. The federal government should itself provide information on what the roles are of these agencies and corporations; what their effectiveness is; what have been the successes and failures – the areas where real progress has been made and those where the situation is worsening, in spite of efforts to contain or improve. This should be presented in an accessible fashion, for the widest possible readership and greatest comprehension.

When, in January 1961, President Eisenhower gave a valedictory speech at the end of his presidency (1953–61), he famously warned of possible tyranny. This might, he believed, come from the influence of an 'immense military establishment ... economic, political, even spiritual' which was everywhere evident. Thus

> we must guard against the acquisition of unwarranted influence, whether sought or unsought, by the military–industrial complex ... we must never let the weight of this combination endanger our liberties or democratic processes ... Only an alert and knowledgeable citizenry can compel the proper meshing of the huge industrial and military machinery of defense with our peaceful methods and goals so that security and liberty may prosper together.[111]

Now, the fear of a 'security industrial complex' has taken the place – or been added to – that of the US military. David Rohde, Reuters's national security investigations correspondent, believes that

> *An odd thing is happening in the world's self-declared pinnacle of democracy. No one – except a handful of elected officials and an army of contractors – is allowed to know how America's surveillance leviathan works … From drone strikes to eavesdropping to torture, the American public is not allowed to know the rules and results of U.S. counterterrorism policies.*
>
> *At the same time, a sprawling secrecy industrial complex does. More than 4.9 million Americans now have government security clearances. Another 1.4 million have 'top secret' clearance.*[112]

The combination of 'ballooning' scale and the accompanying urge to classify very widely is inhibiting discussion about one of the central areas of US policy. In this case, what is required is both a readily available and comprehensible map/explanation of the security complex, together with the same on the oversight and control mechanisms for the 'complex'. This will allow for an informed debate not just among specialists – including specialist security journalists – but much more broadly among the interested public.

Western leaders, heads of security agencies and security experts have warned that the terrorist challenge is increasing: President François Hollande declared, after the Paris attacks of November 2015, that 'we are at war'; President Obama told the summit on nuclear security in Washington in April 2016 that

> *the threat of nuclear terrorism persists and continues to evolve … we know that al Qaida has long sought nuclear materials. Individuals involved in the attacks in Paris and Brussels videotaped a senior manager who works at a Belgian nuclear facility. ISIL has already used chemical weapons, including mustard gas, in Syria and Iraq. There is no doubt that if these madmen ever got their hands on a nuclear bomb or nuclear material they most certainly would use it to kill as many innocent people as possible.*[113]

Bruce Hoffman, director of Georgetown University's Center for Security Studies, has written that a merger between al Qaeda and IS is now increasingly likely,[114] one that would greatly increase the likelihood of WMD-backed attacks.

These are frightening statements: some commentators see them as irresponsible scaremongering. Simon Jenkins, writing in the *Spectator*, called then prime minister David Cameron a 'useful idiot' (useful to terrorists) for saying that 'London is under real threat … from appalling terrorists' and that an attack on the city was 'highly likely'.[115] Idiotic or not, the conviction that terrorist groups are now able to inflict very great damage on Western cities and intend to do so is now a proclaimed belief among Western leaderships and the intelligence services.

It is important that the US government, rightly proud of a better record for openness towards the news media than other democratic states, gives further examples of openness at a time when fear and rapid expansion of security are both growing. The combination of dread of attacks with worries about surveillance may be a toxic one: people need to be able to learn more about both, to make their own judgements about the proportionality, or lack of it, of the state response to terror.

There is a need for a mechanism such as the US Foreign Intelligence Surveillance (FISA) court, which heard applications for surveillance warrants of foreign persons suspected of spying: these hearings are held with only the judge and the government or intelligence official applying for the warrant present. However, the FISA court was the mechanism through which the extension of surveillance to US citizens was passed, and which required the US phone company Verizon to pass all metadata on domestic as well as international calls to the NSA – without the public being aware. Another mediating mechanism is called for, one that mediates between the state, both the administration and the secret state, and the public, and which is tasked with explaining the security-industrial complex to its paymasters. This institution must have the capacity to interrogate those in charge of the complex on the need for secrecy and on the mechanisms developed for bulk collection and examination of communications.

The US is where the most important communications corporations reside – those which have, again very rapidly, revolutionised the nature of communications – and beyond, of work, social interaction, learning, leisure and consumer behaviour. Since the Snowden leaks, the leading tech companies, led by Apple, have strengthened the encryption on their communications products in order to reassure their customers that they can count on privacy. But that has, for the security agencies, a high cost: they often cannot access these communications.

In a speech to Brookings Institution in October 2014, the FBI director James Comey said that the encryption developed for Apple's new operating system, and for Google's Android operating system, will be so strong that encryption threatens to lead all of us to a very dark place:

> the companies themselves won't be able to unlock phones, laptops, and tablets to reveal photos, documents, e-mail, and recordings stored within ... encryption isn't just a technical feature; it's a marketing pitch. But it will have very serious consequences for law enforcement and national security agencies at all levels. Sophisticated criminals will come to count on these means of evading detection. It's the equivalent of a closet that can't be opened. A safe that can't be cracked.[116]

On the technology industry side, Tim Cook, the Apple CEO, has been categorical: in a letter to customers, he wrote that 'I want to be absolutely clear that we have never worked with any government agency from any country to create a backdoor in any of our products or services. We have also never allowed access to our servers. And we never will.'[117] In February 2016, he strongly opposed a Federal judge's order to provide access to an iPhone owned by one of the two killers of 14 people in San Bernardino, California, in December 2015. While the government was trying to enforce the order, a route to unlocking the phone was found, and it withdrew the case. The past practice in such cases has been for the government to alert the company to a weakness in its software: it is thought unlikely to do so in this case.[118] In February 2016, a New York judge denied a government request that Apple hand over data from an iPhone in a drug case, a decision which was seen as a pointer to the San Bernardino issue, and as a reversal of earlier court decisions finding for the government against Apple when data was demanded from the company. Saritha Komatireddy, a Brooklyn Federal prosecutor, said the government's application in this case 'was just a simple routine request for assistance in carrying out a valid search warrant issued by a federal court, as Apple has done so many times before.'[119]

The standoff between government and technology companies is ultimately good for neither, and bad for the public – who are being appealed to by Apple and the other corporations on grounds that they are protecting their privacy, and by the administration on the grounds that they are protecting their security. In a speech at MIT in March 2016, the director of the UK's GCHQ, Robert Hannigan, appealed for 'goodwill on all sides', but placed the onus on the companies to cooperate with whatever decisions 'the democratic process decides – in the area of encryption that must mean some very practical cooperation with the industry – there is no other way to do it. Whatever high level framework, whatever posture democratic nations decide upon will need to be implemented by those commercial providers.' This standoff between corporation and the government must be resolved, and must be resolved with a decision, preferably based on a compromise, which government feels answers the needs of security and law enforcement. Apple is routinely described as the most powerful technology company in the world: it cannot be allowed to determine the way in which the law is administered, or the dystopian vision in Dave Eggers' novel *The Circle* (see Chapter 3) begins to be realised.[120]

3

Down with the State and its Servile Hacks!

We don't understand ourselves as living in Germany, we understand ourselves as living on the internet.
(Andy Mueller Maguhn, a member of the German hacker collective Chaos Computer Club)[1]

The internet has spurred the growth of communities of believers. These communities believe the new technology allows – commands – radically new forms of political and social relationships and that it must be protected as an inviolable space. Some also believe that it can and must be used as a means of shining a harsh light on pre-internet customs and practices, which include governments' secrets. The position of most of these communities is one of deep suspicion of the state, borrowing promiscuously from the new left, anarchists and the libertarian right.

They assume that state institutions – constitutional, democratic and organisational – no longer express real choice in the election of representatives nor provide services efficiently and swiftly. These views, in the US, fit well into existing anti-state reflexes, and are held widely far beyond the communities of those who are immersed in the internet. The burgeoning digital and communications corporations and their agglomerations of highly educated engineers and analysts have as their business model to disrupt established ways, and to create new products and services which in turn create new markets. The rapidity with which new applications are developed and marketed outflanks governments' and civil societies' ability to enfold them into established ways of working, and leave large numbers – the majority – fumbling to understand the new systems. Any state will appear flat-footed when confronted with such a challenge: and as the new devices and systems gain larger markets, so the state loses, and the corporations gain, power.

Where mainstream politics and society see Julian Assange of Wikileaks, Edward Snowden, who leaked the NSA files, Glen Greenwald,

Snowden's most active publisher and others, as alarming people who may present a danger to them, the technology chiefs see them as possible sources of ideas. In June 2011, Eric Schmidt, CEO of Google and Jared Cohen, head of Google Ideas, met Julian Assange for five hours at the country house in Norfolk owned by his friend, Vaughan Savage, a former army officer and founder of the journalists' Frontline club in London. Pierre Omidyar, who founded and owns eBay, created The Intercept investigative news site for Glen Greenwald in 2014. In February 2016, the Apple CEO Tim Cook began a fight with the US administration over the FBI's request that he allow them access to the encrypted phones of the couple in San Bernardino who killed 14 of their co-workers at a health centre in December 2015: Cook has seized the high ground, arguing that Apple cares more for public privacy than the government. Privacy is at the heart of the anti-state argument, hugely augmented by Snowden's revelations which furthered the view that, when you use a mobile phone, you potentially have none.

* * *

The internet has changed and is changing the ways in which we live our lives. The corporations and individuals who are using it to wrench the universe into new shapes are the communications and software companies created in the last three decades in the United States, mainly in California's Silicon Valley, south of San Francisco. It is in the United States that most of the technical breakthroughs were, and are still being, made; where these breakthroughs were, and are still being, turned into enterprises; where the enterprises grew and are still growing until, in the second decade of the twenty-first century, they are among the wealthiest and most dynamic companies in the world. It is in the US where the most concentrated thinking is done as to how these innovations fit into the societies of the world. Naturally, that is aimed at increasing the power and wealth of the corporations developing them; they also revolutionise the societies and the polities of the states which adopt them.

The Americans lead, and they know it: some rub it in. James Woolsey, a former director of the CIA, reacted to complaints from the European Union that the CIA was spying on European companies by writing in the *Wall Street Journal*:

> my continental friends, we have spied on you because you bribe. Your companies' products are often more costly, less technically advanced or

both, than your American competitors'. As a result you bribe a lot … in spite of a few recent reforms, your governments largely still dominate your economies, so you have much greater difficulty than we in innovating, encouraging labor mobility, reducing costs, attracting capital to fast-moving young businesses and adapting quickly to changing economic circumstances.[2]

Others were less blunt: but Wolsey spoke to the view, held by the entrepreneurs and investors who have powered the massive growth of the Silicon Valley intelligence-industrial complex, that the state must remove itself as far as possible, and allow these companies to remould the world. Many European entrepreneurs think the same.

Innovations continue to come from the US and depend on the ubiquity of the internet. The spread of the Uber cab franchise, where people use their own cars to act as cabs, responding to calls or text messages from would-be customers – running in over 300 cities, with 1.2 million drivers worldwide in the mid-2010s – would be impossible without a series of internet relationships: in December 2015, the company announced[3] a deal with Facebook which allows Facebook Messenger users to order an Uber cab while using the chat app. The internet carries the links between the Uber organisation and the drivers, between the customers and the drivers and in the drivers' dependence on satellite navigation to find a route. So, too, with Airbnb, the service which allows householders to turn their homes into hotels, renting rooms to visitors for long or short stays: everything depends on contacts and verifications on the internet.

In both of these innovations, which express the essence of a general approach, the central idea of the service is to turn the individual into an independent marketer of their own space and time – and so gain both more time, free space and income. David Plouffe, the former Obama campaign manager and from May 2015 senior vice president for policy and strategy at Uber, presents the company as a friend of low-income people, allowing the drivers to make extra money at times of their choosing, and allowing customers to take cabs where the price was once prohibitive, thus giving more time for work, personal development or child care.[4] Plouffe is one of many Valley missionaries sent out into the world to convert the masses to faith in the great disruption.

Journalism's internet revolution, as presented by its radicals and their signature actions – Julian Assange's Wikileaks and Edward Snowden and Glen Greenwald's leaks and use of the NSA files – expresses the same, central idea. The journalism of the revolution is a matter of individual action, having a relationship with established corporations which should be in the nature of temporary and suspicious alliances, and a completely distrustful attitude to government and the state. The proclaimed civic duty of the pre-internet press – to act as a sceptical observer and chronicler of power, especially state power, and in doing so to hold these powers to account – is pushed beyond scepticism to aggressive challenge. Assange believes that the state must be disrupted and rendered ineffective through massive and continuous disclosure of its anti-people workings; Snowden and Greenwald believe that the NSA revelations have shown that the state has so routinely and brazenly lied to its citizens, and so obviously seeks to control them through massive and increasingly intimate surveillance, that it deserves only contemptuous disclosure of its egregious activities.

Though they present themselves as outsiders to their societies, they are wholly in tune with, and leaders of, the times, the technology and the spirit which they have helped produce: a spirit of rejection, or at least disruption through acts of forced transparency, of the state. In an interview which is in Chapter 5 of this book, Pierre Brochand, the former head of the French external intelligence service, the DGSE, says that the secret services are the last resource of the state – most others having been whittled down, or privatised. In the past decade, that last resource, has come under sustained attack as an illegitimate actor.

These attitudes come at a time when the corporate centres of the mainstream news media are clearly weakened: many employed in, or observers of, the mainstream media believe it is in a lose–lose situation. A landmark in such opinions was an essay by the sociologist Paul Starr – whose book[5] on US journalism's beginnings and development is at once a history and an affirmation of press freedom in the US. Starr wrote[6] in 2009 that

> whether the Internet will ever support general-interest journalism at a level comparable to newspapers, it would be foolish to predict. The reality is that resources for journalism are now disappearing from the old media faster than new media can develop them. The financial crisis of the press may thereby compound the media's crisis of legitimacy. Already under ferocious attack from both left and right for a multitude of sins, real and imagined, the press is going to find its job even more difficult to do under economic duress. And as it retrenches in the face of financial pressures, [Tom] Rosenstiel [director of the American Press Institute] says, 'More of American life will occur in shadows. We won't know what we don't know'.

Both Starr and Rosenstiel have so far been proven too pessimistic. The mid-2010s internet provides huge amounts of information and opinion; supports (though it may be like the rope of the hanging man) the mainstream press by allowing it to display and augment its wares on the internet, even if at a loss; and is developing new forms of individualistic journalism, more often addressing niche audiences than attempting to aggregate groups into a large readership, as the mainstream press has done for two centuries. Many newspapers, great and small, have shrunk or gone out of business, while others – the *Guardian*, *Le Monde*, or the *Washington Post* – make a large loss[7] and (in the case of the last two) are sustained by wealthy individuals. But that is compensated, for the audiences, by internet journalism having given birth to a vast panorama of journalistic sites – and offering, especially to an Anglophone, a menu of choice of reading and viewing far larger and deeper than anything they will have experienced before the 1990s. More – and beyond the scope of this book – the fact that journalism is now increasingly deployed on the internet breaks down the barriers between the information and opinions it provides and that is available on millions of other sites, from those of lonely bloggers to large institutions, now increasingly developing 'news centres' of their own. To go onto the internet to learn anything is a wholly different experience from reading a newspaper or magazine. It is to experience dizzying choice, a warehouse of information, opinion and sensation compared to what was offered in pre-internet times: a small, neatly packaged box.

The internet is a carrier of journalism, and a supplier of boundless contexts to its narratives. A reporter's story can be complemented by an analysis from a think tank, a scholarly paper, a choice of blogs which may, on occasion, be informative, and background information from government departments and other public authorities. Reading journalism is now active rather than passive, itself an effect of the internet. The journalist Nick Lemann remembered that 'my grandfather, who was a pediatrician in the town of Perth Amboy [New Jersey] would sit in his easy chair on Sundays reading the [*New York*] *Times* in a spirit not dissimilar to that of someone taking the sacrament. After finishing one article, he'd begin the next – who was he to decide what, of the material the *Times*' editors had chosen to publish, he had the right to skip?'[8] Now, the attitude of a reader, especially one on the right of politics, would more likely be: what is the *New York Times* to tell me what to think? Or, is this story or opinion of the *Times* right, or valid? I will check it against other sources and views.

Many believe that one of the biggest losers has been investigative journalism, deprived of the greater resources of workaday journalism which it needs to dig deep and range widely. The point was made strongly by Luigi Zingales, the Robert C. McCormack Distinguished Service Professor of Entrepreneurship and Finance at the University of Chicago in his Wincott Lecture in London in November 2015. Professor Zingales argued that investigative journalism, though precious, appealed only to a minority, did not make money for news organisations and thus, in hard times, was cut. As he put it: 'Before the Internet revolution, newspapers were very profitable and some of them were willing to fund costly investigative reporting and weather any possible retaliation by advertisers. Not any more. Plummeting advertising revenues, disappearing classified ads and dwindling subscriptions have all but hollowed out newsrooms and their investigative reporting teams.'[9]

This reflects a common misconception. Though investigations have been cut in some newspapers (most did not do much), investigative journalism has increased – as other newspapers, broadcast channels and magazines have invested in longer-form journalism and investigative websites spring up both in countries which have had the tradition for decades, and those which have not. Among many others, these include the US Pro Pubblica and The Intercept, the French Mediapart, the Indian Centre for Investigative Journalism, the German CORRECT!V, the Italian Investigative Reporting Project Italy, the British Bureau of Investigative Journalism and the global Consortium of Investigative Journalists, most supported by individuals or foundations. Mediapart even makes a profit. The investigative centre, the International Consortium of Investigative Journalists based in New York, was responsible in the spring of 2016 for the largest revelation of wealth tucked away, both legitimately and illegitimately, in tax-sheltering jurisdictions. The Panama Papers was the work of the centre using journalists across the world, able to keep the work secret for months while a leak of 11.5m documents from the Panamanian law firm Mossack Fonseca was worked through to produce an unparalleled insight into organised greed – this at a time of growing disillusion with societies which permitted huge disparities of wealth and in many cases high unemployment, especially among the young.

One of the by-products of the decline of revenues from newsprint journalism has been the willingness of both individuals and foundations to fill the funding gap – an index of the importance which inquiring journalism is granted. The Intercept, funded by the billionaire Pierre

Omidyar (his fortune made entirely on the internet, with such innovations as eBay, which he created, and PayPal, which he bought, developed and sold), is largely a vehicle for Glen Greenwald and for the publication of further NSA revelations: Pro Pubblica assisted in the publication of the NSA files; the UK's Bureau of Investigative Journalism has published many reports on the use and effect of drone warfare by the Obama administration. All see in Wikileaks and the leaked NSA files a model to at least partially follow, and some – together with many mainstream news organisations – have created safe 'drop boxes' for leaks, with varying results but with a common purpose; that is to further, even if less full-throatedly, that approach to journalism and power pioneered by Assange, Snowden and Greenwald.

The digitalisation of journalism is less important for the decline of what is on offer – there is no overall decline, though there are important niche declines – than for the shift in the relationship between news media, especially newspapers and news magazines, and the state. Both authoritarian and democratic states have needed the news media – the first, to carry the approved opinions and the news that is deemed fit to publish; the second, to act as a pillar for democracy itself.[10] Journalism, even if at times inconvenient and often detested, is too prestigious in democracies to be seriously curbed. Newspapers needed the state – at a local or national level – since they received so much from them in terms of advertising support and information, as well as the services the modern state provides all businesses. Government and the political parties which formed governments needed news organisations for the publicity they gave – even if sometimes bad – and thus appealed to the owners and editors to support them, or at least report them fairly.

This means a vast web of overt and unspoken links, expectations and exchanges of favours. News organisations on the one hand and political parties and administrations on the other, have relationships which can be frankly collusive – especially at local levels, where the newspaper or local TV or radio channel is enfolded into the community and thus finds it hard or simply undesirable to break the skein of mutually supportive links. Or it can be formally independent, where the policy of the paper may be opposed to the government or to one or more of the political parties, but in the end needs access and is constrained to report more or less accurately on the content of policies and programmes, even where in commentary they are criticised. Where this does not happen – the first Obama administration, in its early period, was so stung by the right-wing partisanship of Fox News that it denounced the coverage and said it would counter everything it considered a slur[11] – a brief battle ensues, which the news media usually win, since battling with the government increasingly gives them kudos in the eyes of much of its audience, while the government is open to the accusation of wasting time on trivia. And in the end, the government, and other centres of power, will usually continue to try to influence hostile media to be less hostile.

Internet journalism, most of it with low fixed costs and attracting audiences more with opinion, polemic and revelation than with hard news, needs a collusive relationship with the state much less. It often prefers a hostile attitude: in an age of increased polarisation of political parties and movements in the many democratic states and hostility to politicians, audiences on both the right and left are attracted by denunciation, revelation and mockery of that part of politics they do not like, or of all of it. The relationship Assange, Snowden, Greenwald and others do need – though the need is diminishing – is with the mainstream news media. If newspapers and news outlets had not picked up on the leaks which they organised, they would not have had the effect they did. Papers like the *Guardian*, *Der Spiegel* and above all the *New York Times* command attention because they have for decades dug deep into the societies in which they were created, and in different degrees gone beyond them. That advantage is eroding, though slowly. Even now, those who command troves of secret documents can put them on the internet themselves: a powerful weapon to hold over the head of an editor doubtful about publication. Once 'out there', it will attract other websites and mainstream publications. The loss will be news organisations with the experience, authority in society and a status earned over many years as mainstream publishers. But web organisations, such as the Huffington Post, Vice, Slate, and BuzzFeed, are now carving into the mainstream readerships and proving themselves adept at finding high-profile stories.

A significant part of the audiences for political internet journalism enjoy explanations for governments' actions which are conspiratorial. Devin Nunes, a Californian Republican congressman who is also chairman of the House Intelligence Committee, said politics in the past decade has been radically changed by the rise of online media outlets and for-profit groups which put out false and conspiracy theory-based material to which members of Congress feel constrained to respond.[12]

I used to spend ninety percent of my constituent response time on people who call, e-mail, or send a letter, such as, 'I really like this bill' … and they really believe in it because they heard about it through one of the groups that they belong to, but their view was based on actual legislation. Ten percent were about 'Chemtrails from airplanes are poisoning me' to every other conspiracy theory that's out there. And that has essentially flipped on its head ... [now, only a small proportion] is based on something that is mostly true. It's dramatically changed politics and politicians, and what they're doing.

Conspiracies have, for a considerable part of the politically engaged, replaced discussion of the more formal issues of politics. It also shows that the internet's promiscuous display of conventional journalism, left and right radical investigations, leaks and commentaries, conspiracy theories presented often forcefully and with apparently credible evidential bases, all merge into each other and for many appear to form a view of the political process as a series of moves by a self-interested political oligarchy conspiring against the truth and the citizenry.

As the internet is deconstructing journalism, so it is revolutionising spying – the trade which has been, for the news media, the large black hole at the centre of state power, illuminated first of all by myth, fiction and official releases, later and into our own times by a more determined effort to come to grips with its activities while at the same time (mostly) observing its need to keep a large part of the black hole black. The internet revolution has been, for the agencies, a net benefit, especially for those which, like the US National Security Agency and the UK's GCHQ, have seen their position in the ranks of the intelligence services take the first place, in importance and often in budget.

These and other centres whose business is signals intelligence can now locate people precisely in real time and in the past, through the signals given by the communications they carry – a lap top computer, iPad or most commonly a mobile phone, which can throw off showers of information even when not in use. Savvy terrorists or criminals use either prepaid mobile phones which do not identify the carrier or carry no phone at all: but significant numbers do, or forget for a fatal moment, to observe digital silence.

Emails, wireless calls, texts, Skype calls and social networking records

are treasure troves of information for investigatory agencies. In the bygone era of face-to-face communications, no trace was usually left regarding whom a suspect had talked with. Today, by contrast, an individual would

need to abstain from many everyday activities to prevent the government
from obtaining information about his or her contacts. The identity of
those contacts helps lead investigators to additional targets of interest,
thereby painting a broader and more precise picture of potential criminal
or national security activity.[13]

Both location and information on the network of contacts are part of the
agencies' present and growing ability to create ever-more detailed profiles
of people of interest. The agencies' access to the large amounts of data
stored on personal computers, and on the records of ATMs, security
cameras, store purchases, health records and government departments
can yield, in a very short time, a picture of a suspect which would – in
paper-based days – have taken months or years to compile. 'Data mining'
in 'big data' uses enormously powerful computers to search huge slabs
of information for meaningful patterns and thus identify criminal or
terrorist networks, movements of suspects, meetings of suspicious
groups and the planning and timing of terrorist or criminal acts.

There is a downside for the agencies: much of that lies in the fact that
well-organised criminals and terrorist groups take time to learn what the
agencies' systems are, and not just evade them but adapt them to their
own use. As far back as 1994, a Colombian drug cartel based in the city of
Cali was discovered[14] to have constructed a computer centre whose main
technology was an IBM AS400 mainframe computer, programmed to
correlate the office and private numbers of Colombian intelligence and
police officers and US diplomats, with the entire phone call log of the
Cali phone company. Matching the two, they could discover who were
informants and kill them. Since then, according to US Drug Enforcement
Administration officials, technological sophistication has only grown, with
cartels detailing their own members to acquire advanced software skills –
or hiring experts with huge salaries. The case of Anwar al Awlaki shows
the double-sided nature of the internet, as it both furthers, and targets,
terrorist ends. Al Awlaki and his messages lived by the internet, and died
by it: tracked to his parents' native Yemen, he was killed by a drone in
September 2011.

The agencies' battle with terrorism and crime is complex. Their
struggles with the news media are not violent, and for the most part eschew
any criminal charges, but are more politically and socially complex. The very
large expansion of the agencies' powers in most states, and the rash of laws
passed which greatly increase the capacity of the Signals Intelligence (SIGINT)

centres to make bulk collection of all communications, have raised large legal, constitutional and moral issues, now playing out.

For the agencies and for most governments and many members of the public, their increased powers of surveillance are seen to be in the service of democracy's protection. For civil libertarians – among them politicians, NGOs, journalists and commentators, scholars and members of the public – the increased powers are seen as oppressive in themselves, and could signal a descent, under more authoritarian governments, to at least the outline of a police state. The journalist Misha Glenny puts it simply: 'crime detection and civil liberties have always been uneasy bedfellows, but their co-existence has become significantly more troubled since the spread of the Internet'.[15] In a novel based on a plot to turn the UK into one such police state, another British journalist, Henry Porter, poses, in a short essay after its (happy) ending, the question he believes central to UK citizens:

> *are we building the most advanced systems of surveillance ever seen in a free society because deep down we are so sure of our democratic values, our respect for free speech and legality, that we know that whatever happens nothing will change us? Or does our stoicism, our determination to 'keep on keeping on' and not get too worked up about things, amount to a fatal complacency?*[16]

A quite different fictional dystopia from Porter's is Dave Eggers' 'The Circle', a Google-like corporation in which the staff, highly paid and even more highly pampered, are led to believe that they are the true democrats.[17] Their central project is to make the world and all its peoples and activities permanently transparent, constantly searchable. Mae, the wide-eyed small-town heroine who is persuaded to accept the Circle package, comes up, under insistent but of course well-meaning questioning by one of the leaders, with the slogan (an implicit reference to Orwell's 1984 slogans as 'Freedom is Slavery' or 'Ignorance is Truth') that PRIVACY IS A LIE, a moral absolutism on which the corporation bases its fabulously successful business model. The combination of individual betterment, democratic enlightenment and corporate power clothed in semi-mystic empowerment rhetoric catches much of contemporary techno-capitalism's soaring public promise. One of the triumvirate who are the central power of The Circle, Bailey, tells his senior colleagues ('The Forty') that 140 million Americans (of 244 million) voted in the previous election: while The Circle has 241 million Americans registered with it. This, says Bailey, 'tells you that the Circle has a knack for getting people to participate. And there are a lot of people in Washington who agree. There are people in DC who see us as the solution to making this a fully participatory democracy.'[18] The true purpose is revealed – not the betterment of democratic systems but their replacement by The Circle. These are fantasies in a novel: in the real world, Mark Zuckerberg, founder of Facebook, said in 2010 that 'privacy is no longer a social norm'.[19]

These large issues are not new – democratic systems have, since their development, always and everywhere been vulnerable to authoritarian dilution or outright suppression. The most dramatic of the latter of these, in communist Russia, Fascist Italy and Nazi Germany in the 1920s and 1930s, remain a backdrop to European politics – and, as former German chancellor Helmut Schmidt once remarked,[20] the default image of evil is Nazi Germany, even if fading in the minds of successive post-war generations. But the internet creates a new prism through which to judge how far new threats are unfolding – since they are unfolding on and through the internet.

* * *

The internet's origins lie in the US military. In her revealing history of the US Defense Advanced Research Projects Agency (DARPA), the journalist Annie Jacobsen describes how a civilian psychologist named Joseph Licklider came, in 1962, to DARPA – then, as now, the Pentagon's highly inventive research arm – tasked with updating the military's command and control system.[21] Licklider had a markedly benign view of computing: long before personal computers became ubiquitous, Licklider 'envisioned "home computer consoles", with people sitting in front of them, learning just about anything they wanted to. He wrote a book, *Libraries of the Future*, in which he described a world where library resources would be available to remote users through a single database.'

In his biography of Licklider, M. Mitchell Waldrop writes that, while most in the 1960s see computers, large metal boxes monopolised by the military, government and corporations, as sinister, 'he is almost alone in his conviction that computers can become not just superfast calculating machines, but joyful machines: tools that will serve as new media of expression, inspirations to creativity, and gateways to a vast world of online information'.[22] He sent out a memo to his colleagues soon after arriving, arguing for an 'Intergalactic Computer Network': he left the Pentagon in 1965 (becoming a professor at MIT), but passed on his vision to his colleagues – two of whom, Ivan Sutherland and Robert Taylor, lobbied successfully for the construction of a network linking four different university computers – a network from which the internet, and the development in the 1980s by another visionary scientist, the British Tim Berners-Lee, of the World Wide Web, sprang. It was the most successful invention by DARPA, but as Jacobsen writes, its 'stated mission is to create weapons' and the ARPANET, as it was at first called, did greatly improve the US military's command and control system, though it did not win them the Vietnam War. The origins of the internet give some backing the claim by Russian President Vladimir Putin that 'the Internet is a CIA project' though he was wrong about which agency was to blame.[23]

The network spread to the UK in 1973, via the computer department of University College London; Bulletin Board Systems came in at the end of the 1970s; Usenet – designed for the discussion and passing to and fro of projects and ideas – in 1980. '[B]y the mid nineties and the emergence of Tim Berners Lee's www., the Internet was fully transformed: from a niche underground haunt frequented by computer hobbyists and academics to a popular hangout accessed by millions of excited neophytes.'[24]

As the traffic increased, exponentially once www. was put in front of messages, the largest institution for signals intelligence in the world, the NSA, became involved – and sought to control the system as far as it could. What it most wished to control, and for some time did, was cryptographic information – the systems, constantly being developed, which ensured that the messages sent by the internet would be secure, unable to be read by anyone other than the person(s) for whom they were intended. 'The agency monitored all patent requests concerning cryptography and had the legal power to classify any of those it deemed too powerful to fall into the public domain.'[25]

For the NSA, this was logical, even inevitable. Its double mission was to secure the nation's vital information, and to keep *in*secure, and thus gather, the vital information of other nations and all people of interest to it. It needed to make sure that the first was properly and unbreakably encrypted; and it needed to do all it could to stop everything else being unbreakably encrypted. Thus it sought to stop all efforts to develop encryption whose complexity would be too difficult for even a supercomputer, testing thousands (later, millions) of possible combinations a second, to break. By the 1970s, however, it began to face strong competition.

In the early 1970s, IBM was developing a strong encryption system named Lucifer and in 1974, submitted it to the National Bureau of Standards, which was examining the need for security on government computers. The NSA, which had known of IBM's researches and even taken part in them, was at the time reaping a rich harvest of traffic which was weakly encrypted, easily broken and read. Asked by the Bureau of Standards to comment on IBM's new model encryption, which was a massive 128 bits long and thus quite likely unbreakable at the given level of computer technology, it demanded that the key be more than halved, to 56 bits – after which it recommended it as the state's Data Encryption Standard (DES), which could be exported to other countries and companies. There was a prolonged battle over the decision, in which critics 'charged the NSA with ensuring that the cipher was just long enough to prevent penetration by corporate eavesdroppers but was just short enough for the NSA's own code breakers'.[26]

The NSA, from the 1970s to the present, has had to fight on several fronts. Its relationship with the legislatures had been one in which Congress and the Senate accepted that they should not inquire too closely in its obviously patriotic duty to keep the USA secure. But, spurred by journalism – in this case, mainly by Seymour Hersh's December 1974 revelations[27] of CIA surveillance of anti-war and other dissident groups in the US, ordered by President Richard Nixon – a Senate committee chaired by the Democratic Senator Frank Church took a hard look at the intelligence agencies. Church criticised the NSA (though not at first by name: it was still living up to the alternative meaning of its acronym – No Such Agency), for having the 'capability [that] at any time could be turned around on the American people, and no American would have any privacy left such is the capability to monitor everything – telephone conversations, telegrams, it doesn't matter. There would be no place to hide.'[28] An NSA official described this as 'an indecent exposure';[29] but the era of automatic legislative acceptance of what the NSA did was badly damaged.

Academics had begun to take an interest in cryptography, and resented the NSA's privileged position in judging what they could and could not research and produce. Led by two Stanford University researchers, Whitfield Diffie and Martin Hellman, a scholarly attack on the 56-bit DES was mounted – on the grounds that the NSA had agreed it only because it could crack it – and that soon, criminal networks would develop the capacity to crack it, too. The argument, which the NSA at first won, developed to the point where the agency was forced to abandon its monopoly over what constituted a legal encryption standard.

At the same time, it was expanding its reach over the world – and over America, which it was legally forbidden to do. Much of this was chronicled, years before Edward Snowden's revelations, in a succession of books by a journalist, a former naval officer and lawyer, James Bamford.[30] His *The Puzzle Palace* (1982) is a critical history of the NSA from its foundation by President Truman in 1952. Three more books followed – *Body of Secrets: Anatomy of the Ultra-Secret National Security Agency* (Arrow, 2001); *A Pretext for War: 9/11, Iraq, and the Abuse of America's Intelligence Agencies* (Anchor, 2004); and *The Shadow Factory: The Ultra-Secret N.S.A. from 9/11 to the Eavesdropping on America* (Anchor, 2008). In *A Pretext for War*, Bamford excused Michael Hayden, the NSA director in the aftermath of 9/11, from the harshest criticism, believing he had shielded the agency from the most unconstitutional demands from the Bush White House to spy on everyone. Instead, however, as James Risen and Eric Lichtbau revealed,[31] 'President Bush [had] secretly authorized the National Security Agency to eavesdrop on Americans and others inside the United States to search for evidence of terrorist activity without the court-approved warrants ordinarily required for domestic spying, according to government officials.'

By 2008, with *The Shadow Factory*, Bamford revised his relatively benign view of Hayden, describing an agency that had become increasingly cavalier about what data it would collect, and from whom. As one official told Bamford, 'It's what the N.S.A.'s been doing since 9/11. They're just sweeping the stuff up.' Bamford, regretting his earlier moderate view, wrote that Hayden had been made into 'a three-star sycophant unwilling to protect the agency from the destructive forces of [Vice President Richard] Cheney and [David] Addington, Cheney's chief of staff'. Though Snowden's documents leaked in 2013 supplied the details, Bamford and Risen had got much of the content and established the basic fact that, as a former senior NSA official told Risen, the NSA searches targeted only foreigners.

* * *

None of the pre-Snowden criticism and revelations stopped the expansion of the NSA's reach and grasp, nor even the charges, strongly put by Bamford, that it was not very good at its job, since it had not connected the existing dots to show that the 9/11 attack was being prepared. It faced, however, a growing constituency of highly skilled internet 'intellectuals' who were of a strongly libertarian bent, and who developed into a major force and have remained one – because they helped supply an ideology and a morality both to radicals, and to the communication corporations of Silicon Valley.

For the latter, the soaring success of their technical and entrepreneurial skill has tended to push them towards a view of the state as at best a lumbering, inefficient dinosaur; more often, as a kind of conspiracy against progress and the emergence of a new society. One of the tyros of the Valley, Reid Hoffman, creator and boss of LinkedIn

> *likes to cite a statistic from a United Nations paper on sustainable development goals: the global economy will need six hundred million new jobs over the next twenty years, and existing business can provide only ten to twenty million of them. The rest, he claims, will have to come from startups, so societies everywhere will have to reorient themselves significantly in order to make entrepreneurship easier ... 'I'm trying to get politicians to understand that solving this problem is about facilitation of a network, as opposed to' – sarcastically – 'the New Deal' ... he has concluded over the past year that the American political parties are too entrenched to solve the country's problems ...*[32]

(Perhaps Eggers's 'Circle' dystopia is not so fictional.)

The message from Hoffman is government, get out of the way. This, with a much harsher edge, is also the slogan on the banners of the radicals, who took on the name of 'cypherpunks': a group which has made it their business to oppose those institutions they see as oppressive of human liberty. Their enduring radicalism directly counterposes itself to what they see, with Julian Assange of Wikileaks and his comrades, as state oppression. This world also strongly influenced, if less directly, Edward Snowden who stole the NSA files, and Glen Greenwald and others who have used them as the basis of their journalism. It provides a powerful new charge to that journalism which is now residing, with them, on the internet.

Jamie Bartlett in the UK,[33] Steven Levy in the US[34] and others have produced lucid instant histories of the cultures from which the cypherpunks emerged. These were made up of individuals and ad hoc groups, coming together in the late 1980s and early 1990s, who had worked typically in software development, had advanced mathematics or engineering degrees and in some cases had produced breakthroughs for their companies which allowed them to retire relatively young and rich, and devote themselves to study and activism. Bartlett singles out Chuck Hamill, a mathematician, as one of the first who grasped the need for a new, unassailable realm of the internet by arguing, in a speech to the 'Future of Freedom' conference in Culver City in November 1987, that the internet should be surrounded by deep moats and thick walls of encryption, so complex that it could not be broken 'in less than 100 years by the most powerful computer now in existence'. The link between the radical punks and the libertarian entrepreneurs was best expressed by a group which, individually and together, produced the largest change. It was composed of Tim May, who had redesigned Intel's memory chips in the 1970s, and retired; John Gilmore, who as the fifth staff member of Sun Microsystems and the founder of the company Cygnus Solutions was also able to retire rich; and the mathematician Eric Hughes, who had produced a manifesto arguing for privacy – 'Privacy is necessary for an open society in the electronic age … Privacy is the power to selectively reveal oneself to the world.' For this, strong encryption was necessary, and thus 'Cypherpunks write code. We know that someone has to write software to defend privacy, and since we can't get privacy unless we all do, we're going to write it. We publish our code so that our fellow Cypherpunks may practice and play with it. Our code is free for all to use, worldwide.'[35]

Privacy was used in a particular way. The cypherpunks saw it as a space protected by the strongest, the most unbreakable, encryption – a walled city, in which the citizens lived in complete freedom. Curiously (or not), the best known statement from the heart of the group was one written while its author was attending the annual World Economic Forum, in Davos, the forum for mainstream politicians, corporate bosses, senior officials and journalists. In February 1996, John Perry Barlow, a protean man – Wyoming rancher, lyricist (for the Grateful Dead and others), political activist on both the Democratic and Republican sides and consistent libertarian – was in the Swiss ski resort, there to talk about the internet, then becoming a large factor in government and business, to people who he said, with much New Age condescension, merely wanted to show they were hip, or cool.

At that time, the US Congress and Senate were debating the Telecommunications Act, which had added to it, during debate, a section known as the Communications Decency Act, criminalising material, posted on the internet and thus available to be viewed by children under 18, which 'depicts or describes, in terms patently offensive as measured by contemporary community standards, sexual or excretory activities or organs'. Angered by this attack on free speech, he fired up his computer and typed out 'A Declaration of the Independence of Cyberspace'[36] – 'Governments of the Industrial World, you weary giants of flesh and steel, I come from Cyberspace, the new home of Mind. On behalf of the future, I ask you of the past to leave us alone. You are not welcome among us. You have no sovereignty where we gather.'

In heightened, declamatory prose, Barlow continued

> We have no elected government, nor are we likely to have one, so I address you with no greater authority than that with which liberty itself always speaks. I declare the global social space we are building to be naturally independent of the tyrannies you seek to impose on us. You have no moral right to rule us nor do you possess any methods of enforcement we have true reason to fear.

The burden of the message was to deny both the right of a government formed through the procedures of electoral democracy to legislate for the internet, and to conjure up a realm of beauty and harmony wholly independent both of the laws of the land, and of the physical world itself.[37]

For the most part, and even now, those who share the vision of the cypherpunks and who privilege a realm of secure privacy, deny or ignore that such a realm could be suborned by criminals and terrorists. For those most concerned with the erosion of civil liberties, privacy is posited as a supreme value, a space on which (especially) the state should not intrude lest it initiate what Senator Church called a total tyranny. This protected space is thus seen as necessary for the continuation of an independent civil society. It draws strength from the many examples in the past and present of dictatorial and authoritarian states destroying liberty by destroying privacy. It is given powerful imaginative force by fictional dystopias, among which George Orwell's *1984* is the most cited, the nature of its nightmarish authoritarian society, in which everyone except the sub-class of 'proles' is constantly monitored by two-way telescreens, most dramatically rendered by the image of 'a boot stamping on a human face, forever'. In 2005, an advertisement for an Apple Mac personal computer recreated a *1984* world, with robotised humans marshalled into rows to listen to Big Brother on a screen – which is smashed by a woman athlete, representing Apple. Ten years later, Tim Cook, the Apple CEO, entered into a long-drawn-out fight with the US government over the right to not to be forced by the federal authorities to open a mass murderer's iPhone.

The walled garden projected by the cypherpunks contains much more than their platonic projections. Misha Glenny puts it thus – 'as governments and corporations amass ever more personal information about their citizens or clients, encryption is one of the few defences left to individuals to secure their privacy. It is also an invaluable instrument for those involved in criminal activity on the Web.'[38] A space on the internet has been constructed, which answers to the aim of the cypherpunks to remain outside of state control. That zone is known as 'the Dark Net', described as 'an underworld set apart from yet connected to the internet we inhabit, a world of complete freedom and anonymity where users say and do what they like, uncensored, unregulated, outside of society's norms.'[39]

The criminal gangs, especially those dealing in hard drugs and weapons, and dealing in the hardest versions of pornography, especially paedophilia, work quickly and efficiently. One drugs site, Silk Road, appeared in 2010: by 2013, the FBI reckoned it had an annual turnover of $1.2bn. It is also a space for extremists of every kind, who help groups and individuals link to sites which share their world view, among them aggressively active racists searching for a base from which to transmit their messages.

* * *

Julian Assange, years before he developed Wikileaks, was a corresponding member of the cypherpunks on one of their sites: he imbibed their ideas, but took them further, creating a soaring vision of freedom and escape from earthly restraint. In his book *Cypherpunks: Freedom and the Future of the Internet*[40] – an edited conversation among Assange and three comrades: Jacob Applebaum, Andy Mueller Maguhn and Jeremie Zimmermann, all leading activists at the cutting edge of the anti-surveillance movement – Assange says that

> *The world is not sliding, but galloping into a new transnational dystopia. This development has not been properly recognised outside of national security circles. It has been hidden by secrecy, complexity and scale. The Internet, our greatest tool of emancipation, has been transformed into the most dangerous facilitator of totalitarianism we have ever seen. The internet is a threat to human civilization. [Emphasis added.]*

In this manifestation, Assange is almost mystic:

The platonic nature of the internet, ideas and information flows, is debased by its physical origins. Its foundations are fibre optic cable lines stretching across the ocean floors, satellites spinning above our heads, computer servers housed in buildings in cities from New York to Nairobi. Like the soldier who slew Archimedes with a mere sword, so too could an armed militia take control of the peak development of Western civilization, our platonic realm.

The internet is impossible without a physical infrastructure, the enemy of the 'platonic realm', which Assange believes the cypherpunks need to create and in which they will live. Still, all faiths have mysteries at their heart: and though that is a large one, it is not debilitating – on the contrary, it strengthens the impression of more-than-human powers and insight, and allows Assange to sketch in the outlines of a realm which approximates to paradise, which is 'abstract[ed] away … from its base underpinnings of satellites, undersea cables and their controllers … new lands barred to those who control physical reality, because to follow us into them would require infinite resources'.[41]

That which bars the diabolic forces of the physical world from the platonic realm is encryption, encoding messages sent and received. Assange writes that, 'our one hope against total domination' is that 'the universe believes in encryption. It is easier to encrypt information than it is to decrypt it. We saw we could use this strange property to create the laws of a new world.'[42]

Very strong encryption, unbreakable even by the most powerful computer, protects the platonic realm, just as – on the authority of Genesis 3: 24 – angels with flaming swords were placed by God to guard the Garden of Eden, once he had driven out sinning man and woman, tempted by the serpent to partake of the gross physical world (the apple). Later in the exchange, Assange tells a vividly remembered story to stress his central point. He had walked past Sydney's opera house one evening, and

looked inside the Opera House through the massive glass panels at the front, and there in all this lonely palatial refinement was a water rat that had crawled up in to the Opera House interior, and was scurrying back and forth, leaping on to the fine linen-covered tables and eating the Opera House food, jumping on to the counter with all the tickets and having a really great time. And actually I think that is the most probable scenario for the future: an extremely confining, homogenized, postmodern transnational totalitarian structure with incredible complexity, absurdities and debasements, and within that incredible complexity a space where only the smart rats can go ... it will only be a high-tech rebel elite that is free, these clever rats running around the Opera House.[43]

Utopia, in Assange's telling of it to his friends, is vague: a 'positive trajectory' would mean 'the inability of neo-totalitarian states to arise in practice because of the free movement of information, the ability for people to speak to each other privately and conspire against such tendencies, and the ability for micro-capital to move without control away from such places which are inhospitable to human beings'. A variety of 'political systems' could then be built, 'Utopian ideals' meaning 'a diversity of systems and models of interaction'. Dystopia remains more powerful, though, with 'tendencies to homogenization, universality, the whole of human civilization being turned into one market ... the pessimistic scenario is also quite probable, and the transnational surveillance state and endless drone wars are almost upon us'.[44]

The novelist Andrew O'Hagan had been contracted by the publisher Canongate to help the Australian to write an autobiography (which appeared, in unauthorised form[45]). The ultimately fruitless struggle to get Assange to write it with him is the subject of a long and fascinating sketch[46] of the man, who told O'Hagan that he took seriously his place in an elite of revolutionaries who had seen more deeply into the heart of things than the majority – 'there is a new vanguard of experts, criminalised as we are, who have fastened onto the cancer of modern power, and seen how it spreads in ways that are still hidden from ordinary human experience'.

* * *

Leaking has been the method which Assange, Snowden and Greenwald, and those who are close to them and the many more who follow or seek to follow their example, have used as their attack against the present Western order.[47] The documents which are leaked have the advantage that, when verified, are the genuine article. And though, in the cases of Wikileaks and NSA leaks, the scale of the leaking is now much greater and the documents now define the story rather than act as one of several elements of it, leaking has long been at the core of journalism. Details of a document, note, letter – now an email – which reveal a policy, or a cover-up or a feud appear in the news media, every day. Mild leaking has even been officially supported. Freedom of Information acts have been passed in most democratic states, which allow – even with widely differing degrees of efficiency and political and bureaucratic obstruction – documentation bearing on contemporary issues to be released, often to the embarrassment of some part of authority. So, too, have whistleblowing provisions introduced at various times since the late 1980s in the US, the UK and France.

Leakers act on a variety of prompts. The most ubiquitous is the official leak, sanctioned by one in authority (not necessarily approved by the head of the organisation or administration, and at times in the service of bureaucratic battles). It may be revulsion against the activities of the organisation in which the leaker – more often known as a 'whistleblower' – works, such as Watergate's 'Deep Throat', the Pentagon Papers' Daniel Ellsberg and Edward Snowden all were. It might be in exchange for a favourable coverage in the reporter's subsequent writing, as critics of Bob Woodward's book-length investigations into Washington politics accuse his sources of indulging in. It might be an act of friendship or admiration for an investigative or crusading journalist, coupled often with a desire to be part of an enterprise more exciting than routine departmental work.

Best of all on this list, highest up the ladder of admirable (for journalists) behaviour, is the whistleblower: one whose ethical stance has been affronted by activity they have been asked to undertake, or which they know is being undertaken in the institution of which they are a member, or know about. Because it is done for ethical reasons, the deal is that, in exchange for the information, the journalist satisfies the leaker's moral imperative. It is the best of deals for the journalist, who is thus the handmaiden to the purest form of journalism, with no quid pro quo for the story except its publication, which they want anyway. The whistleblower is a morally driven actor, whose actions bless him that gives and him that takes. In publishing whistleblown material, the journalist constructs or reinforces a public interest pedestal, aligning the material with the noblest of all journalistic projects – that of wresting secrets which the public should know about from the clutches of a government, bureaucracy, intelligence agency or corporation whose reasons for secrecy are at least redundant and pettifogging, more often presented as sinister.

In the pre-internet, post-war age, the most famous investigative story was Watergate, which revealed the criminal behaviour in the early 1970s by the Nixon Presidency, the story being mainly driven by Bob Woodward and Carl Bernstein of the *Washington Post*. The two young journalists obtained and used documents: indeed, the first important breakthrough came not from their work, but from a colleague, the *Post*'s night police reporter, Eugene Bachinski. A police officer acquaintance showed Bachinski the papers and notes taken from the five men who had broken into the Democratic Party offices in the Watergate complex. The letters WH were found in one notebook and 'W House' in another – Howard Hunt, a former CIA officer who worked for Bob Haldemann, President Nixon's chief of staff, was connected to both, a piece of information which greatly strengthened Woodward and Bernstein's early hunch that the break-in trail might lead to the highest reaches of the administration. However, as their account[49] makes clear, most of the information came from interviews by phone or face-to-face – including, in a parking garage, with Woodward's 'Deep Throat', who later revealed himself as W. Mark Felt, then deputy director of the FBI.

Before Assange, the most celebrated leak of documents was that engineered by Daniel Ellsberg, who in 1971 was working as a researcher in the RAND Corporation, a military think tank. The documents he leaked, which became known as the Pentagon Papers, made up a lengthy historical narrative of the Vietnam War, ordered to be written by the then Secretary for Defense Robert MacNamara, to give a full picture of the conflict. Written without knowledge of the then President Johnson or his advisers, it was a full account which revealed that the president and his circle had early believed that the war was unwinnable, while they continued to say it could be and even was going well. Ellsberg thought the professions of the reasons for war and the true calculations were so out of joint that the public had been fooled and had to be informed. Ellsberg had to laboriously and secretly photocopy the thousands of pages over weeks before he had a complete set – which were then published, in installments, in the *New York Times* from June 1971.

The administration sought and received a stay of publication from an appellate court – a stay set aside by the Supreme Court by a majority of 6:3.[50] In the majority was Justice Hugo Black who, in a famed declaration, said that the founding fathers had constructed the First Amendment to the Constitution, prohibiting the making of any law to erect a state religion or curtail the freedom of speech and the press,

> *so that the press would remain forever free to censure the government ...*
> *Only a free and unrestrained press can effectively expose deception in*

government. And paramount among the responsibilities of a free press is the duty to prevent any part of the government from deceiving the people and sending them off to distant lands to die of foreign fevers and foreign shot and shell. ... To find that the President has 'inherent power' to halt the publication of news ... would wipe out the First Amendment and destroy the fundamental liberty and security of the very people the government hopes to make 'secure.' [51]

Black's judgment has, since then, been held by journalists as a canonical statement on the proper relationship between a free press and the state.

Ellsberg, when he leaked the papers, had turned strongly against the Vietnam War – in which he had fought as a junior officer, ending his tour as a lieutenant in charge of a platoon. Before giving the story to the *Times*, he had attempted to have the papers read into the record in the Senate and had worked with Robert Kennedy's office on them before they were published. He was within the system, albeit in the opposition to the administration's policy: he was given covert assistance by a fellow researcher at Rand, Anthony Russo. He believed in the ability of the political system to digest the findings of the study, and to use them to inform debate about the nature of the Vietnam War and the decisions taken in developing and continuing it. He wanted to rally support against a war which he believed to be failing. He thought that the opposition within the political system could help effect that change – as, ultimately, it did.

These actors, and many others up to the present, worked within a tradition set by the rules and conventions of the US, in which the news media had gained an increasingly influential role. The best of the reporters depended hugely on sources, on experience and on their knowledge of the area in which they worked. Many came to journalism with strong opinions – usually, as polls showed, liberal – or were politicised in the course of their work. But they were constrained by the accuracy standards of their own organisations.

These standards were and are higher in some news organisations than in others: the more politically engaged an organisation is, the more careless it tends to be about the standards of evidence for its reportage. These standards and practices were developed for an analogue and paper-based world, and the emerging journalism of the internet is likely to substantially modify them: the leakers of the 2010s are a harbinger of this. They are people of the internet and the screen – men and women for whom the vast space of information flows, and the technology which give access to it, is a great deal of their world.

The relationship between Assange and the publications which carried the Wikileaks material was always fraught and usually ended with the Australian feeling and at times expressing contempt for his collaborators. His dealings with the *Guardian*, the best-catalogued so far, are listed as claims and counter-claims of bad faith: particularly over a release of all of the files Wikileaks held containing the US diplomatic cables, from which a number of publications had been allowed to publish selections.

Wikileaks had put all of the files on to the internet, hidden behind strong encryption. Assange, when working with the *Guardian*'s David Leigh in 2010, had given Leigh the encryption code – which Leigh disclosed in a book he wrote with his colleague, Luke Harding – *Wikileaks: Inside Julian Assange's War on Secrecy*. Assange, claiming that this meant the encryption was no longer valid and could be accessed, dumped all the files on the internet. Leigh said that Assange had assured him that the encryption would decay within hours of its disclosure to him. The files released in September 2011, including tens of thousands on Iraq, contained many names of activists and confidential sources: all of the publications working with Wikileaks condemned the dump.

Whatever the justice or lack of it of Assange's claim against Leigh, the decision to release the whole cache was an expression of Assange's deep belief that everything should be available. Sarah Ellison wrote of him that

> *Julian Assange and WikiLeaks disdain the notion that anything should come between the public and the vast universe of ostensible information you can evaluate for yourself, if only someone will let you. The ideal role of a journalistic outlet, in Assange's view, is to be a passive conduit for reality, or at least for slivers of reality, with as little intervention as possible – no editing, no contextualizing, no explanations, no thinking, no weighing of one person's claims against another's, no regard for consequences. The technology that Assange has worked on for most of his career possesses immense capabilities, and cannot be controlled by a single institution or voice. It is perhaps for this reason that WikiLeaks – ultimately replaceable by the next technologically savvy anarchist – is so disturbing to so many.*[52]

He sees the given press structure – the 'Fourth Estate' – as a problem, in large part because it is 'censored' by legal restraints, and more importantly self-censors. Thus, in order to enlighten the public, a new system must be built – of which Wikileaks is the prototype. In a five-hour session with Eric Schmidt, CEO of Google, and Jared Cohen, the head of Google Ideas and former State Department aide in June 2011, Assange said that

> in a Fourth Estate context the people who acquire information are sources. People who work information and distribute it are journalists and publishers. And people who act on it … is everyone. So that's a high level construct, but of course it then comes down to practically how do you engineer a system that solves that problem? And not just a technical system, but a total system. So WikiLeaks was and is an attempt – although still very young – at a total system.[53]

His inclination to publish without editing has meant he submits to newspapers' intervention reluctantly and erratically. On their side, the newspaper editors know that a gun is held to their head: if they do not publish, or are seen by Assange and his colleagues to be obstructive, he will publish anyway, going direct to that part of the public who wish to be able to read everything on the internet.

* * *

Woodward and Bernstein were general reporters who stumbled on a scandal and had the courage and backing to unpack it. Ellsberg was seized with indignation that a costly war in Vietnam had been mendaciously represented to his fellow citizens and sought an established newspaper to print details of leaked documents detailing its failure. Julian Assange was and is a man of the internet: it is likely that his long asylum in the Ecuadorian Embassy, beginning in June 2012, would have been unbearable had he not, like Mueller-Maguhn, been living not in a tiny slice of Ecuador in London, but on the internet. In a sometimes chaotic childhood and adolescence, he found solace, order and control in the spaces of flows on the internet and found there targets for his anger and his belief in what he saw as a deepening and all-enveloping repression.

He measures himself against a threat to the world, a menace imagined in epic-cinematic terms, as in such popular dramas as *Lord of the Rings* or *Independence Day*, where a lone or a few individuals persevere, against apparently hopeless odds and savage attack, to lift an existential danger. His childhood was nomadic, as his mother sought escape from an obsessive and vengeful partner: he turned, soon, to the cybersphere. In some of his book's most lyrical, even erotic, passages, he describes how, in his mid-teens, his most meaningful communication was with his computer, surrendering himself to its power to bring the world to him, and he to it. To that new life was added, in his twenties, a political attitude that saw all government as a conspiracy, which it became his duty to destroy not by conventionally violent revolution but by breaking into the secret banks of data and networks of power – a pioneer in the new form of crime and warfare which has since become much more common, and threatening. He was an experienced and bold hacker, had the means and, by the mid-1990s, the mission – which became Wikileaks.

The fame of Wikileaks depends very largely on the decision of a young, often depressed and lonely US Army private in a base in Iraq, whose raw and sensitive nature was shocked by the material she was handling and who decided to become a whistleblower, so that the world would know what was going on below the radar of the conventional press. It is quite hard to see Chelsea – previously Bradley, prior to a decision to identify as a woman – Manning as other than a butterfly broken on a wheel, though one largely of her own making. Her parents were divorced. Her mother, who was Welsh, was a heavy drinker and attempted suicide. Aged 13, she moved with her from the small town of Crescent, Oklahoma, to the larger town of Haverfordwest in South Wales; she came back to live with her father and stepmother at 17, left once more after arguments and – following a couple of years of low-paid jobs and temporary stays, she joined the US Army, aged 20. She identified as gay: had come out in her teens, but had kept it relatively quiet because of fear of bullying. Intelligent, she had little further formal education after school.

Manning was a computer whizz. She had, like Assange, retreated into the internet as a child, and when examined by the army, was found to have high enough intelligence and skills to be assigned to duty as an intelligence analyst. Relishing the work, she expanded the scope of it – with supervisors' approval – to weave intelligence information to which she had access into the files she was preparing for the units in the field which she was tasked to support with intelligence products.

Deployed to a base near Baghdad in 2009, Manning was given access to the Secret Internet Protocol Router Network (SIPRNet) and the Joint Worldwide Intelligence Communications System (JWICS) – a huge mass of classified material. Reading the war logs and other material, she became disillusioned and cynical about the US presence in Iraq and Afghanistan.

She was aware of Wikileaks before being sent to Iraq: there, she took part in discussions on the new organisation in internet chat rooms. Reading an army counter-intelligence report on it, she noted, as she wrote (in a statement she made to her trial in January 2013), that – contrary to the critical and hostile tone of the report – Wikileaks 'seemed dedicated to exposing illegal activities and corruption' and had 'received numerous awards and recognition for its reporting activities'. Manning, by temperament and experience accustomed to being outside of whatever form conventional society took, was caught between two sharply differing worlds: that of the military, fighting a failing war, and that of Wikileaks and its supporters, for whom the US Army was at least a virtual enemy. The knowledge she was imbibing through her work, she wrote, 'burdens me emotionally'. Leaking to Wikileaks was to unburden herself: she describes herself as feeling relief after her first transmission of files.[54]

Manning's sworn loyalty was to her first world in which she lived, the army and the US state: her personal loyalty swayed towards the second, the virtual world of Assange: by the time of her mid-tour leave in January 2010, she had stored a great deal of secret information on her laptop (initially to insure against computer crashes) and had come to believe

> that if … the American public had access to the information contained within [the files] this could spark a domestic debate on the role of the military and our foreign policy in general, as well as it related to Iraq and Afghanistan [and] … might cause society to re-evaluate the need or even the desire to engage in counter-terrorism and counter-insurgency operations that ignored the complex dynamics of the people living in the affected environment each day.[55]

On leave, she tried and failed to contact newspapers: hence she went to Wikileaks. For her, the process of persuading a reporter that she had a good story, facing the inevitable series of questions which would verify the information, fearing that the newspaper, a world foreign to her, might report her to the authorities, was much more daunting than clicking the material's way into Wikileaks: the organisation which offered huge exposure required very little effort and security. On her return to base, she began the uploading, and later publication on the Wikileaks site, of material which included a 2007 incident in Baghdad in which a US helicopter gunship shot up a group of men on the ground (they included two Reuters employees, who were killed); Afghan and Iraq war logs; and later, 250,000 diplomatic cables. In May, she contacted Adrian Lamo, a former hacker and occasional journalist – and, in a sudden splurge of confidence to one she did not know and encouraged by a promise from Lamo that he would not betray her, she spoke, disjointedly but in some detail, about what she had done. Lamo, who may or may not have meant to keep the secret, reported Manning to US Army counter-intelligence: she was arrested at the end of May and later sentenced to 35 years. In custody, she came out as a woman, naming herself Chelsea Manning, and in 2014 requested hormone therapy.

Her belief that she should 'spark a domestic debate' is entirely lucid and in itself admirable: yet she could not know how the material would be used, or if, unredacted, it could endanger her army comrades, or others in different branches of US state service, such as diplomats and their sources. She does not seem to have considered it. That insouciance on her part explains the harshly exemplary sentence passed on her, as did the finding that she had violated her oath of service. The sentence said to others who might be thinking of emulation – here is what you can expect.

But the 'butterfly on the wheel' impression remains, because more than any other of the participants in the mass leaks, she was the least protected by any preparation she might have made to steel herself against what would descend upon her. There is nothing of the cold-blooded spy, or one consumed with hatred for his country, about her: just a cat's cradle of contradictions, idealism, self-absorption, inability to understand the loyalty she owed the army, alienation from her environment and thus from the army itself, intellectual curiosity and sympathy for those she saw as underdogs. She denied she had thought of any monetary reward for her leaks, and would not give the material to Russia or China because 'it belongs in the public domain' (where, of course, it could be read and used by Russia and China).

* * *

On first glance, Edward Snowden is closer to the older generation of leakers than to Assange.[56] His is a military family: his maternal grandfather was a rear admiral in the US Coastguard, then a senior FBI official: his father was also a senior coastguard officer. Glandular fever meant he was off school for months: around the same time – in his late teens – his parents divorced, and he moved with his mother to Elliott City, outside Baltimore, within a few miles of his later employer, the NSA. Shy and introverted but described as pleasant, he too was a creature of the screen, taking computer courses – though he never finished high school. It is notable that the three individuals most closely involved in redefining the way in which journalism reports the secret state – Assange, Manning and Snowden – were all highly intelligent but largely self-taught. Assange studied computing, physics and mathematics at Melbourne University, but did not graduate.

As an adolescent, Snowden had inherited his father's patriotism, joining the army to serve in Iraq in pursuit of freedom for its population. Invalided out of Special Forces training because he broke his legs, he found a job on the lower rungs of the intelligence community, then landed a job as an information technology specialist with the CIA, thereafter rising fast because of 'exceptional' IT skills. The CIA sent him to Geneva, where his intellectual and political development accelerated – though in a zigzag fashion. He was then a libertarian of the right, dismissive of social problems such as unemployment and strongly patriotic and hostile to newspaper revelations such as, in 2009, the *New York Times* disclosures of a secret Israeli plan to attack Iran to neutralise its developing nuclear weapon capacity.

Transferring from the CIA to two different civilian contractors working for the NSA – the computer company Dell, then the consultants Booz Allen Hamilton – Snowden found himself, in 2013, first in Japan then in Honolulu, where his advanced computer skills netted him a large salary. He also, in the Booz Allen/NSA post especially, had access to a vast trove of top-secret information which he downloaded onto thumb drives and took out of the underground facility. In May 2013, he told the NSA that he needed time off because of epilepsy difficulties: in fact, he was beginning a new life, as the most comprehensive and disruptive whistleblower in US history. He flew to Hong Kong, checked into a hotel, and began to contact those he wished to help him unload his trove.

He had completed one kind of transition – from a patriot who thought of whistleblowers (as he put it in his guise as trueHOOHA on the Ars Technica site[57]) that 'these people should be shot in the balls', to one who saw his trade as having grossly surpassed its proper limits

when it crosses a certain line, when it becomes serious wrongdoing, when it becomes widespread wrongdoing, we all have an obligation to act.

That's something I feel very strongly and what I witnessed, over the course of my career, was the construction of a system that violated the rights not just of Americans but of people around the world – and not just constitutional rights, but human rights.[58]

Snowden, in both his private and professional life, was as much a creature of the internet as Manning and Assange. Ewen MacAskill, the investigative reporter appointed by the *Guardian* to contact Snowden, with Greenwald and Poitras, in Hong Kong, is quoted as saying after a few meetings with Snowden that 'he's comfortable with computers. That's his world.'[59] Harding also quotes a Hong Kong lawyer whom Snowden consulted, Albert Ho, as telling the *New York Times* that 'he didn't go out, he spent all his time inside a tiny space, but he said it was OK because he had his computer. If you were to deprive him of his computer, that would be intolerable.' From his late teens, Snowden was, writes Harding, 'passionately attached' to the internet.

In a talk with Greenwald which was part of *Citizen Four* – the film which Laura Poitras did on Snowden, much of which focused on his conversations in the Hong Kong hotel with Greenwald and MacAskil – he said, in response to a question of why he had leaked the material, that

for me it all comes down to state power – and people's ability to meaningfully oppose that power. And I was sitting every day getting paid to design methods to amplify that state power. I realized that if the policy switches ... [Snowden here probably means, if the governing politics became more authoritarian] you couldn't meaningfully oppose that power.

He said he believed that 'the promise of the Obama administration' had been betrayed, significantly by the use of drones: he had been able, at the NSA, to watch drones hit their targets in real time – and that had 'hardened me to action'. He said that

I remember what the internet was like before it was being watched and there has never been anything in the history of mankind like it. You could have children from one part of the world who could be having an equal discussion, granted the same respect for their ideas, with experts in the field ... it's become an expectation that we're being watched ... and that limits the boundaries of their intellectual exploration. I'm more willing to risk imprisonment than I am willing to risk the curtailment of my intellectual freedom … [and] I feel good in my human experience to be contributing to the good of others.

Snowden, the centrepiece of Poitras's absorbing film, reveals his line of descent from the cypherpunks' recoil from the state and all its works – and also uses highly idealistic, even romantic, images of the internet.

Passionate – even moderate – attachment to the internet is prompted by the freedom it offers: Sherry Turkle writes that, on the internet, 'we are encouraged to think of ourselves as fluid, emergent, decentralized, multiplicious, flexible, and ever in process'.[60] For the internet-adept, as Manning, Assange and Snowden became from an early age, barriers to the freedom to search and to read or watch, run against the grain of the internet life, where everything should flow. In paper-based, behind-steel-doors days, state secrets were clearly inaccessible: now, they are 'on' the internet – if only they could be accessed. For those of a libertarian bent – and that both fosters 'passionate attachment' to the internet and is encouraged by it – the fact of non-accessibility is an affront, a denial of the contemporary age.

Snowden chose three journalists to whom to leak his material – Barton Gellman of the *Washington Post*, who had covered the uses and failures of intelligence before and during the Iraq War; Glen Greenwald, a lawyer who blogged for Salon and wrote columns for the *Guardian*, his writing also concentrating on methods of surveillance, especially by the NSA; and Laura Poitras, an award-winning documentary maker who had, among others, produced two films on different theatres of the war on terror. Snowden chose them because of their choices of subject: significantly, only one was from the mainstream press. Gellman has said that the full story of his contacts with Snowden has yet to be told, and that he may not tell it. Greenwald later said that Snowden did not contact the *New York Times* because of the decision it took to hold James Risen's warrantless eavesdropping story for a year – publishing it in 2005, because Risen was about to publish a book which told the story, thereby scooping his own paper. The story anticipated by many years some of the details which Snowden's files revealed.

Gellman, who had been one of the stars of the *Post*'s security reporting, has a much more nuanced view of the Snowden revelations than Greenwald or Poitras. He is a strong believer in disclosure: when contacted by emissaries from the intelligence community not to run a story on the fact that communication companies were providing data to the NSA – a fact that both the companies and the secret services very much wished to remain secret – he replied that 'if the damage that you're worried about consists of the companies being less willing to cooperate or suffering a blow to their businesses because the public or their customers don't like what they're doing or don't approve of the program, that's exactly why we have to publish it. That's the core duty we have in terms of accountability reporting.'[61]

At the same time, he also believes that

I have no doubt from reading through some of these files that the surveillance has achieved very important goals, has found very important facts that have served American security. It's not all ... in the field of counterterrorism, but we care a lot about the spread of nuclear weapons; we care a lot about certain activities that are undertaken by foreign governments. So I am absolutely not making the claim that this stuff does not serve American security.

But you know, in the preamble to the Constitution there are six major purposes that are set out for the design of our government. One of them ... is to secure the national defense. It's not the only interest we have and there has to be a balance, and the balance has not been debated by an informed public because there was an absolute dearth of information. And what we're seeing now, what a lot of Americans say they appreciate, is enough transparency to enable Congress and the American public to decide where they want to draw the lines.[62]

Snowden's contacts with the initially uninterested and distrustful Greenwald and Poitras bore fruit when Greenwald, having been instructed in encryption techniques by Snowden, received from him a handful of files formerly in the sole possession of 'one of the world's most secretive agencies in the world's most powerful government'. One of these files was a description of a programme under which some of the most highly valued and coolest corporations in the world – Google, Microsoft, Apple, YouTube and others – allowed NSA collection of billions of messages from their servers. Then and later, Greenwald was too elated to keep reading without breaks of delirious joy: after panhandling for little traces of gold for years, he had been gifted a fabulous, world-changing, mother lode. He and Poitras, having enlisted the backing of the *Guardian*, set off for Hong Kong, their delighted celebrations over the files they were reading on a sleepless flight waking other passengers.

In a memoir-cum-polemic Greenwald summarises what he glimpsed in these first minutes of delirium – a joy prompted by the realisation that the issues he had blogged about for years now had a material base, and that his suspicions about the 'security state' had been confirmed. The 'mountain' of documents

indisputably laid bare a complex web of surveillance aimed at Americans (who are explicitly beyond the NSA's mission) and non-Americans alike. The archive revealed the technical means used to intercept communications: the NSA's tapping of Internet servers, underwater fibre-optic cables, local and foreign telephone systems and personal computers. It identified individuals targeted for extremely invasive forms of spying, a list that ranged from alleged terrorists and criminal suspects to the democratically elected leaders of the nation's allies and even ordinary American citizens. And it shed light on the NSA's overall strategies and goals ... crucial, overarching documents at the front of the archive ... disclosed the agency's extraordinary reach, as well as its deceit and even its criminality.[63]

Poitras, with Greenwald and a clutch of others, mainly investigative reporters, later joined the staff of The Intercept, a website which concentrates on revelations and investigations, and is funded by Pierre Omidyar, the creator and owner of eBay. Gellman, who had left the *Post*, returned to write and oversee stories drawn from the Snowden cache. In a story written on 5 July 2014 with Julie Tate and Ashkan Soltani, Gellman used some of Snowden's purloined documents to show that 'ordinary Internet users, American and non-American alike, far outnumber legally targeted foreigners in the communications intercepted by the National Security from U.S. digital networks'.[64] The story contained the statement that 'The *Post* will not describe in detail, to avoid interfering with ongoing operations', the contents of the Snowden-provided files. It also says that 'At one level, the NSA shows scrupulous care in protecting the privacy of U.S. nationals and, by policy, those of its four closest intelligence allies – Britain, Australia, Canada and New Zealand': it then qualifies this with a paragraph which points out that some individuals are not so protected. It is evidence of a journalistic style which wishes to avoid the charge of marshalling facts in a purely polemical fashion.

Glen Greenwald, who has mixed polemic with reportage since beginning his journalistic career, is by some way the most prominent of the Snowden group, in part because of his much less constrained style and because he takes an aggressive stance to all critics, most of all to those within the journalistic community who have been critical of the Snowden leaks, and of the newspapers, especially the *Guardian*, which publish them.

Greenwald and Chris Blackhurst, then editor-in-chief of the *Independent* titles in the UK, had an exchange on the issue in October 2013 which makes clear Greenwald's aggressive distrust of most mainstream journalism. Blackhurst, while making many genuflections to the importance of whistleblowers, wrote[65] that he would not publish because he could 'not get wound up' about the fact 'that the security services monitor emails and phone calls, and use internet searches to track down terrorists and would-be terrorists … what [is it], exactly, that the NSA and GCHQ, are doing that is so profoundly terrible?' He added that he did not publish the material the paper did get from the Snowden files because the government had asked him not to, on grounds of national security.

Greenwald replied in white-hot mode. Blackhurst, 'a career journalist', had in obeying the state's request not to publish, 'perfectly encapsulate[d] the death spiral of large journalistic outlets'. Blackhurst was 'subservient, obsequious'; he was 'a good journalistic servant' (of the UK state);

> *what Blackhurst is revealing here is indeed a predominant mindset among many in the media class. Journalists should not disobey the dictates of those in power … it does not surprise me that authoritarian factions, including (especially) establishment journalists, prefer that none of this reporting and debate happened and that we all instead remained blissfully ignorant about it. But it does still surprise me when people calling themselves 'journalists' openly admit to thinking this way. But when they do so, they do us a service, as it lays so vividly bare just how wide the gap is between the claimed function of establishment journalists and the actual role they fulfill.*[66]

Greenwald believes that most journalism and most journalists ('establishment' or 'career' journalists) have either gone, or more likely have always been, soft – in the sense that they are amenable to the blandishments and commands of the state and of corporate power, and have lost or never had a sense of journalism as in permanent opposition to these powers. Greenwald is a journalist of the internet; Blackhurst (formerly business editor of the *Evening Standard*) a man of institutions.

Of all of those who have spearheaded the mass leaking movement, Greenwald has been the most explicit in his contempt for the existing media, and the most explicit in believing what all in the leaking movement, in one form or another, believe. That is, that the US, with its subaltern state the UK, has lost any legitimacy because it has enthusiastically embraced surveillance technology which they use to oppress both their citizens and foreigners. That being so, Greenwald thinks of the journalism he and his close colleagues on The Intercept practice as the most vital in the world today, and their journalistic approach as the only one journalists who deserve the name should adopt.

In his memoir, Greenwald contrasts the 'iconic reporter of the past [as] the definitive outsider' on low wages, when 'a career in journalism virtually ensured outsider status', with the present corporate creature, 'peddl[ing] media products to the public on behalf of that corporation ... those who thrive within the structure of large corporations tend to be adept at pleasing rather than subverting institutional power'.[67] (In fact, the journalists of pre-war years were more completely under the thumb of proprietors and editors, and often much less scrupulous in ensuring accuracy, as well as more careless of the feelings of those about whom they wrote, especially if they had no power within the establishment.)

Greenwald came from a middle class family living in Lauderdale Lakes, Florida, a town of some 34,000 people. His grandfather, L. L. Greenwald, had served as a feisty member of the city council: at 18 and still at school, the younger Greenwald stood for the same council, on a ticket which emphasised that – as he told the local daily, the *Sun Sentinel* – the issues 'quite simply, all concern the neglect and imperviousness the present councilmen have displayed toward the needs of the city': early evidence of the absolutism he practices in his politics and journalism.

A straight 'As' school student, he attended the private George Washington University in Washington, DC, an institution constantly credited with being among 'most politically active' colleges in the country, with a high proportion of its graduates entering politics. He took a degree in philosophy, then a further degree in law at a second prestigious institution, New York University, where he majored in law. As he wrote in 2006 – to answer 'childish ad hominem attacks' from 'followers ... of the Bush movement' after he had begun blogging against its 'extremist impulses and authoritarian mindset' – he received 15 offers from the foremost law firms in the land, choosing the most 'prestigious and selective among them', Wachtell, Lipton: he interned at the firm while completing his degree, and worked there for over a year after graduation, receiving 'uniformly and enthusiastically positive' performance reviews. He then set up his own, successful practice, which over a decade grew to a firm employing six lawyers with a US-wide practice specialising in constitutional issues. He published three books – *How would a Patriot Act?*; *A Tragic Legacy*; and *Great American Hypocrites*, all vigorous, and often popular, attacks on Republican politics in general and the Bush presidency in particular. The fourth book is *No Place to Hide*, recounting his relationship with Edward Snowden and the publication of the files Snowden had stolen from the NSA.

Greenwald has been explicit in seeing journalism as in permanent opposition to political and, to a much lesser extent, corporate, power and that it should eschew any pretence at objectivity. In a dialogue with Bill Keller, then executive editor of the *New York Times*, in October 2013, Greenwald endorsed the need for 'strong, highly factual, aggressive adversarial journalism', and dismissed 'this suffocating constraint on how reporters are permitted to express themselves, produc[ing] a self-neutering form of journalism that becomes as ineffectual as it is boring ... [it] rests on a false conceit. Human beings are not objectivity-driven machines. We all intrinsically perceive and process the world through subjective prisms. What is the value in pretending otherwise?'

Keller replied that

> I believe that impartiality is a worthwhile aspiration in journalism, even if it is not perfectly achieved. I believe that in most cases it gets you closer to the truth, because it imposes a discipline of testing all assumptions, very much including your own. That discipline does not come naturally. I believe journalism that starts from a publicly declared predisposition is less likely to get to the truth, and less likely to be convincing to those who are not already convinced. (Exhibit A: Fox News.) ... this pursuit of fairness is a relatively new standard in American journalism. A reader doesn't have to go back very far in the archives – including the archives of this paper – to find the kind of openly opinionated journalism you endorse. It has the 'soul' you crave. But to a modern ear it often feels preachy, and suspect.[68]

Most radically, Greenwald believes – a belief which puts him close to Assange – that journalism should be an act of aggression against the government. The 'check' which the notion of a Fourth Estate is supposed to provide to government 'is only effective if journalists act adversarially to those who wield political power': the largest sin is to be 'subservient to the government's interests, even amplifying rather than scrutinizing its messages and carrying out its dirty work'. This is vague (what is 'dirty work'?) but it seems to mean that *any* government policy should not be approved or supported ('amplified'). Greenwald's extended critique of the news media in *No Place to Hide*, from which these quotes are taken, is to a significant extent drawn from his own and his close colleagues' experiences, and is a sporadic rather than a fully coherent critique: but it is clear where he stands, which is for journalism to live in the strongest opposition to the state and to the governments which administer it.

Keller, and journalists in his mould – liberal, professionally sceptical, practitioners and/or editors of investigative reporting – are at least as much suspect in Greenwald's eyes as journalists and commentators of the right. The characteristic which O'Hagan had seen in Assange – 'he expended all his ire on the journalists who had tried to work with him and who had basic sympathy for his political position'[69] – is not wholly true of Greenwald, who expends a lot of ire on the right. But he does see mainstream journalists, like Blackhurst of the *Independent*, as traitors to a cause which, as he defines it, should mandate root and branch opposition to government. Keller believes in revelation: but he has, when *New York Times* editor, held back stories and cut details in others, because of government requests.

In a joint declaration with Dean Baquet, then editor of the *Los Angeles Times* (and since May 2014 editor of the *New York Times*) in July 2006, Keller affirmed the identity of interests between journalists and other citizens in defeating terrorism; and attested to occasions when, after discussions with administration officials, they had held or cut articles. They affirmed the basic credo – that freedom brings responsibility, 'a corollary to the great gift of our independence' and also affirmed that

> the virulent hatred espoused by terrorists, judging by their literature, is directed not just against our people and our buildings. It is also aimed at our values, at our freedoms and at our faith in the self-government of an informed electorate. If the freedom of the press makes some Americans uneasy, it is anathema to the ideologists of terror.[70]

When he was *LA Times* editor, Baquet had killed a story, brought to the paper in 2006 by an AT&T technician Mark Klein, about NSA 'surveillance rooms' being installed in AT&T centres across the country: he decided not to run it after talking to administration officials, but said the conversation did not materially affect his decision. When Baquet was appointed *New York Times* editor, Greenwald, recalling the AT&T affair, commented in the Huffington Post[71] that the new editor

> *does have a really disturbing history of practicing this form of journalism that is incredibly subservient to the American national security state, and if his past record and his past actions and statements are anything to go by, I think it signals that the* New York Times *is going to continue to descend downward into this sort of journalism that is very neutered and far too close to the very political factions that it's supposed to exercise oversight over.*

However, when Baquet, in an interview in June on National Public Radio, said that 'I am much, much, much more sceptical of the government's entreaties not to publish today than I was ever before', Greenwald used a piece on his new medium, The Intercept, to pat the new editor on the head for his 'epiphany' on the administration's exaggerations of the danger of publishing secret information – '[it] is long overdue, but better late than never. Let us hope that it signals an actual change in behaviour.'[72]

Greenwald joined The Intercept, published by Omidyar's First Look Media, in 2014, leaving the *Guardian*, for which he had written regularly. Omidyar was already owner of a website, the Honolulu Civil Beat, which covers Hawaii. The New York University journalism academic and commentator on the media, Jay Rosen, wrote in October 2013 that Pierre Omidyar – with whom he had talked, and whose First Look Media he briefly joined, then left – had been strongly attracted to Greenwald's journalism as the revelations poured out. He met with Greenwald, and learned that he, with Poitras and *The Nation* magazine's Jeremy Scahill, had decided to set up their own news organisation. Omidyar persuaded them to 'join forces' with him, and The Intercept – the name came later – was born.

Rosen wrote that

> *Omidyar believes that if independent, ferocious, investigative journalism isn't brought to the attention of general audiences it can never have the effect that actually creates a check on power. Therefore the new entity ... will have to serve the interest of all kinds of news consumers. It cannot be*

a niche product. It will have to cover sports, business, entertainment, technology: everything that users demand.[73]

It has not done so: a project to develop investigations into business through an internet magazine, Racket, using (as Greenwald and others described it in a long narrative about its failure) 'merciless ridicule, humor, and parody',[74] with the *Rolling Stone* journalist Matt Taibbi in charge, was tried, and closed after much argument.

Omidyar, who had been approached about buying the *Washington Post* (which Jeff Bezos of Amazon did buy) said that he was concerned by the growing pressures on journalism round the world and wanted to support 'independent journalists with expertise, a voice and followers' to come together to do their journalism in concert. He believes it important to have a well-funded organisation, with a strong legal team behind them because (again according to Rosen) 'the kind of journalism [The Intercept] intends to practice is the kind that is capable of challenging some of the most powerful people in the world'.[75]

With Greenwald at its centre, Omidyar pledged $250m to build up The Intercept as an online investigative news site specialising in security and privacy issues: other well-known names were hired, including, the reporter Jeremy Scahill and, as editor-in-chief, John Cook, who had run the Gawker site. For the first months of its operation, its main output was twofold: more stories crafted from Snowden's files and blog posts by Greenwald. Perhaps worried by the hostile messages from readers disappointed that the site hosted so little, Cook wrote in a 14 April 2014 message on the site that most of the basic questions had 'not been worked out' and that, until they were, the output would remain largely NSA revelations, and Greenwald's opinions. In November 2014 Cook resigned, and returned to Gawker as Investigations Editor: Taibbi had resigned the previous month. Cook, who had been said to be deeply unhappy at The Intercept, nevertheless left a statement saying that 'I was convinced that The Intercept would become an innovative and influential force in adversarial journalism. The last year hasn't been easy, but I am convinced more than ever that this is exactly what The Intercept is fast becoming.' Taibbi, by contrast, left bitterly, after rows with Omidyar, president John Temple, formerly of the *Washington Post* and the chief operating officer Randy Ching, a former eBay executive. He had received a complaint from a staffer of the Racket, of bad behaviour towards her exacerbated, she said, by the fact that she was a woman: he denied the charge. Greenwald, with Poitras, wrote a lengthy account of the issue, mostly blaming First Look management for the disputes.[76]

In a piece in *Vanity Fair* in January 2015, going over the same ground as Greenwald and Poitras, Sarah Ellison concluded that

> it's ... likely that the misunderstandings at First Look derive from a fundamental philosophical divide between two groups. The journalists saw themselves as freethinking, independent, and adversarial, and felt hemmed in by a process-driven management structure. For its part, management thought it was simply providing some much-needed organisation – a system – within which the journalists could operate. The hubris that each party brought to First Look probably meant that self-awareness was not at the top of the list of personal attributes.[77]

* * *

The challenge which, most explicitly, Greenwald has thrown down to the 'corporate creatures' working in newspapers, broadcasting and for news websites is this: that governments, in the first instance those of the US and the UK, have lost any right to be believed and thus that journalism must pass beyond scepticism to aggression and to confrontation. The security systems increasingly being strengthened in both authoritarian and democratic countries will increasingly demand – and get – licence to collect all communications data from anywhere, and use it in ways hidden from everyone, including most people in government.

The German sociologist Wolfgang Sofsky believes that 'surveillance has always been one of the most effective methods of control. Fear of the Other keeps people submissive ... but today power is unwilling to rely on fear of discovery, obedience and loyalty to laws and principles alone. Its suspicions of its subjects are too deep for that. It wants to know everything, all the time, everywhere.'[78]

That last line is close to the truth of the most advanced secret services. They do not, of course, want to 'know' everything, but they do want to be able to search all communications data to find links between those they deem suspicious, and they have wished to keep that ambition secret. Sofsky believes that 'these measures not only destroy the freedoms that they are supposed to defend but also drive individuals apart and sever social ties. In the end, no one feels safe with others.'[79]

This belief – of universal collection of communications data as the corridor to the realisation of an authoritarian, wholly controlled state – underlies the new journalism proposed by Greenwald and others who hold similar beliefs. It takes investigative journalism, seen for much of the past century as the most civically and politically active brand of journalistic enquiry, and adds to it distrust-in-principle, going beyond a discipline of checking to an assumption of bad faith – which needs to be discovered, described and exposed.

4

The Breaking of Freedom's Back?

The thing is that you don't know what you're giving away. People now think it's all about transparency and not about security.

(Meta Ramsey, former MI6 officer)

When, from soon after the war to the 1970s, Chapman Pincher was the dominant figure in security journalism, much of the news media took more or less the same view as he did: that the security services – minus a few rotten apples who had been exposed, or were still to be exposed, as traitors – were a bulwark against communism. At the age of 94 (he died a few months after his 100th birthday, in 2014), Pincher wrote a piece for a volume of essays[1] which were, in the main, sceptical or even distrustful of the agencies. It was as unapologetic as ever. He recounted, with obvious pleasure, that he had persuaded the *Daily Express* to run a false story, on the front page: this was to fool Japanese protestors, who were expected to sail in their thousands to Christmas Island in the Pacific, where the latest British nuclear test was to be carried out in May 1957, to stop the test by their presence. Pincher's story said the test had been delayed from May to June, and was picked up by wire services everywhere. In fact, the test went ahead in May and the Japanese protestors were confounded. Pincher went to observe a second test later, and 'received some special facilities from the chief scientist there – my old friend Sir William Cook – for my assistance, which was acknowledged by the task force commander Air Vice Marshall Wilfred Oulton, who became another lunch companion.'[2]

This was in a collection otherwise written by experts and scholars, with a title suggesting dishonesty on the part of the secret services and the news media, at a time of cynicism, sometimes hostility on the part of an influential minority, towards the military-intelligence complex of which Pincher had made himself an ornament. He made clear, as he had all his journalistic life, that the country's security was a responsibility of the press as well as of the intelligence agencies, and that the former's duty was to aid the latter. Journalism, in this area, had no claim to guard its own reputation for trustworthiness and independence: when called, it must be subaltern to the demands of the nation's security.

Something of Pincherism still adheres to the British press, or at any rate is thought to. David Davis, a Conservative MP and since July 2016 Secretary of State for Exiting the European Union and who has taken a high-profile position as one concerned by the erosion of civil liberties, told me that 'most of the press doesn't want to appear unpatriotic, and they don't want to be blamed' for publishing facts or opinions which might assist terrorism. The grief the popular press gives to the security services and the government, however, differs from that which Pincher gave: it lies now less in the accusation that communists have penetrated the secret services, more in the reflexive hunt for the guilty men whenever any project goes wrong or attack occurs, and the assumed softness of the British Foreign Office to which MI6 is accountable.

Pincher, the *Daily Express*'s star reporter, wrote for a paper which dramatised issues in order to have them attended to and when these stories were situated within the sphere of intelligence, there was a simple, obvious, powerful enemy in the shape of the Soviet Union and its satellite states (Pincher claimed in the *Spinning Intelligence* essay that a Soviet diplomat in London, certainly KGB, tried to recruit him, naturally over lunch, by waving a wad of pound notes under his nose). The popular papers of today are at least as easy to outrage should a jihadist atrocity occur, but though critical at times, most are fairly steady in their support for the growth of both the staffs and the budgets of the secret services, and do not hunt within them for moles.

Pincherism no longer defines coverage. The most patriotic paper would be unlikely to lend its front page to assist an atomic bomb to be tested free of inconvenient Japanese. The deals which Pincher made with his lunch companions from various parts of the government and the secret services – access and scoops as rewards for coverage which reflected well on the state – would no longer be a reportorial badge of pride, even as they are still done, for personal advancement rather than patriotic duty. Pincher thought of himself, at least in retrospect, as 'an investigative reporter throughout my journalistic career' – and in a sense he was, for he used his array of lunching, shooting and fishing companions to good purpose, wringing or charming from them stories which were usually at least partly true and at times embarrassing to the government. But embarrassment was easier then, when the mere fact of referring to the agencies was daring, given that they did not officially exist.

Now, investigative journalism is harder-edged, depending less on lunches with the chiefs (though that happens, and is more widely dispensed than simply to one reporter – who, unlike today's guests at intelligence tables, picked up the bill). Instead it works through the evidence of whistleblowers and disaffected or former employees – as well as, increasingly, using data sets to search for connections between institutions and individuals. Pincher got his scoops, genuine and planted, from the vanities and battles within the government, scientific and intelligence establishment, as reporters do today: but he and the *Express* knew which side they were on, and however many waves they made for the government, they sought to serve it. No nonsense about objectivity.

What developed from the 1960s on was a form of investigative reporting, much aided by the editorial energy of Harold Evans at the *Sunday Times* (from 1967–1981), which was demotic, covering the frauds and impositions on ordinary people, with glimpses into the malefactions within corridors of power, where large decisions were made, gross errors committed, and both often concealed. Evans, son of a railwayman, saw on a family holiday to Rhyl hundreds of soldiers who had been evacuated from Dunkirk, and had been transported there to recuperate: they were lying on the beach, exhausted and traumatised. His father, congenitally curious and sociable, went among them, asking them for their stories of retreat and rescue, and heard stories of fear, humiliation, death of comrades, poor weaponry and near misses – quite different from the stories the newspapers were telling.[3] Philip Knightley, in his account of war reporting, writes that 'Above all, the stories [in the press] stressed the high morale of the evacuated troops, itching to get back into France and into the fight again. It was not until the late 1950s and early 1960s ... that a fuller, truer picture of Dunkirk began to emerge.'[4]

Evans wanted to close that gap – between comforting myth and historical examination – with a journalism which dug deep into the present, rather than leaving the forensic work to historians two decades later. In his first large investigation by the team – Insight – which he created, the *Sunday Times* published the story of the betrayals of Kim Philby, the most proactive of the Cambridge spy ring and the most deadly, responsible for the deaths of many anti-communist activists and would-be defectors: the story of the investigations by the Insight team and others on the paper is one of lengthy efforts to pull at threads of the story, some of which snapped, but more of which finally yielded an illumination.[5] This exposed both the scope of Philby's ruthless treachery, and the inept, class-prejudiced handling of his case by colleagues who either could not believe that a gentleman could behave as Philby did, or were more concerned to cover up the signs that he was doing so than investigate.

There were other influences: indeed, the *Sunday Times* had essayed some investigations before Evans, such as the uncovering of the slum landlord empire of Peter Rachman centred in London's Notting Hill. But it was Evans's championing of the form, explicitly based on what he regarded as a model, the American approach to uncovering issues of importance with long-form journalism, which was most influential and which stimulated imitation and set a tradition in place. The *Sunday Times* revealed that Israel had a programme that had successfully developed nuclear weapons – though this was under the editorship of Andrew Neil, after Evans had been persuaded by Rupert Murdoch to edit *The Times*, and then been fired. It was an important story, obtained in part by chance but teased out over time with skill and persistence – like a successful intelligence agency investigation. To Neil's distress, it resulted in the capture, through a honey trap, of the leaker, Mordechai Vanunu and his imprisonment.

There is, however, an inescapable truth underlying the UK's intelligence services: as in the UK's nuclear defence, it is very closely tied to the US, and though there is much mutual irritation, on the British side there is more necessary submission to strategies and choices largely determined in Washington, even where sometimes influenced by the UK. This is not a relationship of equals, and cannot be: however good the British services are and however valuable they can be within the 'five eyes' consortium, they have not the resources, the global scope nor the self-imposed task of informing the world's policeman. One of the delights of James Bond was that he, a British agent, continually saved the world from disaster, with occasional, often laggard, help from the CIA. John Le Carré's fictions emphasised the reverse.

* * *

British journalism on the spy world, and every other world, has tended to take a more partisan edge than that of the US. Though it has, in the BBC, the model of a public service broadcaster which strives – with lapses but with a recurring commitment – for neutrality and balance, Britain's newspapers are generally partisan, and in the case of the dominant tabloid press, strongly so. The kind of training in objectivity to which

Warren Strobel referred at the University of Missouri journalism school, and duplicated in every other such school in the US, has no such powerful equivalent in the UK press. Reporters are influenced by the culture of the paper they work for – and the papers are influenced by their choice and promotion of reporters and above all commentators by their political leanings. Many investigations, especially in the popular papers, tend to take on a partisan form, where particular targets of the left or right are the object of investigations and commentary in papers.

There are however several British reporters whose work on issues of security and the contemporary forms of war are as vivid and closely reported as anything available elsewhere. One of those, whose work is close in style and scope to that of the US, is Stephen Grey, a former head of the *Sunday Times* Insight team, who then moved to Thomson Reuters. He had done a lengthy and largely one-man investigation into rendition – the taking of jihadist suspects to countries where they could be tortured for confessions: an early draft of what became a much longer story was published, titled 'America's Gulag', in the *New Statesman* in 2004.[6] The much longer account, in his *Ghost Plane,*[7] is as harsh an exposure of the 'dark side' as anything written. Grey followed the flight of a Gulfstream V jet which was one of the principal shuttles used by the CIA between the US and the countries to which the suspects were rendered, and found that it and others like it had transported suspects, usually shackled, from the US, Africa, Germany and elsewhere, to countries where they then disappeared into prisons, in whose dungeons they were kept in appalling conditions and regularly tortured.

In the opening pages of *Ghost Plane*, Grey describes a prison in Damascus, Syria, named Palestine Branch, where prisoners 'rendered' by the CIA were put in cells measuring 3 feet wide by 6 feet long by 7 feet high – little larger than a coffin. One prisoner was a Canadian-Syrian called Maher Arar, who had left Syria for Canada when a teenager with his parents, and had become a Canadian citizen – graduating with degrees in computer science, working for a software company in the US, then returning to Canada to set up his own business. Arar had been arrested in New York, interrogated then deported to Damascus. In addition to his close confinement, he was beaten and shown a particularly painful form of torture called the German chair (so-called because it had been learned from the East German Stasi), which stretches the spine to near breaking, but not used on him. He was interrogated ceaselessly, then left in a cell where he could hear others screaming. He was lucky in having a determined wife back home – who pressured the Canadian government to insist on consular visits which, when won, ensured relief from beatings – but he was kept in the cell, where he nearly went mad. He was released after a year and flown back to Canada, and he was later pronounced innocent.

Other likely innocent men had the same treatment, or worse, than Arar: others were guilty of taking part in terrorist acts, or of being members of terrorist groups. It is not clear yet – there are quite contradictory accounts – how far the torture produced useful intelligence.

Grey parsed carefully President Bush's declaration on rendition, at a press conference in April 2005, the first he had given on the subject. Bush said that 'we operate within the law, and we send people to countries where they say they're not going to torture people'. Grey said that the sentence 'had the appearance of a lawyer's draft': to say that 'they say they're not going to torture people' doesn't mean that 'they don't torture people' (as the President had incautiously said some months earlier in comments to the *New York Times*). Grey writes that 'for more than a decade, under both Presidents Clinton and Bush, the rendition programme had sent prisoners to foreign jails in the full knowledge they would be tortured'.[8]

Where Grey has plumbed the depths of the effects of the loosing of the dogs of war on those who wished destruction on the US, Jason Burke of the *Guardian/Observer* has for over more than two decades produced a narrative in articles and books which have closely followed the rise, and rise, of Islamist militancy in its heartlands of Afghanistan, Iraq, Syria and elsewhere in the Middle East and Asia. It is an area also covered, with similar requirements for experience and steady nerves, by reporters (among others) Patrick Cockburn of the *Independent*, Antony Loyd of *The Times*, Christina Lamb of the *Sunday Times* and Marie Colvin, also of the *Sunday Times* (killed with the French photographer Remi Olchik in February 2012 in the Syrian city of Homs).

Burke has provided some of the most closely observed insights into the spread of militancy, the nature of its threat, the reception the various groups have within the Muslim world, their success (or lack of it), in spreading militancy, especially in the new enlarged Muslim communities of Europe and North America and the quality of the Western response to Islamist violence.

Like Grey, he is able to focus a reader's attention through vivid reporting, including that gained from interviews with sources of events at which he could not have been present (or if he had, would not have been left alive). In his 2015 book, he describes the blitzkrieg launched by IS on the Iraqi city of Mosul in the early summer of 2014, a complete military success which saw the rout of the Iraqi forces: he quotes (from a Reuters despatch) an Iraqi officer as saying, while in flight – 'We can't beat them. They're like ghosts: they appear, strike and disappear in seconds.'[9] Burke, able to contextualise an action which he sees as the decisive entry of IS into contemporary terrorism, writes that

> the four-day campaign in June 2014 was unprecedented in the annals of violent Islamic extremism. Militants had seized cities before. Some, such as the Taliban in Afghanistan and Al-Shabab in Somalia, had even managed to bring significant swathes of territory under their control. But none had taken on a state's army in this way, nor acted with such speed or astonishing efficacy. Hasty appraisals of the attack on Mosul as 'opportunistic' were rapidly revised as intelligence analysts and experts recognised a reality that had escaped them over previous months: that the campaign had been meticulously prepared over two years or more.[10]

The ability to deduce trends and patterns from events which he has often himself covered has made Burke into an influential commentator as well as a reporter. In an analysis of the strength of al Qaeda, written when its leader, Osama bin Laden, was still at large, Burke was clear about the leader's importance and limits:

> Bin Laden still plays a significant role in the movement as a propagandist who effectively exploits modern mass communications. It is likely that the United States will eventually apprehend bin Laden and that this demonstration of U.S. power will demoralize many militants. However, much depends on the manner in which he is captured or killed. If, like deposed Iraqi President Saddam Hussein, he surrenders without a fight, which is very unlikely, many followers will be deeply disillusioned. If he achieves martyrdom in a way that his cohorts can spin as heroic, he will be an inspiration for generations to come. Either way, bin Laden's removal from the scene will not stop Islamic militancy.[11]

His advocacy recommends courses of action to Western military and governments – always on the side of their recognising complexity, rather than seeking popularity or revenge through singling out one course of (usually military) actions as a panacea:

> if Western countries are to succeed, they must marry the hard component of military force to the soft component of cultural appeal. There is nothing weak about this approach. As any senior military officer with experience in counterinsurgency warfare will tell you, it makes good sense. The invasion of Iraq, though entirely justifiable from a humanitarian perspective, has made this task more pressing.[12]

Burke is sceptical (but not dismissive) of the ability of jihadist groups, including IS, to posing a WMD-enabled, 'existential' threat to a Western country – but sees the distrust that terrorism has sown as the larger casualty. This is distrust not just by non-Muslims of Muslims, which has risen quite sharply, especially in America and France; it is also distrust, even hatred, of non-Muslims by Muslims. Burke wrote that 'Around two thirds [of Muslims] said they thought people in the West were selfish, greedy and violent while more than a half thought they were immoral, arrogant and fanatical.'[13] Less than a third of people in the Islamic world believed that Arabs had carried out the 9/11 attacks, and more than two-thirds and rising thought the West fundamentally hostile.

The imperative which moves US reporters – that the United States, especially under the presidency of George W. Bush and to a lesser degree under that of Barack Obama, had sacrificed some of its founding principles in pursuing the war on terror, and that the ways in which this has happened need to be described and exposed – is much less felt in the UK. Both Grey and Burke, in their most extended reporting and analysis (and implicit or explicit criticism), centre much of their attention on the US.

Lengthy accounts, in journalism and in books by journalists and others, have been and are still being written, especially in light of the Chilcot report published on 6 July 2016, about the decision Prime Minister Tony Blair took to form part of the invasion of Iraq with the US forces – most of that unfavourable to Blair. John Kampfner's *Blair's Wars*,[14] a highly critical account, is a prominent example. But British journalists have not felt the moral urgency which comes through much of US journalism on the aftermath of the Iraq invasion: instead, they concentrated fire on the decision to unseat a mass murderer, seeing the project as imperialist in conception, mendacious in representation, shambolic in execution and disastrous in effect within the Muslim world.

Though Britain and the British secret services cast themselves as the closest of allies to the Americans, they stood apart in the matter of torture: though how far apart is still a matter of sharp debate. The claim was that the secret services did not torture, nor did they profit from torture – in the sense that it did not use intelligence derived from torture. At a speech she gave in 2010, I asked the retired head of MI5 (2002–7) Eliza Manningham-Buller, if there had been British protests when the use of torture became known: she said 'the government did lodge protests' to its US counterparts.[15] She and colleagues had known of the techniques of waterboarding and other techniques of pressure while she was director – and had disapproved. 'Nothing – not even the saving of lives – justifies torturing people … the Americans were very keen to conceal from us what they were doing.' In her talk, she took sideswipes at the hawks in the Bush administration, saying that 'Bush, Cheney and Rumsfeld certainly watched *24*' – the Fox television drama that has run since late 2001 and features an agent, Jack Bauer, saving people and sometimes cities from terrorist destruction, often with the use of violence on suspects. In the second of the Reith lectures she gave in 2011, she repeated that torture must be 'utterly rejected even when it may offer the prospect of saving lives'.[16]

Yet the picture is more complex than only one of principled opposition. In an investigation commissioned in 2010 on British involvement in torturing suspects, the retired judge Sir Peter Gibson produced, in 2013, an interim report which concluded that

> *in some instances UK intelligence officers were aware of inappropriate interrogation techniques and mistreatment or allegations of mistreatment of some detainees by liaison partners from other countries … the Inquiry would have wished to examine whether that reporting was adequate and, in particular, whether the Agency Head Offices then responded adequately or, in some cases, at all … in some cases, documents indicate that the Agencies continued to engage with liaison partners in relation to individual detainees where treatment issues may have justified withdrawal or the seeking of appropriate assurances. The Inquiry would have wished to investigate whether the legality of the detainees' detention abroad and the Agencies' own methods of questioning were subject to sufficient scrutiny and consideration.[17]*

Gibson uses the past conditional case because his inquiry was terminated and passed to the parliamentary Intelligence and Security Committee – which has yet (2016) to complete it. Human rights organisations, who treated the appointment of the Gibson Inquiry with suspicion because of his earlier post as an Intelligence Services Commissioner, have said they do not believe a full report will ever be made.

A document obtained by the *Guardian* in 2011 – its origin is not stated, but it appears genuine – gives legal advice to the intelligence services on how to treat evidence which may have been obtained, by foreign agencies with which the British services are working, by torture.[18] The advice stresses that – as the first paragraph states – the intelligence agencies do not 'participate in, solicit, encourage or condone the use of torture or inhuman and degrading treatment'. The greyer area is when information which is valuable and could save lives is known or suspected to have been obtained by torture: in paragraph 38, agents are instructed on the need to balance the 'level of mistreatment' with the possibility of obtaining 'life-saving intelligence'. In a speech[19] he gave while still head of MI6, John Sawers asked his audience to

> suppose we received credible intelligence that might save lives, here or abroad. We have a professional and moral duty to act on it. We will normally want to share it with those who can save those lives. We also have a duty to do what we can to ensure that a partner service will respect human rights. That is not always straightforward. Yet if we hold back, and don't pass that intelligence, out of concern that a suspect terrorist may be badly treated, innocent lives may be lost that we could have saved. These are not abstract questions just for philosophy courses or searching editorials, they are real, constant operational dilemmas.

The situation as it most probably is – that British agencies do not torture but may at times use information which has been so obtained if it is deemed urgent – leaves grey areas, but not (as far as it is known) black ones. The overt prohibition on torture appears strict; and while it is unlikely to stop rough treatment of the kind that remains common in some police stations, the probability is that it is effective in drawing the line some way before waterboarding and rendition to countries whose propensity to torture is the reason they are chosen.

There is thus much less perceived damage to British democracy and civil society, which hard investigation should uncover. It is unlikely that subterranean, 'black' activity has gone on in secret dungeons overseen by British intelligence officers, or flights out of British air bases have been hauling suspects off to the chambers of agony in the Middle East or

Pakistan. There remains dispute over whether or not MI6 officers colluded in torture: a Libyan Islamist militant, Abdel Hakin Belhadj, alleged[20] he had been delivered to torturers in Libya by MI6: an allegation covered fully by both newspapers and NGOs. Britain's journalism and human rights organisations cannot be fairly accused of either complicity or negligence, since there was much less pressure to comply, or to neglect to investigate programmes designed to break the spirit by traumatising the body.

There is another level of accountability, however: one which, in the US (though not in France) usually works much more aggressively and proactively than in the UK, and which provides a significant part of the content and context for American journalists. The Senate and House committees on intelligence routinely inquire into the conduct of the agencies – 17 in all – in the US intelligence community; they have large and expert staffs and are free from any institutional (though will have unofficial) ties to the political parties, or to the administration. They were certainly part of the surge of patriotism after the war, which chilled any serious inquiry into secret service wrongdoing: and a few of the members knew about it, at least in outline. But they recovered, belatedly, and have produced grimly critical reports.

In the UK, the Intelligence and Security Committee (ISC) was first appointed under the Intelligence Services Act in 1994. It is perennially criticised – by journalists and human rights NGOs for being too compliant and by the intelligence services for being too nosy and careless of the need for operational secrecy. Stephen Grey, in interview, is relatively indulgent to the ISC:

> *you can't blame them for everything: there are some good people on it. But the people on the Congressional and Senate committees on the secret services are in a different league. There are many of them, and they are often poachers turned gamekeepers. And their investigations go deep into the agencies – where in the UK the committee talks only to the heads of the agencies. And they have very little in the way of staff.*

Grey, who has worked in both the US and the UK, is a severe critic of US actions in the war on terror – and an enthusiast for the openness of the people who speak for the agencies and the administration, and of officials. He contrasts the British approach to the latter's disadvantage.

> *MI5 set up a press office to widen the circle of those they talked to in the newspapers [as did MI6, later]. They confined themselves at first to the editors*

of the broadsheets – not the tabloids – though they spoke to the editors of the tabloids. There was only one who dealt with the press. They would talk to journalists on general issues, not on operational matters. Though they said they didn't talk about operational matters, but they did if it suited them, and if the operations were over.

They were cloistered people. For example, they would say, 'We have gay officers', that is, they had dropped a ban on gay officers: and we wrote stories about that. The relationships were based on 'cherished access'. They didn't like dealing with newcomers or freelancers.

The big difference between the US and the UK is that the US people were always very straight. They took criticism. I had written a book on rendition which was very revelatory of the CIA. The next time I asked for a briefing it was given without hesitation, and as fully as ever. The agencies here don't want to deal with critics. The US is much more grown up in speaking to journalists. There is a professional concept. A reporter in the UK can't do a fully good job. There's a culture clash. The secret services just don't want to be held under scrutiny. The secret services in the UK have the reporters too close – in the sense that they become 'mitarbeiters' – co-workers. So those that are in the know are inhibited. It's not just the attitude to journalists. It's a measure of the difference in cultures. Stories on security were tremendously powerful in the newsroom. So of course there was a pressure not to be critical – because then you would lose access and a fund of good stories.

In a later book, Grey dug deep into the evidence of WMD brought by 'Curveball', the code name for an Iraqi source who had told the German BND domestic security service that Saddam had mobile laboratories to make biological weapons. It turned out to be a wholly false revelation which was believed, and formed a substantial part of the 'proofs' which Secretary of State Colin Powell presented to the UN to prompt a move to war. In the same book, he gave a fine definition of what makes a good spy – 'they must be patriots but their patriotism should be rooted in serving their society's and humanity's wider values … what is most needed is total independence of thought, allied to accountability of action'.[21]

Few others in the UK have the experience to give status to that observation: though several work the same theme. Nick Hopkins reported for the *Daily Mail* and the *Guardian* (at the time of writing he is an investigative reporter on BBC *Newsnight*) where he wrote, in 2014, several pieces on the effects of the Snowden revelations, broadly supportive of the

Guardian's decision to publish a selection of the stolen documents. He highlighted the greater willingness of President Obama to overhaul US intelligence following the leaks, while 'the UK government remains closed to a real privacy debate'.[22] He wrote of the 'periods of indifference, heavy-handedness and blind fury[23] with which the British political class reacted to the leaks, but in the end were forced to admit that he 'had a point'. He also gave the view of a barrister, Jemima Stratford QC, that the British surveillance system was 'probably illegal'.[24] While at the *Guardian*, he reported on his own editor's view that oversight of the UK agencies' work was 'laughable' and that the claim that the Chinese and Russian intelligence services had probably obtained all of Snowden's files was 'theatrical'. This was in contrast to the then Foreign Secretary, William Hague, who had said that 'we have probably the strongest system [of oversight] in the world. Not only do I and the Home Secretary oversee these things, but we have commissioners who oversee our work and report to the prime minister. No country has a stronger system than that.'[25]

The BBC, which has by far the largest staff of journalists (c. 5,400 in April 2016)[26] of any news medium in the UK and one of the biggest in the world, had in the 2000s and 2010s reporters covering the intelligence and defence world who were academically well-qualified for their posts: in two cases they have experience as army officers. The leading correspondents are: Gordon Corera, Security Correspondent, a history graduate of Oxford and a graduate student at Harvard on US Foreign Policy, who had a brief spell as an aide in Bill Clinton's campaign but has otherwise worked only for the BBC; Frank Gardner, also a Security Correspondent, with a degree from Essex in Arabic and Islamic Studies and a career in marketing and investment banking before joining the Corporation; and Mark Urban, a graduate in International Relations of the London School of Economics, Diplomatic Editor on BBC's *Newsnight*, who joined the BBC after university, left soon after joining to spend three years as a Defence Correspondent on the *Independent*, before rejoining and remaining with the BBC.

Both Urban and Gardner served in the Territorial Army (Urban also had a nine-month short-term commission in the regular army). Gardner, in Saudi Arabia with a cameraman in June 2004, was shot several times by an al Qaeda sympathiser and left for dead; his cameraman was killed. Still in great pain, he recovered, but was left semi-paralysed and unable to walk. Interviewed in 2014, and asked if he could forgive his would-be assassin, who was executed, he said: 'Forgiveness is not really an option

[but] … I don't feel any kind of triumphalism at all. This is no one-nil moment. Justice has been served. The court has looked at the evidence. My understanding is that he has not offered any defence for what he did. It was inexcusable.'[27]

Energetic broadcasters, Corera and Urban are both successful authors. In 2015, Corera published a book which displayed an apparent mastery of the swift transition in computer technology from primitive text messaging among scientists to a vast worldwide field of information where control of that information, and of others' use of it, has become the focus for personal, commercial, political and military battles. Mindful of the demand for balance by the employer he has served all of his working life, Corera insists on the complexity of dilemmas which are often posed in sharply polemical, black and white frames:

> the fundamental questions of the crypto wars – privacy versus security, anonymity versus identifiability and the place of encryption – remain unanswered. Some people ask if we should be more scared of our governments or those that they are there to protect us from. The answer to that may well be where you live, and what your politics are … you might want your data to be secure in order for it to be private from prying eyes. A company may encrypt it for you but also scan it themselves to sell you things. A state may demand the data for its definition of security. But you might rely on the same state to protect your data from cyber criminals and foreign cyber spies. And to do that the state may want to scan information going in and out of the country to spot them … the choice may not be simple in a global, interconnected world.[28]

His 2011 book[29] on spies has a careful and quite detailed rehearsal of who did what when to whom in the political run-up to the Iraq War – including the crucial evidence provided by the Iraqi known as 'Curveball' to the German secret service – where (as Grey had also concluded) he was 'clumsily debriefed' with 'leading questions' put to him. Experienced in the medium of television, which has as much performance and presentation in it as substance, Corera was able to catch the political world's sweat, deadlines and tension of both the behind-the-scenes suppliers of texts and the principals who had to present and be held to account for it. 'There are only', he concluded, 'a handful of secret services which aggressively practice the recruitment and running of human sources around the world – the Americans, the Russians, the Chinese, the Israelis, the French and the British' – a claim often made by the British intelligence officers (though at times they place themselves second only to the US), and also one which gives status and relevance to those who, for the national and world broadcaster, are tasked with illuminating the secret world.

Urban is more attached to the military, more knowledgeable about them and – like Anthony Loyd on *The Times*, a former army officer – more successful in cultivating and benefiting from relationships with them, including the special services. Loyd, who had been the first to break the story that Syrian President Bashar Assad had used chemical weapons on the insurgents fighting him, was captured and shot in the legs near Aleppo when trying to escape – then tried again, and did escape, to Turkey. In a recapitulation of his capture, he vividly conveyed[30] both the suddenness of being taken when he thought his mission was nearly over and the clarity of thought he was still able to muster, working out that when one of his capturers returned to him the inhaler he used to calm his asthma, he might have a chance:

> *that moment was an epiphany: We were hostages whose lives had value. They were not going to kill us. Instead, they likely were planning to sell us to a jihadi group – an increasingly common practice among rebel groups in Syria. At that point, of course, all bets would be off. Still, this was key information that I was determined to exploit. If these men could be made to believe I was sick with some condition they only half-understood, I figured, they'd underestimate me, providing me an edge when I got the chance to run.*

For his bestseller,[31] Urban wrote an account of the British troops, especially those in the SAS, in the southern Iraqi port of Basra from 2003. It was a story which, among much else, brought out the difference between the American special forces who worked by the take-no-prisoners rules of the Iraqi War and the British equivalents. The British, in spite of their toughening training and tougher experience, were said by Urban to be deeply divided on the extremity of the violence they were commanded – from the supreme commander in the country, US General Stanley McChrystal – to deploy.

Unlike a piece written around the same time in the US weekly *Rolling Stone* about McChrystal and his aides in Afghanistan,[32] Urban's reportage is generally admiring, an account of soldiers under great pressure, faced with competing, and ultimately incompatible, demands upon them – written by one who had some personal sense of what soldiering meant, even if never in such extreme circumstances (he had briefly commanded a British Chieftain tank, but not in battle). His earlier book[33] on espionage in the UK includes a passage in which he illuminates the reluctance with which the services approached the press, even when forced to by being 'avowed' and having parliamentary oversight which pushed them to have a means of explaining themselves directly to the press.

On the day in October 1994 when the Intelligence Services Act, which gave a legal basis for the first time to MI6 and GCHQ, was passed, MI5 and MI6 participated in a unique press conference in the Foreign Office. The then head of MI6, Sir Colin McColl (1989–94) banned cameras: he explained, in response to a question, that he had done so because

> *Secrecy is our absolute stock in trade, it is our most precious asset. People come and work for us, risk their lives for us sometimes, risk their jobs often, because they believe the SIS is a secret service ... I am very anxious that I should be able to send some sort of signal to those people that we are not going to open up everything, we are not going to open up our files, we are not going to allow ourselves to be undressed in public with their names as part of the baggage.*[34]

Urban concludes – it is a theme much stressed by UK journalists writing on their country's security services – that 'more than anything else, British intelligence is a system for repacking information gathered by the USA. Most intelligence relates to foreign or defence policy, most of that intelligence is sigint and the vast majority of sigint processed at Cheltenham [GCHQ] has been obtained from the USA.'

In a short book[35] published in 2015, Urban sounded an alarm that the West was disarming, while the East was arming: as the *Daily Telegraph*'s Chief Foreign Correspondent David Blair wrote in his review[36] of the book, Urban 'lays out the way in which an entire continent has chosen the path of wholesale disarmament ... impossible to read this authoritative book without feeling a deep sense of alarm, indeed of wonder, that our leaders have chosen to take such breathtaking risks'. In interview, Urban was explicit about his view that 'it's all over for the West: in 30–50 years, the US must either decide to default on its debts to China, or go to war with it. The inability for democracies to live within their means is chronic and it doesn't seem as if it can be solved.'

Like any reporter who must inform an audience on a (sometimes) daily basis, Urban has close links with sources, including the intelligence services, and has had for three decades. This is now seen by a new generation of radical reporters, powerful in the US, as collusion: aware of the changed ecology in which he works, Urban says that

> *the security services were drawn increasingly into court cases, as that of Cathy Massiter.[37] They were forced into having a more functional relationship with journalists. So those of us covering the beat had an identity of a spokesman, and a phone number. You could negotiate the terms of openness. Often when they briefed they were also lobbying through us – for more money. At times I felt they were spinning us dodgy stories and took the decision simply not to use them. The relationship with Security Service was first – then with the Secret Intelligence Service. But the relationship with GCHQ remains completely non functional.*
>
> *The charge made against us was always, 'You are a stooge'. But in fact we were told quite a lot of useful stuff. The relationship between us and the services varied as to their helpfulness: the SIS [MI6] did more to shape the narrative during and leading up to the Iraq War.*

Urban, who with his colleagues reported extensively on the Snowden leaks, told me that

> *Snowden and Glen Greenwald and the others did do us all a favour; it was important to get out some of this stuff and to have a public debate. I think that Snowden had to show he had the real stuff in the form of files when he went public – wouldn't have been enough to resign without leaking, and then claim that the NSA was hoovering up all this stuff. He could have taken the black budget of the secret services – no reason why that should be kept secret, people should know what they're doing with their money.*
>
> *It should only be that stuff about which there should be a public debate. Yet they came out with so much more. And the reaction of the people, the authorities, who should have pushed back against that was quite feeble. The arrest of the partner of Glen Greenwald was the one time they were proactive and thought, 'Maybe he has the stuff'. They were very passive otherwise. I understand Alan Rusbridger was upset that there wasn't more of a reaction to the revelations – so the* Guardian *published more and more. It was right to publish the public interest stuff: but then it got into areas which were not in the public interest, and publishing that could have been dangerous.*

If you ask me, 'Do I believe this caused damage?' – yes I do. A US journalist who writes a lot about these issues said to me, 'It's probably true that Russia and China have got his stuff' – not necessarily from his computer, which may well be empty of it – but at a prior stage. Alan Rusbridger and the others can't have it both ways: they can't say, 'This is terribly important to get out', and then say, 'It had no effect on operations'.

The pessimism which Urban shows about the future of the West is based, in part, on his perception that authority is declining – and this, too, he believes, is perilous, because the public does not listen to, believe, or trust well-founded warnings on the growing dangers of the world, some of which the secret services must attempt to thwart, or at least moderate. He is more alert to the dangers confronting the country, and the world, than he is to the challenge the secret services may offer to civil liberties. Like his colleague Corera, he knows that 'some people ask if we could be more scared of our governments or those that they are there to protect us from'. He decisively chooses the latter fear as a more rational one to have: 'I think there is a widespread distrust for all authority. But if people who criticise or dismiss the security services knew what the situation was, they would think again.'

The most influential among British journalists who believe that the publication of Snowden's material is not just irresponsible but wholly dangerous, even treacherous, is a senior editor of *The Economist*, Edward Lucas. For many years a correspondent in the former Soviet Union, Lucas has long been strongly anti-communist and opposed to the authoritarian, post-Soviet regime of President Vladimir Putin. His *The New Cold War*[38] argues that, in contemporary Russia, 'repression at home is matched by aggression abroad' – a judgement written even before the seizing by Russia of the Ukrainian province of Crimea, and the support, with weaponry and troops, of the insurgents in eastern Ukraine. In 2014, he published a long essay,[39] *The Snowden Operation: Inside the West's Greatest Intelligence Disaster*, in which he argued that the theft of the material 'weakens America's relations with Europe and other allies; it harms security relationships between these allies, particularly in Europe; it corrodes Western public opinion's trust in their countries' security and intelligence services; it undermines the West's standing in the eyes of the rest of the world; and it has paralysed Western intelligence agencies'. Lucas continues, 'All these are bad. And as it happens, they are also all Kremlin priorities:

if Vladimir Putin were writing a "to do" list of his officials, it would have all these five points on it'.

This *cui bono* argument leads him to speculate that Snowden may have been a Russian agent. He reasons that had he been a concerned or morally outraged whistleblower, he would simply have leaked the document which showed that Verizon, the US mobile phone company, must hand over its customers' phone records, an arrangement which is legal and time-honoured, but unknown and, in Lucas's words, 'still shocking … there are reasonable grounds for worrying about a single government agency creating an automatic, perpetual, searchable warehouse for all such information'. That he did not do so, and instead seized huge amounts of material which he could not have read before taking, allows Lucas to moot the possibility that 'something more sinister than mere naiveté and carelessness is afoot'.

Reconstructing his subject's pre-leaks biography, Lucas finds that Snowden, who turned rapidly from a right-wing patriot to one who organised the largest intelligence leak in history, might have been turned by the Russians since he was, according to the former NSA analyst John Schindler, 'intelligent, highly naïve and totally uninformed',[40] and thus a perfect target for the Russian SVR, its MI6/CIA equivalent. After giving more circumstantial evidence, Lucas concedes that there is no proof – but leaves hanging the possibility, draped with the many loose threads of Snowden's life. Whether or not he is a Soviet agent, or as he has also written a 'useful idiot' (though the two can coexist in one person), is thus unclear. Lucas told a conference[41] in March 2014 that 'if Snowden had approached me with these documents I would have marched him down to Bow Street police station and asked them to arrest him'.

Lucas says that the secret services should be held to close account, and thinks that those working for the services should, if found to be digging improperly into people's private lives, be severely disciplined. But he also believes that they are

> *a special case. They break the law. They steal secrets. They cannot be judged on the same criteria as other institutions. If you have them you must expect that they are different. But in reporting them, you must be very careful that the services really are doing something way off their mission. You must have a very high bar in deciding to report on their activities. And the journalism you do must vary according to the*

level of the threat. When you are dealing with terrorist cases – you must aim off a bit. In the case of Northern Ireland, for example [Lucas had reported from there] I would cut the spies some slack. It's all about judgment at the time and in the context. You must think: how big is the wrong doing.

Lucas does not take the same position as Chapman Pincher had: he would not suborn journalism to security by falsifying the former to assist the latter. He argues instead that, because of the particular nature of intelligence work and its importance in maintaining security, revelation must confine itself to major dereliction of duty or fundamentally aberrant behaviour.

That last is an important condition, which divides reporters everywhere. The current assumption in journalism is that what is discovered should be uncovered (or, in journalism's use of the word, 'covered'), and that the public interest which is ascribed to the publication of the story overcomes almost all appeals for it not to be covered. The default position on security stories has shifted from a respectful acquiescence to the need for secrecy to one where such acquiescence is seen as backing away from a journalist's responsibility – including by journalists who would previously have agreed not to publish. This is especially the case in the US: Dean Baquet of the *New York Times*, who had acquiesced in holding stories after requests from government, said in an interview that 'I don't think I was hard enough earlier on … I think I am tougher now and hold them [the administration] to higher standards.'[42]

In the Snowden case, Lucas runs against the direction Baquet has taken – and which, since it is the *New York Times*, will serve as something of a model worldwide. Where Baquet argues for increased scepticism about the intelligence services pronouncements, stemming from a sense that he had been played as a sucker before by the CIA, Lucas argues that the scope of any revelations about the work of the secret services must always be calibrated to the danger posed to that work by the revelations. He also dismisses the case made by Glen Greenwald, the journalist closest to Snowden, that the bulk collection of data on communications is a step towards authoritarianism – a view which others, such as the British journalist and novelist Henry Porter, and Alan Rusbridger, former editor of the *Guardian*, partly share. Lucas says: 'Glen Greenwald thinks that we are on the way to an authoritarian society. He also believes that the US is at the root of all evil in the contemporary world – but there is little evidence. It's a faith which they have. If he had simply been an investigative reporter and uncovered a lot about the NSA – there's a distinguished tradition in the US doing this. But he is after something else.'

David Omand, a former head of GCHQ, says of Lucas's suspicion that 'there's no evidence that Snowden was a plant. Rather that he was a naïve man who fell into the hands of bad journalists. Especially Laura Poitras.' But he adds

> She must have had an arrangement with Assange – he sent his lawyer out to Hong Kong to talk to Snowden. She bought him the ticket to go there – which was a strange choice, since it's very much watched. She introduced him to the Russian consul there. Assange told Snowden that he had to go to Russia because if he went somewhere else, like Cuba or Venezuela, the US would assassinate him.

The newspapers and websites, which take the view that the intelligence services are increasingly essential to the security of the British public, can be helpful to them, if less directly and proudly than with Pincher. This support is wise marketing – for the intelligence services are popular with the public, and are not feared by the majority. Polls show that 64 per cent of the UK population think the intelligence services have enough, or too few powers to protect the UK public – with only 19 per cent saying they have too many (the rest do not know).[43] Nearly 60 per cent are not worried by surveillance by the security services (though half of that number thinks it is wrong); while a further 7 per cent also think it right, but are worried). Less than a third are worried and think it wrong.

In a move which had at least one member of the Intelligence and Security Committee 'stunned' by the amount of detail disclosed, The Times, in October 2015 did a short series on GCHQ, with a picture of its recently appointed director, Robert Hannigan, atop the first piece.[44] The writer was Ben Macintyre, an associate editor and columnist of the paper, an expert on espionage, with a series of books on spies throughout history: his 2015 book on Philby[45] received a chorus of praise from reviewers. Macintyre explained the sudden opening of GCHQ doors by pointing to

> the explosion of the internet, the astonishingly rapid evolution of communications technology and the revelations of the NSA whistleblower Edward Snowden [which] have changed [GCHQ secrecy] for ever: GCHQ is opening its doors, at least a crack, to reveal what it does, if not exactly how it is done. This is the first time that GCHQ has allowed its most

senior officials to be interviewed, on the record, and even, in the case of those with a public profile, by name. 'GCHQ has to be out there,' one of the senior officials says. 'We can't operate behind veils of secrecy any more'.[46]

'Out there' is not very far out. On Macintyre's tour of inspection, he was not allowed to inspect much: officials, alerted to his presence, blanked their screens or showed a screen saver. He is reassuring:

> GCHQ is not in the business of routinely reading your emails. The myths that Britain is subject to mass surveillance by GCHQ, or that certain trigger words set off alarm bell … are just that. The data harvested is foreign in focus; given the global nature of internet traffic, this may well include communications to and from people in Britain. To investigate an individual in Britain any further, an additional warrant would be required. … at each stage, the hunters must clearly explain and justify why the action being taken is both 'necessary' and 'proportionate' … as one GCHQ official put it: 'The challenge is how do we fillet out information without looking like the Stasi? The mission is about saving lives but also obeying the letter of the law'.[47]

The reassurance continued in the second piece, a day later.

> [R]epeated by almost everyone I meet at GCHQ is that everything is done under the strictest legal framework. Every stage of an investigation must be justified as 'necessary and proportionate'; legal training is mandatory for anyone who accesses, handles or makes decisions about operational data, and is repeated every two years. Two commissioners inspect the books twice a year. 'There is rigorous oversight,' the senior legal adviser to GCHQ says. 'Lawyers look at everything we do.' That insistence on demonstrating legal oversight is not just PR; nor is it a direct response to the perception, again largely powered by the Snowden revelations, that GCHQ routinely invades the privacy of ordinary citizens without controls or hindrance, although the spectre of Snowden still hangs over GCHQ. 'The Snowden leaks were an attack on our community,' one analyst said. 'It was really upsetting. On the day it happened, there were people in tears'.[48]

There is no reason why journalism should not be reassuring about systems which the reporter is convinced are robust, both in seeking to protect the British public and in complying with the law. But it was seen as outrageous by some, including Shami Chakrabarti, former director of Liberty, who expressed herself as amazed that the GCHQ would go so far as to open itself up merely, as she thought, to gain a victory in the propaganda war – and thinks the opposite of Macintyre, that is, that GCHQ *is* practising PR. Interviewed, she said:

> *I do think the agencies should be more public: but there's a difference between transparency and spin. They've gone on the front foot for PR, post Snowden – there's been a PR offensive. The agencies have always seen that their work will involve propaganda – no problem with that in principle, but they're not being honest with themselves, and they're not honest about the difference between PR and transparency.*

She thinks that the news media have an 'essential problem' with the coverage of the secret services:

> *they have to be secret: even I have to accept that. But that's a huge problem because there's a lot of pressure to cover them in a heroic light. I was in the Home Office, and I know that there is something inherently exhilarating about being given access. After 9/11 they created secret institutions or strengthened the existing ones – and for politicians, lawyers and journalists, a psychological trap is set: when you have privileged access, you are grateful.*

Chakrabarti, daughter of Bengali immigrants, a barrister who left the Home Office to lead Liberty (which had evolved from the National Council for Civil Liberties), is the highest-profile critic of the agencies among the several civil and human rights organisations in the UK, and the one most likely to be featured on, or quoted in, the news media. Giving the Reading Agency lecture[49] in December 2015, she asked, rhetorically, 'when will our leaders truly learn from the misjudged, misnamed "War on Terror" and the language trap that both dignifies the enemy and undermines our own democratic doctrine?' She set this beside another misnaming, that practised by IS, which 'can dehumanise the Parisian victims of its recent barbarism as long as they are "crusaders" or "pagans" gathered for a concert of "prostitution and vice" rather than the easy innocent civilian targets that they plainly were'. It was a parallel criticism which ran the risk of arguing a moral equality between democratic politicians and Islamist terrorists, underscored by her excoriating, in the same lecture, UK politicians for 'rush[ing] to

Paris to say "Je suis Charlie" [after terrorist murders at the French satirical weekly *Charlie Hebdo*] ... only to return to London with promises of crackdowns on debate in mosques and universities as part of their "domestic extremism" agenda'. (Chakrabarti resigned from the leadership of Liberty in 2016.)

Her critique was all the more influential because it was legally backed, sharing the qualms many lawyers have of the extension of legislative powers and curbs on speech as well as on action. Ken (Lord) MacDonald, Director of Public Prosecutions from 2003–8, warned in the CPS Lecture[50] just before he retired that

> we need to take very great care not to fall into a way of life in which freedom's back is broken by the relentless pressure of a security State. ... technology ... gives the State enormous powers of access to knowledge and information about each one of us. And the ability to collect and store it at will. Every second of every day, in everything we do ... we need to understand that it is in the nature of State power that decisions taken in the next few months and years about how the State may use these powers, and to what extent, are likely to be irreversible. They will be with us forever. And they in turn will be built upon. So we should take very great care to imagine the world we are creating before we build it. We might end up living with something we can't bear.

MacDonald conjures up the 'slippery slope'; the view that legislation, and the acts of police, intelligence services and the decisions of the courts based on the legislation, will make the state steadily less liberal and more authoritarian, each descent from the main tenets of a liberal order accelerating the shift to an intolerant and repressive state. It is one of the most important elements in the coverage of the response to terrorism, and in particular in the response to Snowden, since its power proceeds as much from an implicit fear as an explicit threat – a fear that illiberality has a momentum which, beyond a certain point, will be both unstoppable and empowering of a governing and security class who together cow the population in the name of protection from an evil whose force is exaggerated in order to support the security state. In this context, it is instructive to compare Henry Porter's monitory novel, *The Dying Light*, in which malign security service people collaborate with populist politicians to close down British freedoms, with the novels of the former MI6 officer Alan Judd, in which the secret services are staffed by men and women who are fallible but dedicated, in an understated British way, to the protection of the public and the preservation of a liberal society.

MacDonald's critique is amply shared in what has seemed a surprising quarter. It is a curiosity that the most ardent critic of the government's – any government's – tendency to choose hard responses to terror threats should be a Conservative MP, and one who has spent much of his parliamentary career on the right of his party. David Davis, who had been a Foreign Office Minister in the Major-led Conservative government, had a working-class upbringing, enrolled briefly in the SAS, went to business school and became an executive in the sugar industry. In Parliament, he revealed himself as opposed to the European Union – though he was Europe Minister in the Major government from 1994 to 1997. Strongly opposed to Britain's membership of the European Union, he was created Cabinet Minister for Exiting the European Union in July 2016.

Davis retains many of these views, but in one area has emerged into an area generally reserved for liberals and the left, as a strong supporter in parliament of human and civil rights, and of free speech. It is a position which sees him oppose not just his own party, but also Labour, and, when they were in a coalition government with the Conservatives from 2010 to 2015, the Liberal Democrats. In 2008 he resigned from his seat (while he was Shadow Home Secretary) in order to prompt a debate in the country about the erosion of civil liberties – this was on the day after the passing of a parliamentary vote on the Counter Terrorism Bill, extending the period in which a terror suspect can be held from 28 to 42 days (the measure was later dropped). In a speech to the Hay Festival in May 2009, he said that the left had been a champion of civil liberties, initially because of its interest in securing freedom for trade union organisation; but had ceased to care. Quoting the former Labour Home Secretary Jack Straw as saying that 'Britain is not a police state', he agreed – then asked rhetorically, 'when do you become a police state: when is your freedom really eroded? When the government knows everything about you?' – an argument, some years before the Snowden revelations, that data bases on every citizen and ubiquitous CCTV cameras were the preconditions for the conclusion of such a state, and were taking the UK closer to it.

For Davis, a police state is a real, alarming and approaching condition. When I asked him what – aside from the evidence that bulk collection of communications data was common – showed the advent of such a state, he instanced the forced resignation of the former BBC journalist Martin Sixsmith from the post of Director of Communications at the Department of Transport – after Sixsmith had opposed the actions by Jo Moore, an adviser to the then Transport Secretary Stephen Byers, in 'burying' bad news on railway performance on the day of Princess Margaret's funeral;[51] the allegations that Pam Warren, a survivor of the Paddington train crash, and a fierce campaigner and government critic, had had her sex life investigated on the suggestion of a Labour special adviser – a charge Davis made on the floor of the House of Commons in May 2006, and was criticised for lack of evidence by Labour's Ed Miliband, then a junior minister in the Blair government; and the arrest, in November 2008 of Damian Green, then the Conservative opposition spokesman on immigration, for publicising information leaked to him from the Home Office on illegal immigration. Green was not held after his arrest and no charges were brought against him or the leaker, Christopher Galley – who was, however, dismissed. Galley, an official at the Home Office, had contacted both Davis and Green two years before the arrest, angered by the failures on immigration policy which were, he later said, 'at least as bad as Mr Davis had thought, possibly worse'.[52] When I asked if he thought these were major breaches, Davis said the incidents were evidence of a mindset which could descend to more severe restriction of liberty.

The British government does try to restrict publication, and thus arguably liberty, in some cases – with a system which attempts to limit publication of material it thinks would be dangerous if put in the public domain. It did think this about the stories the *Guardian* published from Snowden. A Defence Advisory (DA) notice was issued on 7 June 2013, the day the paper published the first story on the NSA's Prism programme, asking all other news media not to pick up on the story. Editors were asked not to publish information that may 'jeopardise both national security and possibly UK personnel'.[53] Most followed the guidance.

The DA notice – still often called by its pre-1993 name, D-notice – is a voluntary system under which news organisations can check with the secretary of the DA-notice committee – a senior diplomat – on something which may be dangerous to report or reveal; and which issues advisory notices in an effort to stop publication of sensitive material. At the *Guardian*, Rusbridger determined to ignore the committee – though as the stories continued, he did turn to it for guidance. David Omand said in an interview that the *Guardian* editor 'first made the decision that he would be capable of choosing what did and what did not go into the paper. Then he joined the D notice system – implicitly admitting he didn't know. He never admitted to that.'

Rusbridger disputes Omand's view.

> We didn't tell the D-notice man about the first story because we weren't
> confident that the British state in some form wouldn't move to injunct us.
> That turns out to have been a reasonable fear. After the first story I spoke to
> [Air Vice Marshal Andrew] Vallance [director of the D-notice committee]
> and we agreed we would have an ongoing relationship. That turned out to
> be fruitful. He came into the Guardian at once point and talked to the
> newsroom [off the record]. I have admitted that I've spoken to the committee
> – I've spoken about it on numerous occasions, including I think before
> the [Keith] Vaz [Home Affairs] committee.

In October 2013, the then prime minister David Cameron said in the House
of Commons that continued publication by the *Guardian* could result in a
court injunction to stop publishing: he said that the paper should show
social responsibility. His statement came after the Conservative MP Julian
Smith quoted a report in an edition of the *Sun* that said Britain's intelligence
agencies believed details from the NSA files leaked by the US whistleblower
Edward Snowden had hampered their work.[54]

Davis is a strong critic of journalism on the issues which have come
to define him: he said that

> the press is bloody awful at doing its job. There are two syndromes – one,
> in a world where news is both secret and glamorous there's a huge
> premium on access and the stories access brings. The journalist becomes
> too close to his source, and is unwilling to upset them, and you can't verify
> what is written. See the Sunday Times *story quoting Downing Street*
> sources on the belief that the Snowden leaks – all – are now in the hands
> of the secret services of China and Russia. Some of it is demonstrably
> wrong. Some of it was altered on the web after being printed.[55] Second,
> government can silence critics through the press: see the NGOs being
> ambushed by a member of the Intelligence and Security Committee:[56]
> asked if it were worth losing lives to uphold civil liberties. That was a trap.

* * *

Davis allows the *Guardian* an exception from his general contempt for the
British press: indeed, he shares the paper's distress that other newspapers
did not more fully support the paper (they did not have the Snowden

material: but the charge is that, having seen it and having ensured that it was genuine, they could have more robustly interrogated the security services and the government). The *Guardian* did not just take a lonely lead among British papers, it pushed harder than any other publication on the stories – except, in some cases, the German weekly *Der Spiegel*. Under the editorship of Alan Rusbridger (1995–2015), the paper went further to the left than it had before, but retained a mix of approaches in its many columns – from the often angry Marxism of Seamus Milne (who left in the summer of 2015 to be director of communications for the newly elected leader of the Labour Party, Jeremy Corbyn) to the often angry liberal conservatism of Simon Jenkins, through the often angry social democracy of Polly Toynbee – together with centre-leftists like Rafael Behr, Jonathon Freedland, Martin Kettle, among others. However, on the Snowden revelations, the main journalists involved were, when separately interviewed, largely of one mind. They were strongly for their publication, and strongly supportive of the way in which the newspaper handled it.

Their agreement rested on several factors, important among which was a sense that they could handle the stuff. Janine Gibson, who was head of the *Guardian*'s operations in the US and was then appointed head of BuzzFeed UK – having just missed out on the post-Rusbridger editorship, though she was his candidate – said that

> because we had all worked on Wikileaks, we were well versed in the ways to make these decisions. Most other journalists have not been faced with a massive data dump. Nor faced with a situation where, in the case of Wikileaks, your boss is going to get on the phone with Hillary Clinton [then US Secretary of State] and have a discussion about American lives being lost. And most other journalists haven't had to look at a leak repeatedly and ask – have we identified anyone here who could be at risk? What category of risk could this be?
>
> Alan and Ian [Katz: then deputy editor, left in 2013 to edit the BBC news programme Newsnight] made the decisions on Wikileaks – but I was around enough to know the criteria on which decisions were made. And at various times I had to make a decision to say – yes, that can go. Had I not gone through all of that the speed with which we moved on Snowden would not have been possible. It was like being at a finishing school.

The *Guardian* staffers shared a common belief that what Snowden's leaks revealed were an affront to civil rights. Henry Porter, with others including

Simon Jenkins and Richard Norton Taylor, the paper's first security correspondent, advised Rusbridger on publishing the material. He says that 'I do think that targeted surveillance is necessary, but mass surveillance can be abused – and has been, by GCHQ, when it listened to conversations between a lawyer and clients. I believe strongly in privacy – in its giving a sense of individual, internal freedom.'[57] Gibson, more graphically, said that when they had downloaded the material, 'we sat on the couch with a cheap computer we had bought so it couldn't be traced – and went through the documents – and all you could hear was "fucking hell" – just swearing – and "Look at that! Look at that!"'

Ewen MacAskill, the paper's intelligence correspondent with two decades on the paper, was sent with Glen Greenwald and Laura Poitras to check out Snowden in Hong Kong, so that the paper could be reassured that – as Gibson put it – 'this was not going to be a rerun of the *Hitler Diaries*'.[58] He relates the ubiquity of private information in state hands to his own situation.

> *I'm glad the intelligence agencies are there and doing what they do – but the onus is on them to justify bulk data collection. The problems with that for journalists are horrendous. Supposing someone tells me they don't like something about Faslane [the UK's nuclear submarine base in Scotland's Holy Loch], which happens. Then they [the security services] can say – well, that's a matter of national security. We have to find out who's been giving Ewen MacAskill that information. In a nanosecond they can go back through my emails and calls – and I wouldn't know. I'm pretty sure I was under surveillance post-Snowden – I've no evidence for that – the only thing was that for six months when I entered the UK I would be stopped at the airport. Something flagged up on the computer and they'd ask me to step out for a while, 15–20 minutes. They didn't ask questions, gave me some bullshit reasons, 'Sorry, we had to stop you, because your passport has been lost or stolen', that is, they lied to me.*

The *Guardian*'s former Moscow correspondent Luke Harding – who was effectively expelled from Russia (visa not renewed) after a series of pieces about the Russian secret services – followed MacAskill to Hong Kong and spent some time with Snowden and others in the Hong Kong hotel: he later wrote a fast-paced account of the leaks, with the first insights into the characters of the main protagonists, including, crucially, Snowden: the book became the basis of *Snowden*, a film by Oliver Stone. He said that

> I think you have to say that what the secret services can do has galactically increased in the last 10–15 years. Ewen and I wrote about Tempora[59] – the bulk data collection, trialled in Cornwall with money from the NSA, where they take everything they can, store it for 30 days, then review it. It's a new capacity because technology can do it. It's clear that the ambition, which came through from the Snowden documents, was full take. All message data from everybody globally. The powers are extraordinary – the problem is that the conversation about this and the regulatory framework have fallen behind.

Both MacAskill and Harding, with others, believe that the Intelligence and Security Committee is bad at its job of holding the agencies to account. MacAskill said that

> Someone from the security services said to me, 'Why are you going on about us? All that is old now.' And I said, 'I'm a journalist – if we don't hold you to account who will?' And he said, 'That's not your job, that's the job of parliament. And the judges.' I said, 'The problem is they're not doing it – the ISC under [Sir Malcolm] Rifkind, they're illiterate about the technology, they don't have the staff. If the media aren't doing it who is?'

Alan Rusbridger, interviewed after he had left the *Guardian* to become Principal of Lady Margaret Hall College in Oxford (many of his former staff – Gibson, Harding, Jenkins, Katz, Norton Taylor as well as the new editor, Katharine Viner – were Oxford graduates; he graduated from Cambridge), was the capstone of the operation: another point of agreement among those concerned with the Snowden material was that his leadership was central. By the time he went, he was among the most admired editors of a British general newspaper of his day, inside and outside of his newspaper, sharing the (unofficial) accolade with Paul Dacre of the *Daily Mail* (they have largely – not wholly – different groups of admirers). His reserved, self-composed manner was in strong contrast to Fleet Street's noisy tyrant stereotype – and reality, in some papers. Norton Taylor, the security reporting trade's doyen (he still writes on the issue, part time) said that 'he agonised over the decision about running the Snowden material, and how to run it: when he had made up his mind, he was steely'.

Like Gibson, Rusbridger believes that the Wikileaks episode was a necessary learning experience – and it helped give him a sense of the size of the scoop he got: 'Wikileaks helped in a number of ways – it gave us some experience in handling difficult material. And it's obviously the most secret stuff that our generation of journalists had seen, so it was obviously going to be difficult to handle. We agonised. I discussed it with colleagues, such as Simon Jenkins – showed him a bit.'

Jenkins is among the strongest opponents of an increase in state powers to combat terrorism of any commentator writing in the UK. A column written after the House of Commons voted to join the US and French air forces in bombing IS targets in Syria, claimed that

> bombing Syria has nothing to do with terrorism, except possibly to increase the likelihood of it in Britain. It has nothing positive to contribute to Britain's national security, which is not currently under threat. The idea that ISIS might undermine British values is an insult to those values. That it might attain a caliphate in the Mile End Road is a fantasy of men shut up too long in a Cobra bunker [an expanded acronym for the Cabinet Office Briefing Room, a secure chamber where the response to crises are discussed].[60]

Jenkins' belief is that the dangers to the UK from terrorism are wildly overblown by governments seeking popularity through wrapping themselves in the national flag, and intelligence services seeking more money for operations which are of little use. His advice would be certainly to publish.

Rusbridger said that

> The elements were – who was going to work on this? How would keep it be kept secret? How much to publish? How much to talk to governments? What was legal, what was not? Was the British government going to move against us? Was an injunction likely? Politically, organisationally, legally, this was the most complex story we had ever done. It never occurred to me not to look at. Maybe there would have been journalists who would have said: this is too secret – can't even look at this. But after taking the decision that I would look at it, I was going to publish it – and do it on a story by story basis.

He took the paper to a Pulitzer in 2014 (shared with the *Washington Post*) and came to admire the US press culture more than his own. One of the learning experiences he underwent during the Wikileaks publication with the *New York Times* was

> to learn from them how they regarded national security stories, which was generally a bit more robust than some of the Brit press.
>
> There's no official secrets act in the US and it's impossible to injunct a newspaper – which is something that's been under-examined. As a result of the Pentagon Papers case, every lawyer thinks it's almost inconceivable that the US government would ever move against a newspaper in advance – and that leads to a better conversation. You can lift the phone and discuss things with the administration in a more adult way – with the government or the agencies. You can say, 'We've got this stuff – we're going to publish it, what do you want to say?' The British government was not like that at all.

Rusbridger met Stewart Baker during a debate, a lawyer and a former General Counsel of the NSA in the Bush administration. 'He said, "Look, once the stuff is in the hands of journalists, the journalists are absolutely protected. But if I met Snowden tomorrow he'd be in jail for the rest of his life". His line was, "I completely understand why you publish this."'

All of those on the *Guardian* who worked on the story were disappointed in the response of the rest of the British news media: Harding said that

> I'm most disappointed here in the BBC – no one followed us up. We had a sensational story and no one did it. You can understand why the Murdoch papers didn't, for political reasons, and for hatred of us because of our phone-hacking investigation [led by the Guardian's Nick Davies, centred on the News of the World, Britain's most popular tabloid, which News International felt constrained to close]. In the BBC, I know from friends that there was this notice that went round – top-level meeting about what to do about it – and the decision was, not to do anything about it. Ignore the story. We had the absurd spectacle of an interview with William Hague after another major piece – Evan Davis [the main host of Newsnight] interviewed him – not a single question on Snowden – that was cowardly. The BBC did eventually come round – it took them six to nine months. Gordon Corera finally did some stuff – Panorama did an interview with Snowden last week [October 2015: the interview was done by the long-time journalist-specialist on terrorism, Peter Taylor] – after practically everyone else – I think he was quite reluctant to see them.

For the BBC, James Harding (no relation of Luke), when asked by the *Guardian* writer Charlotte Higgins about the lack of coverage, said that

> *I think the thing that is really tricky on Snowden is where you get yourself straddling a line between reporting a story and campaigning on a story ... obviously we cannot campaign. We cannot use the public's money to make an argument. And the nature of that kind of leak and that kind of story was that the person who held the information wanted a certain story and to roll it out in a certain way. That deal, the deal between, if you like, the media organisation and the source – I'm not sure we could have done that deal ... So in my last job [as editor of* The Times*] I ran a campaign on something you may think as innocuous as cycling safety. You couldn't campaign on cycling safety at the BBC. And that's where things are different.*[61]

The BBC did do the story, long before six or nine months had elapsed and noted that their coverage was much more popular in the US than in the UK, where the public were largely indifferent. A major objection within the senior ranks of BBC News was that the *Guardian* had entered into close relationships with Snowden, Greenwald and others: they could not, they insisted, be or be seen to be any part of such relationships.

Rusbridger said that

> *the attitude here spreads to the rest of the press who didn't grasp the need to publish – a surprising degree of muddle. It was surprising to me that the NSA official counsel was more enlightened about the protection the press needed than the papers here. In America the press was bipartisan for publication, and the libertarian right was appalled by what the documents revealed. That was true to an extent here – the libertarian right, David Davis, Dominic Raab [in 2015 a junior Justice Minister], David MacLean [formerly the Conservative Party's chief whip, resigned from the House of Commons, now a peer under the name of Baron Blencathra] came out early on to say that 'this was the first time I felt sympathy for the whistleblower'.*

Bill Keller, editor of the *New York Times* when the paper published the Wikileaks material, said that he would lie awake at night sometimes, worrying that a source had been identified and killed. Alan Rusbridger was also conflicted: a reason for his wide consultations with colleagues – though many, as Jenkins and Henry Porter, were likely to be strongly for publication. No one else I spoke to on the *Guardian* said they were so worried: all believe that the intelligence services and the government were deliberately and grossly exaggerating any such risk arising from the Snowden disclosures. Rusbridger is again less certain: he points to past instances where they have been certain of damage and none occurred, and cites – at times off the record – several conversations with senior officials who confided that the dire warnings were exaggerated. One senior secret service officer said to him that Wikileaks 'was nothing', leaving Rusbridger to say, 'Well, that was not what you said at the time'. The former *Guardian* editor said that the then Home Secretary, Theresa May, was 'the person who has revealed most when she revealed[62] (in early November 2015) what the services could do, including what they do with phones, on questionable legal authority'. But his position is: 'I don't know, it's possible that the Russians and Chinese have the material.'

In a number of these conversations, he says, senior officials have admitted that the regime under which they were working, because it was not made public and thus was unknown to nearly everyone, was bound to be uncovered. 'I spoke to another guy in the heart of security, in Whitehall, and he said – well, GCHQ would of course say, we wish Snowden hadn't done it, but we had probably had gone a bit further than we should have done and we couldn't have carried on like this, this was something that had to happen.'

Rusbridger went further still, saying that, if the government were able to get new legislation on the statute book, which made the system less hidden, brought in a judge to deal with warrants allowing investigation but yet also gave an explicit legal underpinning to bulk collection of data,

> they may say, 'Well we've had a bit of debate about it, the sky didn't fall in, and now it's OK'. I'm sure they won't credit Snowden with this, but it wouldn't have happened without him.
>
> On this being in Chinese/Russian hands – no-one has come out and said, it's in the Chinese or Russian hands – they said it's a threat. I mean, we didn't lose it, they lost it – so before you lecture us ... let's have some humility. I don't want to give the wrong impression. They didn't say 'OK'. They said, 'We wish you hadn't done it, you did cause damage'. I don't want to claim that they gave us a clean bill of health – but in private, it was not, 'the terrorists are rubbing their hands with glee' which you got publicly.

All the people who cried blue murder at time of Wikileaks – the sky didn't fall in. There may be something in what the secret service say, that we've made their jobs harder for a while, but if in the historical sweep this has meant that we've got things on a legal footing, historians might write, 'That was uncomfortable but it was right and proper to have it revealed'.

I think the services will soften. I think they have to. Even in the UK they had to help us a bit. At the moment, they say: we will never confirm or deny. But I don't think that can last'.

He does not believe, as does Glen Greenwald, that journalism must now pass from scepticism to outright hostility to governments and agencies. Yet while he does not believe that the UK is, or will soon be, a police state, he will not deny it could happen.

It certainly makes me anxious. I think when you pass laws, you have to pass laws that will assume anything can happen in the future. Why do we think that the digital world and the analogue world are so different? If I arrived at your door – I'm a policeman, and I say, 'I'd like to collect all your papers; we're just going to lock them up – we won't look at them unless we have to'. And people don't realise that that's exactly what they've done, and what they will do under the new law. Why should it be different with electronic records? It's the same thing with professional privilege of doctors and lawyers and priests etc., which will not be protected. And it's a big thing to say, we don't recognise that. In the analogue world there would be shrieks of horror. And people have got no idea of how revealing metadata is. Stewart Baker told me, 'The metadata is everything, we can build up a complete picture from that'. But they get on the Today Programme *and they say, 'Don't worry! We're not going to read your content!' And people are reassured by this.*

I asked him if he thought the UK public had been insufficiently alarmed.

Well, there's something to discuss there. In my experience – I've talked to lots of groups – they understand what this is when it's put to them. People I meet, as at the opera, will say: keep it up. It may be we're complacent because we've never had a Nixon or Hoover or the Stasi or the Nazis – that may be one bit of it – but we're complacent generally. Maybe the media have not done the greatest job of explaining. And I think the political framework – if the Labour Party decides to sit it out and the Liberals won't help – then the debate in UK will not be lively.

You can't have these agencies taking advantage of technology without having a debate. If the debate happens and it's accepted then fine, I've done my duty as an editor. That seems to me what the press is for.

* * *

Alex Carlile, son of Polish-Jewish immigrants, a Queens Counsel (senior barrister) from the age of 37, a Liberal Democrat MP in Wales from 1983–97 then a member of the House of Lords, was appointed the independent reviewer of terrorism legislation by the then Labour Home Secretary David Blunkett on 11 September 2001, that is, the day of 9/11. He had little exposure to the intelligence world and had been told that the job would be a relatively light one. On the afternoon of the day which changed much in the world, in particular that of security and intelligence, Blunkett's office rang him and said this may involve a bit more work than we originally thought. It did: 'in fact, it became my main work', and his period in that office – nearly ten years, being reappointed twice for three-year terms – was one in which he grew to be less of a mainstream Liberal Democrat and more a security liberal: seeing security as the necessary precondition for the survival of democracy and civil rights. 'I very quickly came to the view that terrorism was a very dangerous threat which changes all the time. People haven't grasped the scale of the problem. Shami [Chakrabarti] hasn't seen the evidence. I have. By contrast the [US-based human rights group] Human Rights Watch[63] has been tough, but in the end responsible.'

The view that the intelligence services are democracy's bulwark is one strongly held. One of the key recent texts for intelligence officials is by David Omand, the security services' public intellectual. Omand, educated at Glasgow Academy and Cambridge University (in economics), joined GCHQ from university, then made a rapid career through the ranks via, at first, the Ministry of Defence. He returned to GCHQ as director in 1996, carrying with him, according to the historian of GCHQ Richard Aldrich, 'a fearsome reputation … tough management and intellectual rigour'.[64] In his brief 18-months stay, he reordered the agency to fit the diverse threats in a post-Cold War world, greatly developing its new SIGINT systems (in a programme called 'Sinews') and moving it out of dilapidated quarters into the 'doughnut', a circular building with a space in the middle in the Benhall district of Cheltenham, a few miles from its previous home.

Omand's book, *Securing the State*, uses the great series of fourteenth-century frescoes by Ambrogio Lorenzetti in Siena's Palazzo Pubblico – 'The effects of good and bad government in town and country' – to make his central points. In these paintings, he writes, 'we see the intimate relationship between external and internal security, between collective and personal security, between security and privacy ... Security, as a sense of public confidence that it is safe to go outside, work and play and get on with one's life, is at the heart of good government.'[65]

Carlile grew to share the belief as or more strongly: it makes him angry with the news media, for precisely the opposite reasons professed by David Davis: where the Conservative sees them as complicit with the state in its repressive acts, the Liberal Democrat sees them as insufficiently apprised of the threat and unwilling to grasp its full dimension.

> *The largest problem with the news media is ignorance. The journalists are incredibly lazy about detail. There's a scant understanding of the security services. We need a much more balanced view of the protection they give us. They must focus on the detail. They should understand much more.*
>
> *Snowden is an illustration of this. There is no doubt that there were genuine issues. The story of Prism [the programme under which the NSA collected data from the major communications company: the programme was shared to a degree with GCHQ] needed to be known. But the way in which the information has been dumped has made it easier for the child abusers who are savvy about the way in which they access material and about the ways in which they are stopped. We do not want terrorist groups to know the ways in which the secret services are incompetent – the things they don't know or don't do. 95 per cent of the material that the security services keep secret is already in the public domain. It is crucial that the terrorists don't know the 5 per cent.*

Carlile is certain that increased surveillance will not damage the British democratic system: 'I don't see the agencies here as presenting a danger. They are just people doing a job. Also the nature of our parliament is a contrary one. If any government took an authoritarian trend they would be pulled up sharply.' He says that the Counter Terrorism Act of 2015 – which significantly extended surveillance powers to monitor internet traffic, requires public authorities to take measures to prevent terrorism and allows for warrantless interception of mail – is a 'transitional' measure: as were the jury-free ('Diplock') courts in Northern Ireland, a measure taken to prevent intimidation of jury members, initiated in 1973 and phased out in 2007.

Nothing is more firmly stated by security professionals than the belief that they are securely within the democratic ambit, and would not and could not trespass beyond it. Omand ends an interview with a catechism – of the 'three Rs' – a checklist which he believes has been strengthened and modernised in the Investigatory Powers Bill, going through the legislative process at the end of 2015/early 2016:

> *Rule of law – the law must be clear. The real mistake of the security services before, was that it wasn't. The tribunal looking at this here found that the government was guilty – it was unlawful – because it had not been explained. That's been fixed [with the new legislation]. It's now clear.*
>
> *Regulation and oversight: nothing fundamental changes here – it can be made to look smarter. A new Intelligence and Security Committee should be appointed with sharper members. Some of the judges should be younger and more aggressive. But it's essentially PR. And third, restraint. The security services must do things with restraint and care, as they do.*

Omand's comment that the changes to the legislation are 'essentially PR' is an irritant to journalists, but reflects a mindset which holds that oversight, and the efforts of the news media to hold the services to account, may be an essential part of a democratic society but are less important either than the management of the services and their insistence on the rule of law, or the temper and character of the employees of the agencies.

In a talk with the former head of MI6, John Scarlett, he responded with moderate indignation to a question about the possibility of the services degenerating into an instrument of civil repression:

> *Well, if we had serious attacks every fortnight for a year – then we'd be in a different situation. But the idea wouldn't be authoritarian measures, the concern would be the attacks. Anything like that would be more likely to come from politicians. But anyway we're not in that situation and one of the reasons we're not is because we have had very good intelligence which has prevented such attacks. That's the irony. The talk as if we're living in a state on the edge of authoritarianism is nonsense. And it needs to be clear that it is so. As we've said – this is a liberal society. And where do you think the officers come from? The services have never opposed oversight. We need it.*

In his valedictory speech in October 2014, Iain Lobban, head of GCHQ from 2008 to 2014, said that 'the people who work at GCHQ would sooner walk out the door than be involved in anything remotely resembling mass surveillance. I want to make it absolutely clear that the core of my organisation's mission is the protection of liberty, not the erosion of it.'[66]

* * *

For all their determination to be at the cutting edge of technology, the British services remain conservative in their relations with the news media. Alan Petty, better known under his nom de plume of Alan Judd, has, since he left the service, become a successful novelist, writing a series of novels with his old employer as the context, within which he deploys a character, Charles Thoroughgood, who is made to move excitingly between public and private life (and who really is a thoroughly good man). In *Inside Enemy*[67] Thoroughgood, by then chief of MI6, has performed heroically and is induced to play up his actions by the urbane Foreign Secretary who asks – 'If you could bear to do it, Charles? You'll hate it, of course.' The 'we hate it' is the general view that officers claim to take of press exposure, even that sanctioned by the government and organised by them, even when they gain, as they often do, good copy from briefing correspondents on an issue in which they had succeeded in foiling an attack.

Petty joined the intelligence service after a spell in the Parachute Regiment where, on a tour of duty in Northern Ireland, he was appointed as the officer who dealt with the press. He became one of the first MI6 officials to perform the same function – soon after the ending of the fiction that the agency did not exist, in 1992, one of the first acts of the John Major premiership, designed to be a large statement of modernisation.

Under the then leadership of Sir Colin McColl, the service began a contained and discreet programme of briefings, which Petty organised. Interviewed, he said that 'They were with editors and specialised journalists: we talked about what we were about, the way we operated, not of course about actual operations. We would give some views on the threats to the country. Many of the contacts we made continued in a relationship with the service. It was more about getting rid of myths than anything else.'

And it was controlled. Petty had suggested that Daphne Park (1921–2010), who had risen higher than any other woman of her time in the service and who was an expert on Africa, should be the subject of a documentary (women have done better since: though none has risen to the top job, as two have in MI5 – Stella Rimington (1992–6) and Eliza Manningham-Buller (2002–7)). The programme was made – and Petty sat in on the interview with her, and 'as I remember it, I had the right of veto on any part of the programme judged to be overstepping a line of security' – which was well for the agency's reputation. Park, who had been ennobled as Baroness Park of Monmouth, later told a fellow peer David Lea, a former TUC Assistant General Secretary, shortly before she died in 2010, that she had been deeply involved in the assassination of Patrice Lumumba, the prime minister of Congo, in 1960. The agency briefed only the upmarket newspapers at first – later including BBC *Newsnight*, and then the *Sun*, when it was realised their editorial line was strongly positive to the service.

Petty's fiction suggests that the internal conversation about the news media and journalists was based on the assumption that the former could be manipulated: if a personality-based narrative could be confected and held before the journalists, they would snuffle along obediently on that trail. Iain Mathewson, a former director of security and counter-intelligence, who followed Petty in taking on the press, says that

> the PR was always done by an official – no professional PRs. We don't record meeting with journalists – to safeguard the latter – otherwise they could become the target of charges that they collaborated. We briefed the newspapers, not the broadcasters. That changed with the advent of Newsnight.
>
> But it was mainly print media because we were going for the elite. Then when the Sun emerged as a defender of the services – we briefed it as well. The Sunday Times always caused us most bother, because of their investigations. The people who briefed were very few – and they reported to the Chief. A lot of people in the service hated the fact that we were briefing: their point, and it was a good one, was that we had a reputation for saying nothing – those people who might come to us might say, 'Well, they're talking to the press, they might talk about me'.

John Scarlett was head of MI6, in which his working lifetime had been passed, from 2004 to 2009. His one period out of the service was between 2001 and 2004, when he was chairman of the Joint Intelligence Committee (JIC), – the body, within the Cabinet Office which brings together the heads of agencies and departments concerned with security issues. His period there put him even more squarely in the public eye than he had been when expelled from Moscow, where he had been MI6 bureau chief in 1994. When he was JIC chairman, the progress of the US–British invasion of Iraq prompted ever more violent fighting, both with the foreign troops and between Shi'a and Sunni groups. Further and with a more damaging effect on the politicians and their officials, weapons of mass destruction, the possession of which by Iraq had been the main cause of the invasion, were not found, contrary to the belief of their existence in the country by the UK, and all other major, agencies. Scarlett was accused of having been politicised and of bowing to the will of the Blair administration – especially Alastair Campbell, the Director of Communications – in assisting in the production of a dossier on the reasons for the invasion which was held to be 'dodgy', that is, exaggerated or even mendacious.

The review[68] by (Lord) Robin Butler, a former Cabinet Secretary and then Master of University College in Oxford, found no deliberate distortion of evidence, but criticised MI6 for too credulous reporting, especially of a claim that Iraq could fire rockets within 45 minutes of an order being given. He blamed no named politician nor official, specifically exonerated Scarlett, and recommended that he be made head of MI6 (he had already been – controversially – named so by the prime minister). Nevertheless, his return to MI6 was at first a rocky one: Ian Mathewson said that 'the dossier period was a bad one; and when John Scarlett came back a lot of people didn't like it and he had a difficult time at first. I was shouted at for defending him. But he worked hard at relationships and was accepted in the end.' After retirement, Scarlett has joined a number of boards, and created a security consultancy[69] with Carlile, SC Strategy, working mainly with the leaderships of the Gulf states. The Chilcot Inquiry, harsher on the main actors than previous inquiries, criticised the Joint Intelligence Committee, then headed by Scarlett, for presenting the evidence on WMD 'with a certainty that was not justified'.[70]

When chief, Scarlett tried to reach out to the public domain, at least with regard to the past. Notably, he developed plans started by his predecessor and commissioned the first official history of the service, written by the Queens University, Belfast, Professor of British History, Keith Jeffery.[71] The historian was allowed access to all files in the service archive up to the end of December 1949. His final draft was subject to pre-publication review by the service. Part of the reason for the history, and for developing a website, was the dislike by Scarlett and his colleagues for the 'myths' which encrusted MI6.

The big change came with the end of the Cold War and ideological confrontation and then avowal – *the word we use for admitting its existence –*

of the Service. The staff was operating under cover. I didn't talk to anybody; I was apparently a diplomat; but the point is nothing was admitted. The vast majority of officers don't go round saying what they do – nor can they. In my particular case, the fact that I was kicked out of Moscow, that was public and had to be acknowledged. But it was very unusual.

In my mind there's a clear line between what happened after avowal, and before. It wasn't trouble-free before by any means – and one of the problems, because no one could acknowledge the Service existed, was that there was a complete lack of official information available. So, of course, we're heavily into legend and myth land.

Bond did create a romantic image: I'm very aware of the history of the service and how different it is from the myth. As a general view, Bond was looked at as good fun. [John] Le Carré ... sought to present things as realistic, a world of plotting and intrigue and mistrust. Also the constant line that Britain was in decline. But ... he was a great novelist. The fantasy was filling a vacuum. They [the Service] weren't talked about officially. No government minister would ever say anything, even acknowledge its existence. It did make things difficult.

We'd got to the point where the difference between fact and fiction became blurred because of all the fuss and bother. Remember that in the eighties it really was pretty frenetic. We had the Peter Wright Spycatcher book and so on; the Blunt affair; then the theories about Roger Hollis being a Soviet spy. I can't be completely sure it didn't affect the quality of the decision-making.

So when it came to 'avowal' – late 1980s in the MI5/Security Service case, early 1990s in our case – there was very broad acceptance of it – I think probably for that reason, so that fact and fiction could be separated. And that was right. There's now a vast amount of information out there – much, much more than most journalists will get round to reading – and there's a much better understanding of what we do and don't do (though not as good an understanding as there might be). The key difference for me, when Head of the Service, was: yes, there was a good deal we could put out in the public domain to explain what we were doing, and it was increasingly necessary to do that because the service only functions properly when supported by a public consensus. You have to have that to operate – and it's been retained.

You go up to any British citizen and you tell them who you are and ask them to work with you – most people will say yes. That's always been true and it's still true. But it does depend on a consensus that you are *doing the right thing. So we could do something: it was in my time that we brought in the website, in 2006. That was a big move. Some retired officers were worried. Once you start where will it end? But that wasn't a good reason. Once started, it was perfectly possible to manage it.*

The distinction we make on openness is between what the Service does, what its functions are – and what the operations are, day by day. That still remains absolutely secret – your operations, your sources. And there's been no change there; it's the same as it always was. We still don't release files, we have no time release. Once you're on the file you sit on it forever. From 1909 on, the file is closed.

With 'avowal' it became official policy to have relations with the media. The whole thing became more open and the director who was responsible for overseeing that – the director for security – became the director for security and public affairs. So, we had a concept of public affairs, including the media. We never expected journalists to be nice to us all the time. There was never a price like that. It was more – if we said, you mustn't publish this and they did, then that was a breach of trust. But it hardly ever happened. It was more usual that people just made things up. If that happened, you stopped dealing with them.

I only once did a public event. I also did a few private seminars in Oxford. The only public event was a BBC radio interview with Gordon Corera in July 2009 – to mark the centenary of the Service. The first and only time. There was an argument that it set a precedent. But we said. Yes, it does. And in another 100 years I might do it again.

The issues which plagued both MI5 and MI6 in the 1980s and 1990s were, as Scarlett mentioned, the memoirs of the MI5 agent Peter Wright, which recorded the suspicions he had that Roger Hollis, chief of MI5 (1956–65) was a Soviet agent – together with suspicions that the prime minister, Harold Wilson (1964–70, 1974–6), also was or had been a Soviet informant: neither charge was remotely substantiated. In 1979, Prime Minister Margaret Thatcher revealed that the art historian Anthony Blunt, who had worked for MI5 in the war, had spied for the Soviet Union, but had been given immunity in exchange for his confession and naming of other spies. David Shayler, an MI5 officer, was prosecuted in the 1990s for passing secrets to the *Daily Mail*: he also alleged that MI6 had tried, and failed, to assassinate President Muammar Gaddafi of Libya. Richard Tomlinson, an MI6 officer, was prosecuted under the Official Secrets Act for trying to publish a memoir about his life in the service.

All of these found large coverage in the press – in part because, in the cases of Shayler and Tomlinson, they actively sought coverage. It could, however, have been much worse. Shayler, according to a journalist who worked with him at the time, had offered huge files on the IRA – files which, the journalist said, would have been deadly for a number of people, detailing as they did informers and police and intelligence service contacts. The editor of the *Daily Mail* and the reporter himself would not countenance publication.

Scarlett notes that 'in the 1990s ... a lot of people said, because social mores are changing, you'll face a lot more cases like this. I didn't really accept that and it's not been true. Neither Shayler nor Tomlinson were an index of changing social habits.'

The innovations from this time – the official history, the website – were major steps to Scarlett and to his colleagues. In other institutions they would have been either inevitable (creating a website) or prestigious (an institutional history) – neither a case for the close personal attention of the Chief Executive. That he should see them as major steps reveals the depth at which concern for secrecy operates, and underscores the distance it keeps from the news media, and the difficulty the media have in penetrating to the roots of any of the service's actions – or even of fully understanding what these actions are, a major problem in a democracy which increasingly depends on their effectiveness.

Even today, officers – at least some former officers – express regret that too much about MI6 is demanded to be in the public domain. Meta Ramsay, a former senior officer, now a member of the House of Lords and a former adviser to the Labour leader John Smith after retiring, was in favour of avowal in the late 1980s/early 1990s.

> We were getting hammered in the press and a lot of stories were made up. People thought we were nasty cowboys: that was the influence of James Bond. We lobbied for avowal in Westminster. But Mrs Thatcher was dead against it: and Michael Joplin, the chief whip, was also very much against and advised her accordingly. Prime Minister Thatcher was an admirer of the service and wanted to keep her relationship with it exclusive. But we kept up the pressure and Prime Minister Major agreed.
>
> Now I've changed my mind. I think I was wrong. Look at the Intelligence and Security Committee. I was on it for some time, and I could see that it didn't work. and I have serious doubts about how it was working then and these doubts have increased since its role has in many

ways expanded. An average MP has difficulty in getting in to the agency mindset and understanding the overriding need of complete secrecy about agents and operations. The Heads of the Agencies when they appeared before the ISC certainly never lied and actually revealed more than I thought they would.

If people are going to risk their lives in order to give information they must be assured that the services won't leak. They won't have that trust if they think a lot is being told to a parliamentary committee, or if former officers write books. The fact that we didn't leak works very well for us – and people felt their security was safe when working for us. This is a big plus when recruiting agents for a Service that is much smaller than the Americans'. The problem for non-professionals is that you don't know what you are giving away in seemingly very minor details.

People now think transparency is all important instead of security.

The services, especially MI6, may, as GCHQ did, use journalists to create a favourable impression in the aftermath of the Snowden leaks, and at a time when new legislation will extend the scope of bulk collection of data. But that is the limit. Secret is secret – in the service of an open society.

* * *

Rusbridger is correct that the follow-up to the Snowden leaks by the British press was unenthusiastic and should have been much more active. This for the most part reflects its culture: in this instance, a dislike of being scooped, and crediting, even implicitly, another paper with an exclusive. The BBC, however, did not have these concerns and the argument that it could not mount a campaign is thin: reporting and analysing and doing further investigative work along the lines which Snowden's leaks indicated would not have been a campaign, but part of the remit of a public broadcaster.

US papers, largely city-based, have not got the same competitive pressures – and the story was big enough for all other news organisations to follow up energetically on the revelations, first of all in the *New York Times.* Yet many of the US journalists, while conceding that Snowden had done a service by revealing the wide scope of the unannounced and massive collection of communications data, were doubtful or even hostile to the apparently random seizing of so many files whose content he could not have known, and the publication of those which could impact negatively on intelligence gathering overseas, or even put agents and sources in danger.

Perhaps as a result of the much wider news media coverage, the response in the US has been greater, especially on the part of the big communications companies, such as Google, Apple, Facebook and others, who now fight to restrict the access to customers' data which they hold. The availability of that data to the NSA embarrassed the corporations and thus impels them to be much more protective – probably the most serious negative effect, for the agencies, of the Snowden leaks. In the UK and in France, the response has been more muted, and now (2016) is only a matter of public debate when legislation to give a legal basis to the agencies capture of communications data – in the UK the Communications Data Bill, in draft form at the time of writing – comes before members of parliament.

The larger consideration is whether or not, however much media coverage the leaks got, British public reaction would have been greater. It is likely not. The lack of any experience of authoritarian rule for centuries and the generally good image of the secret services are both probable causes of this indifference; but so, too, must be fear of terrorist attacks – of which there is some experience – and a desire for security, even at the cost of the secret services being able to collect large amounts of information on private communications, contacts and activities. While many commentators, and no less an authority than President Obama, have argued that the terrorist threat is not 'existential' – that is, it does not threaten the fundamental safety of the US, or the UK, or any other major state – anecdotal evidence suggests that many believe in the possibility that the increasingly sophisticated terrorist groups – especially IS – could sooner or later acquire a WMD and use it. Indeed, according to George Tenet, it was a constant nightmare not just of him as a former CIA director but to the presidents he served. Such possibilities sway public opinion towards support for the security they believe the intelligence agencies provide.

It is also the case, however, that neither France nor the UK have taken action against the publication of the Snowden leaks (though in the internet age, what counts as national media is much less defined than before it). In this, they are following the US example: leakers may be hunted and punished – and in the US, the main leaker to Wikileaks, Chelsea Manning, was severely punished in 2013 with a 35-year sentence (though with the possibility of parole after eight years). Snowden, fearing a long sentence, remains in Russia, where he has decided not to criticise his hosts. But journalism is left alone.

* * *

How could the UK agencies open up more?

The British were until recently so secretive about their secret services that they officially had none. They were not admitted to exist until near the end of the cold war in the case of MI5 (1989) and after it had ended in the case of MI6 and GCHQ (1994). The Acts – the 1989 Security Service Act and the 1994 Intelligence Services Act – gave the services a legal standing, the lack of which had been the subject of a number of legal challenges under the European Convention on Human Rights. At the same time as GCHQ and MI6 received legal underpinning and under the same Act, a parliamentary committee, the Intelligence and Security Committee, was created, with a brief to examine the policies, management and spending of the three main services. The remit differed at first from other parliamentary committees; until 2013, it reported to and was appointed by the prime minister. It now reports to parliament, reporting to the prime minister only on security sensitive issues.

The interception of communications requires a warrant, issued by ministers – the home secretary and foreign secretary – and is open to judicial review. The law which regulates these activities is the Regulation of Investigatory Powers Act 2000 (RIPA) which is to be replaced by a new Investigatory Powers Act, which as this is being written is still before parliament. The Bill, in essence, seeks to put on a legal footing that which was revealed by Snowden: that all communications will be open to tracking.

Communications firms will be compelled to hold a year's worth of a person's communications data. This will be details of services, websites and data sources connected to when online – an 'Internet Connection Record'. It does not include the detail of subsequent activities within each service. Police say they want to be able to get at these records, going back a year, so that if they get a lead on a suspect, they can establish more about their network or conspiracy.

Under existing law, agencies can already ask firms to start collecting this data – but they cannot access historic information because companies do not keep it. Police argue that this means many investigations into crime with an online element go cold because they cannot link activity to specific people or devices. Police or other agencies can already access communications data such as historic phone bills but there is a ban on them asking firms to hold and hand over information detailing which online services have been used.

The Bill also brings together all other investigatory powers which involve intrusion into communications or private lives, including:

- The interception and reading of communications – this can only be carried out if approved in person by the Home Secretary.
- 'Interference' with computers – including hacking – to acquire information or for some other investigative reason. Companies are legally obliged to assist in these cases.
- The collection of very large amounts of internet or phone data so that they can be later sifted looking for leads and patterns.

The legislation includes an existing power to compel a company in the UK to hand over an encryption key so that scrambled messages can be read, where there is a legal reason for the police or other agencies to access that message. This could include, for example, asking a company to help unscramble chat messages which may reveal where a missing person – or their kidnapper – can be found. However, this legal duty cannot be imposed on overseas companies, such as Apple, that use a form of encryption which they say they cannot themselves breach (though that may now be in dispute).

Safeguards include a new 'Investigatory Powers Commission' (IPC), led by senior judges who will act as a 'double lock' on interception warrants. When a minister signs off an application to monitor communications, the operation will not begin until the commissioners have also agreed. The IPC will be expected to be public and explain how powers are used. If the new commission finds a serious error in how powers have been used, the Investigatory Powers Tribunal, a special semi-secret court, could then rule that the targeted individual has the right to know. A new offence of unlawfully accessing internet data will be created – and it will also be a crime for someone who works for a communications firm to reveal data has been sought.

The Bill, which had been mooted during the Conservative-led coalition government (2010–15) but not brought forward because of opposition from the minority partners in government, the Liberal Democrats, is still unpopular with civil libertarians, and thought to be both unnecessary and a product of panic. In a *Guardian* interview,[72] the Conservative libertarian (he prefers 'rule of law enthusiast') David Davis said that the 'double lock' procedure, where an interception warrant must be signed by both a minister and a judge, presented as an extra safeguard, was pointless because judges would object only if the secretary of state did not follow the proper rules, not on evidential grounds – 'As long as the home secretary has followed the correct procedure, the judge will go along with it. Judges hate overturning the executive, and it happens very rarely.'

Davis also admitted that there was little public pressure against the measure, saying that 'because for the past 200 years we haven't had a Stasi or a Gestapo, we are intellectually lazy about it, so it's an uphill battle. Even people who are broadly on my side of the political spectrum in believing in privacy and liberty tend to take the state at its word too often.'

Davis is right that, in this area at least as much as any other, the public, politicians and the news media cannot take the government at its own word. This is not because it lies or spins – though that can happen – but because the basis on which legislation is introduced, and the practices based on it, can go badly wrong. Even when accepting that the services strive to remain within the law and have no designs on a democratic polity, the comforting blanket of secrecy could allow deviation from the rule of law, civic norms.

To combat that, the UK needs a more powerful, more generously staffed Intelligence and Security Committee, which can be more active in investigating possible lapses and abuses on a sounder factual basis than it has been able to do in the past. Services should be tasked with developing ways of sharing their information and analyses with the news media, and thence to the public. This must not stop at public relations demonstrations of present rectitude and past successes. Adherence to democratic and civic behaviour has been a mark of the British agencies (as far as is known), but both government and the services themselves have been reluctant to move to a proactive policy of explanation.

5

Le jour de guerre est arrivé

Entre démocratie et renseignement, l'histoire nous apprend que les rélations n'ont pas toujours été sereines.
(Francois Fillon, Prime Minister of France, 2007–12)[1]

In matters of security, as in politics and the economy, French commentators and politicians like to draw a distinction between the French approach and that of the 'Anglo-Saxons', which includes the US and the UK, as well as Australia, Canada and New Zealand (in security circles, the 'Five Eyes', who share information among themselves). It has traditionally been a strong distinction: it was behind the opposition of Charles de Gaulle to Britain's several efforts, during his presidency, to join the European Economic Community (as it then was), since he wished to create a Union free of US influence and saw the UK as a Trojan Horse for the Americans.[2] That view is now weaker, as succeeding presidencies have themselves moved closer to the US (and to the UK), and the 'French exception' has become less exceptional: but it remains important and well-based in matters of intelligence.

The relationship of the French with the secret services whose public duty has been to preserve their security has been conflictual and suspicious, with some justice; and this has strongly affected the way in which the services have been, and until recently still were, reflected in the news media. To say 'until recently' is to take account of two events which shook France, and much of the Western world, in 2015: the murderous Islamist attacks on the weekly satirical paper *Charlie Hebdo* in January, and the still more bloody attacks on various sites in Paris in November. More was to come in 2016, with several attacks – such as the 'truck killer' in Nice, in July, with 84 dead; and later the same month, the murder of a priest in his mid-eighties in a church in Rouen, by having his throat cut. These drew from President François Hollande the heartfelt claim,[3] made to a joint meeting of the two Houses of Parliament after the November attacks, that 'France is at war … in a war against terrorism, jihadism, which threatens the whole world.' The echo of President George W. Bush's announcement of 'a war on terror' after 9/11, much mocked in France at the time, was widely commented on: that, and France's increased commitment to bombing IS strongholds in Syria and Iraq, brought the country much more into line with the 'Anglo-Saxons' and further diluted its exceptionalism. The 2000s and 2010s have been a period in which the secret services have undergone extensive reforms, and are now seen as at the top tier of Western services: a former British intelligence official who had a working relationship with the French services says that 'you get all sorts of stuff written about them in the British press, but the fact is that they are brilliant in counter terrorism, at times the best in the world'.

Charlie Hebdo habitually insulted religion, much more often doing so to Christian figures than Muslim. However, for devout Muslims in France and worldwide, the magazine and its insistence on the right to parody, lampoon and insult was seen not as an expression of a right in a liberal society, but as an offence: for jihadists, a mortal offence. Jason Burke writes that the attack on the paper stimulated a few refusals by schoolchildren to take part in the minute's silence decreed in memory of the victims and that there was 'a 500 per cent rise in Islamophobic attacks on mosques in France in the first quarter of 2015, while one survey in the UK three months after the attack suggested that more than half the respondents felt there was a fundamental clash between Islam and the values of British Society'.[4] Burke also draws attention to Amedy Coulibaly, the terrorist who – having earlier killed an unarmed policewoman and shot and injured two others – entered a Jewish supermarket at the Porte de Vincennes, in eastern Paris and killed four customers: the attack, he had claimed, was calibrated with the separate murders at *Charlie Hebdo*. Coulibaly was wearing a GoPro camera, a device which can be affixed to a helmet or a jacket to capture the activity in which the wearer is engaged: they are often worn by sports people. Burke writes that 'the next step for the terrorists is obvious and inevitable. It is a live stream of a terrorist attack, the ultimate combination of terrorism and the media. The question all of us will face is: will we watch.'

After the two 2015 attacks the militant reaction of the president was, on the evidence of the polls, well received publicly; while the new powers and resources given to the police and the secret services, including powers to collect data on communications in bulk along the same lines (as the Snowden leaks had demonstrated) as in the US and the UK, were also well received. One of the main reporters/commentators on security, Jacques Follorou of *Le Monde*, reminded the readers of his paper on 14 December that the ex-defence minister, Hervé Morin, had warned against the new powers of surveillance brought in after the *Hebdo* killings, saying to his fellow deputies that 'What I don't want is that one day, in France, in 2017 or 2022 [the years of presidential elections] an arbitrary regime will use these surveillance tools without any control … I would doubt the ability of a director of the central administration to resist pressure from the head of state.'[5]

Follorou wrote that 'the risk is real … state power … [can] respond to the emotion of public opinion in overturning, before our eyes, the fundamental balances which guarantee our liberties'. Both Morin and Follorou had in mind, as the head of 'an arbitrary regime', Marine Le Pen – who had demonstrated the growing strength of her far-right Front National by taking more votes nationwide than any other party (nearly 30 per cent) and coming first in several parts of France in the first round of the regional elections, held a few weeks after the Paris attacks (the right and left joined forces in the second round to defeat her candidates).

According to Natalie Nougayrede, a former chief editor of *Le Monde*, Follorou's voice, in a time of heightened fear and anger after the murder of 130 people, mainly young, was a rare protest – 'the newspapers have not given sufficient scrutiny to the new laws, especially that on the collection of data; it was passed before the November attacks and of course there was even less examination then. *Le Monde* should have taken the lead on this; but Follorou's piece was almost the only one.' In this, too, France drew closer to the US: several US journalists stressed that critical or probing pieces of journalism on the measures taken, in law or for the security services, were largely unwelcome at news desks, since the editors believed they would be unwelcome with their audiences. A poll[6] conducted by Ifop two weeks *before* the November attacks showed that 40 per cent of those polled would favour an authoritarian government dedicated to crushing terrorism, while 67 per cent favoured a government of unelected experts who would put in place an effective anti-terrorist policy.

The differences, however, remain strong and the history of espionage in France explains some of them. In an essay on attitudes to espionage,[7] Anja Becker says that the authorities – in dictionaries and in encyclopedias – generally considered spying as a 'vile' (*infâme*) trade, certainly not one for a French gentleman. Becker quotes Montesquieu, from his *De L'esprit des Lois* (1748), to the effect that 'espionage might be tolerated if it was exercised by honest people: but from the necessary vileness of such a person one can infer the vileness of the occupation'. The Revolution and its sequel might have caused a shift in attitudes: Republican France, and Napoleon, needed and made use of intelligence about their many enemies.

Napoleon especially made use of, and was used by, Joseph Fouché, one of the most extreme and bloodiest of the revolutionary leaders who developed into a Napoleonic spymaster. Becker writes that 'he might be one of the reasons why in the course of the nineteenth century the French seriously developed an understanding of spying as something inherently abject'. She believes that

> for the French, espionage seems to be a foreign affair, one that could not possibly earn an individual much glory, one that, consequently, is best not talked about. In France, espionage might be considered a negative myth, and a reluctance to discuss the topic systematically can be traced back to the Ancien Régime ... after the French Revolution, disdain for the spy-business developed into a predominant theme in society and eventually culminated in the Dreyfus affair.[8]

That affair might have prompted a serious study of intelligence, the more because the French were so decisively outmanoeuvred by the Germans in the matter of intelligence, which the latter took seriously. But it did not. Instead, Becker believes, the engagement of writers and other public figures in the affair, both for (as Zola) and against (as Maurice Barrès) Dreyfus, created the figure and the role of the intellectual, with a duty to take a position on affairs of the day and to attempt to set the tone and the parameters of the national conversation.

Fouché's position at the ear of Napoleon set a fashion which was followed in the twentieth century. As the post-war leaders of France sought to restore its status, economy and military prowess, they needed to know at the same time, in a restless and divided society, what the powerful movements and individuals in and around politics were doing. To this end they relied heavily on figures who came from, or worked with, the secret services, both domestic and foreign. These figures were 'hommes de l'ombre' (the title of a popular 2012 French TV series, not featuring spymasters but political communications consultants, translated as *Spin*), 'shadowy', but powerful and while in power, untouchable and protected, averse to any kind of press attention except that which they constructed themselves.

Phillipe Hayez, a former intelligence officer, then a Professor at Sciences Po, with his co-author Jean-Claude Cousseran believes that all political leaders suffer from the temptation to have close relationships with secret service officials, turning them to serve their political ends. They enumerated[9] some of the counsellors who served powerful figures in successive French governments: their actions, often opaque and the stuff of rumour rather than hard information at the time, were generally beyond the reach of news media which had not, in the main, seen the secret services as an area open to inquiry, or even much worth inquiring into, as against providing the stuff of scandal. Their activities deepened the sense that the secret state was one of intrigue, corruption and danger, often allied to far right-wing forces at home and abroad, closely tied in to the dictatorships of the Francophone states, a series of no-go areas – or rather, areas which could yield up their secrets only through the patient digging of investigative journalism, of which there was little in the French press up to the 1990s.

De Gaulle had formed a secret service accountable to him while in exile in Britain during the war – with the opposition of the British, who tried to recruit the French escaping from occupied France into their own services, the Special Operations Executive and MI6. As president he relied on Jacques Foccart, who oversaw his policies in Francophone Africa as well as liaising with the newly formed secret services, especially the external intelligence service, the SDECE (Service de Documentation Extérieure et de Contre-Espionnage, whose name was changed to the present DGSE, or Direction Général de la Securité Extérieure). Foccart acquired the reputation of being second in power only to de Gaulle and performed the same services for the latter's successor, George Pompidou; he was pensioned off by Pompidou's successor, Valéry Giscard d'Estaing, but came back to serve again under Jacques Chirac, until he died, at the age of 83, in office.

Michel Debré, one of the most active and powerful of de Gaulle's prime ministers (1959–62), had as the coordinator of the secret services Constantin Melnik, who was deeply involved in the war in Algeria. He was strongly anti-Soviet – his father had been an officer in the Russian Imperial Guard, and his grandfather, a doctor, was physician to the last tsar, Nicholas II and was killed with the imperial family in 1918. Melnik wrote and edited several books, both documentary and fiction, on dictatorship and, shortly before his death in 2014, a poorly received book, *Espionage à la Française* (2012), which harshly criticised the intelligence services' record over the past four decades.

Francois de Grossouvre, like Mitterrand (and Melnik), a former Vichy official who joined the Resistance in the last two years of the war, had joined the SDECE in 1950 and organised a section in France of

Gladio, a semi-underground military group established in several European countries, whose purpose was to resist a communist takeover. Gladio has been the subject of much speculation about its links both with mainstream politics and the new secret services being established on the continent from the mid-1940s, as well as charges, as yet unproven, that it contributed to the growth of right-wing terrorism, especially in Italy. De Grossouvre's post as general manager of a large sugar production company – his father-in-law's business – gave him a cover for his work, as he was required to travel frequently and develop a large acquaintance: he became more widely known, and was introduced to François Mitterrand in the late 1950s, later assisting him in the development of the Socialist Party and being entrusted by him with negotiations on collaboration with the still-powerful Communist Party. He was also godfather to Mitterrand's 'secret' daughter, Mazarine Pingeot (now Mazarine Pingeot-Mitterrand) whose mother was Anne Pingeot, Mitterrand's mistress; he entered the Elysée with Mitterrand in 1981, and was given a wide-ranging brief for oversight of the secret services, and relations with a range of Middle Eastern and Asian states.

Close to the president on most sensitive and intelligence issues, he was alleged[10] to have been part of a meeting at the Elysée at which Mitterrand agreed to the bombing of the *Rainbow Warrior* (see below). Of all the many 'men in the shadows' (he was given the nickname by the press), de Grossouvre was among the most complex and most effective for his political master. Mitterrand, whose own nickname was 'The Florentine' – an allusion to Machiavelli – had a labyrinthine approach to politics, for which de Grossouvre seemed well attuned. His death by a gunshot in his room at the Elysée – which he had kept even after his official post in the presidency had ended – was said to be suicide, but has been the subject of speculation that it was a murder attached to a past feud.

The three-star General Philippe Rondot was a former parachutist, veteran of the Algerian War and an Arabist; he was also an adviser to the Ministry of Defence and especially to Michelle Alliot-Marie, Minister of Defence in 2002–7. Rondot, through his many connections in the Arab world, played a large part in the arrest, in 1994 in Khartoum, of 'Carlos the Jackal' – the widely sought anti-Israeli terrorist Ilich Ramirez Sanchez, who had committed a series of murders and attempted murders in the UK and France, generally against Jewish targets. He was caught up in the 'Clearstream' affair – in which claims had been made of corruption against

Nicholas Sarkozy and others connected with the sale of six La Fayette class frigates to Taiwan in 1991. Asked by the Ministry of Defence to clarify the issue, Rondot reported[11] that Dominique de Villepin, when prime minister, had been told of the list of allegedly corrupt politicians – and had allowed the list to be published in order to stain the name of Sarkozy, with whom he was soon to be locked in a battle for the presidency. Rondot was himself investigated over the incident – in which he, with all the principals, was cleared. In a statement[12] to *Le Monde* years later, Rondot said that he had 'contempt' for the political world and that 'we in the intelligence service are not a gang of hooligans, broken by twisted attacks, which can happen in the world of politics'.

Finally in Cousseran and Hayez's list of shadows is Christian Couteau, the only one of the shadow men still alive, the son and himself an officer of the Gendarmerie Nationale. He had created a much-decorated Groupe d'Intervention de la Gendarmerie Nationale in the early 1970s, then entered Mitterrand's Elysée in 1982 to found the Groupe de Sécurité de la Présidence de la République. This group combined both intelligence and protection of the president, separate from the established presidential protection detail: their duties also included protection for Mazarine Pingeot.

Prouteau's group was involved in two large scandals, which ran for months – in the latter case years – in the press. The first[13] was the arrest of a small group of Irish citizens in Vincennes – Michael Plunkett, Stephen King and Mary Reid, all classified by the Metropolitan Police in the UK as members of the Marxist-inclined Irish National Liberation Army. When brought to trial, however, both examining magistrates and the press revealed that the explosives and weapons 'discovered' in the apartment where the Irish arrestees were living had been planted by the presidential protection group: later, it was alleged that the weapons had been obtained for them by a French ally, hidden in Paris then planted in the flat, before the ally denounced his erstwhile friends to the police.

Second, and another malign part of Mitterrand's legacy, the presidential protection group was assigned the task of tapping the phones of those considered by the president to be his present or future enemies, among whom were numbered several journalists. Around 150 individuals and 3,000 calls were tapped: some of these were undertaken for security reasons, but the largest part were personally ordered by Mitterrand and were undertaken in pursuit of his own private interests, especially those concerning Mazarine. Many others were involved – including senior politicians, such as Gilles Menage, chief of staff to Mitterrand and Michel Delebarre, chief of staff to the prime minister, Pierre Mauroy; as well as Louis Schweizer, a classic Enarque (graduate of the elite Ecole Nationale d'Administration) whose career spanned the civil service, politics and top appointments in the automotive company Renault, where he was chief executive from 1992 to 2005.

One of the journalists tapped was Jean-Edern Hallier, a prolific and outspoken editor and author who attacked many figures in the establishment (of which, as the son of General Hallier, a hero of World War I, he was part), both in his books and in his newspaper, *L'Idiot International*, which ran from 1969 to 1994 (his son Frederic revived it in a more moderate form in 2014). Hallier, a far leftist in the early part of his career, went over to the right, even far right, in later life. In the mid-1980s he announced he would publish a book named *Mitterrand and Mazarine*, revealing the existence of Mazarine Pingeot: the book did not appear until 1996, and then under the title of *L'Honneur perdu du François Mitterrand*. Another in the tapped roll of honour was the *Le Monde* reporter Edwy Plenel.

Mitterrand was never brought to book for these taps: the dossiers of evidence were declared 'defence secrets', and were not made available to the courts until 1999, three years after his death; while a court did not hear the case against those who had carried out his will, and collaborated with him, until 2004. Mitterrand was most concerned with the press and most intrusive on their privacy: but it seems that tapping, if on a much reduced scale, continued after him. Under the presidency of Nicolas Sarkozy, from 2007 to 2012, a journalist, Gerard Davet of *Le Monde*, was also wiretapped while engaged in an investigation whose results had already been embarrassing to Sarkozy – allegations that he had been funded in his presidential bid by the L'Oréal heiress Liliane Bettencourt without declaring it. Davet had published a book, *Sarkozy m'a tué*, composed of interviews with 27 officials and politicians who had been dismissed from their posts by the president. One of these, an investigating magistrate named Isabelle Prévost-Desprez, had been relieved of the Bettencourt case after, she claimed, two witnesses had told her that substantial sums in brown envelopes had been delivered from Bettencourt to Sarkozy (she admitted, however, that the witnesses had talked to her outside of the framework of an official investigation; one of them, a nurse, later denied that she had said it).

The interior minister, Géant, a close associate of the president, initially denied that the journalist had been tapped – then admitted that the list of his calls had been obtained, but only to identify the whistleblower who was his source: he was identified, in the Ministry of Justice, and was sent to a new posting in Cayenne, French Guiana. Had Davet been tapped, it would have been an illegal act on the part of the authorities since a law had been brought in early in Sarkozy's presidency which banned such a move.[14]

France is not alone in having politically engaged services, and in possessing politicians who seek confidants among intelligence officials. Prefacing Cousseran and Hayez's list is Winston Churchill, who relied before and during part of the war, for intelligence on the intelligence services, on Desmond Morton. Morton was a former MI5 officer who was early alarmed by Germany's rearmament and who assisted Churchill – whom he had met during World War I – in the latter's speeches and writings on the theme. According to a recent biography,[15] Morton was active in publicising the Zinoviev letter, a forgery purporting to be from the head of the Comintern, Grigory Zinoviev, urging British communists to sway the Labour Party towards signing a British-Soviet treaty: the letter was published in the *Daily Mail*.

In February 1973, an attempt was made, apparently under government orders, to bug the satirical weekly *Canard Enchainé*: ministers wished to know who the informants were for a range of embarrassing stories.[16] The 'plumbers' were discovered by a cartoonist for the paper, who had passed the building late at night, saw lights on and went in to investigate: he recognised two of the policemen who were accompanying the agents. *Le Canard* took the case to court and to appeal, but successive judges ruled against incriminating the agents of the domestic security agency, then the Direction de la Surveillance du Territoire (DST), in spite of strong evidence of their involvement. The Watergate investigation by the *Washington Post*, reaching its climax as *Le Canard* scandal broke, led to the DST agents being called 'plombiers', the affair itself gaining the name of 'Watergaffe'. The main immediate political effect was the replacement, by Prime Minister Pierre Messmer, of Interior Minister Raymond Marcellin by the up-and-coming politician Jacques Chirac.[17]

The record shows both a very strong personalisation of the security officials closest to the president – especially Mitterand. The formal structures of security were circumvented by men whose large power derived from their offices in the Elysée, and underscores that the secret world has been, for French leaders, both a prop to rely on and a network of groups to suborn.

* * *

Journalism in the US, and to a growing extent in the UK, can use the output of scholars of security and intelligence which, in the past 20 years, has greatly increased – the more as signals intelligence (SIGINT) has come to the centre of intelligence work and (as we saw in Chapter 2) the academy in the US became engaged in defending its own work on encryption from the overbearing presence of the NSA. In the US, the tradition of senior figures in the intelligence world moving into the academy is well established, especially in the Ivy League universities: the UK is more hesitantly following suit. Two of the interviewees for this book, John McLaughlin, former deputy and briefly acting Director of the CIA, and David Omand, former director of GCHQ, are professors in Johns Hopkins University's School of Advanced International Studies, Washington, and King's College London, respectively. In the past two decades, intelligence studies have developed strongly in US and UK universities, with more than 100 departments and schools in the US and in Britain, some 15 university departments (2016), including in the universities of Aberystwyth, Buckingham, Glasgow, Salford and Warwick, and a major presence at King's College London, part of its defence studies department. The doyen of academic writing on espionage who is also a popular author, Christopher Andrew, is at Cambridge.

Anja Becker writes[18] that 'the recent studies [on French intelligence] tend to apply formulas borrowed mainly from American and British contexts. Jean-Paul Brodeur [a French-Québecois scholar of the police and intelligence], for example ... argues that one reason for the near-absence of research is the fact that there has never been a demand on the part of the French public – nor among French politicians – to learn more about the operations of the French secret services.' The demand, however, has grown, as has the supply: Hayez was part of the creation, in 2010, of the Paris School of International Affairs (the title is, significantly, in English, as is the bulk of the teaching) within the elite, internationally highly ranked Sciences Po, with courses in security and intelligence.[19]

That there should be other sources for journalists than within or around the agencies themselves will relieve some of what many French journalists see as the narrowness of their references. One of these is Christophe Deloire, director of Reporters sans Frontières, formerly head of the Centre for Journalism Training in Paris and a senior reporter on *Le Point* magazine, later head of the non-fiction department at the publisher Flammarion. With another investigative reporter, Christophe Dubois, he published a book in 2004[20] on the growing danger of terrorism; and in 2006, the same pair published *Sexus Politicus*,[21] a bestseller, which did much to end the decades' long tradition of *omerta* on the sex lives of politicians, and attracted no writs because, as Deloire later said:

> We haven't been attacked, because to be really honest, often we knew more than we wrote. No politician wants to run the risk that more stories will come out in court. We never based our claims on rumors, but on information that was given to us by people who were in the room. So when we talk about something that happened in a bedroom, it is because one of the two people talked.[22]

The book reveals a number of affairs – with both Valéry Giscard d'Estaing and Jacques Chirac contributing disproportionately to the size of that number – but also makes the point that the seductive quality of a president or a senior politician, is, or was, a prized possession both by him (the few female politicians are different), and by most voters, including women voters.

The aphrodisiac of power, to which several ex-presidents, including Giscard, Chirac and Sarkozy, both openly and obliquely, referred went along with a marked sexism towards the few women who made it to the top of politics. Ségolène Royale, for many years the partner of François Hollande with whom she had four children before he became president in 2012, was asked, when she made a bid for the presidency, by a fellow socialist grandee, Laurent Fabius, 'who will look after the children?' As Dubois and Deloire write, many of the liaisons between the men of power and women were with female journalists[23] – a tradition which Hollande, when president, retained when in 2007 he left Royale (they were never married), for the journalist Valerie Trierweiler, who became the first lady for a few years – she later left the Elysée when Hollande began an affair, at first secret then revealed, with the actress Julie Gayet.

Deloire, now head of Reporters Sans Frontières, one of the most militant of the organisations defending freedom of the press, says that

> in France the tradition of journalism is a bit different from the Anglo Saxon approach. You have journalists here who are against leaking. You have journalists here who, for example, cover the police; and are very close to their sources. Being close to the sources is a particular thing in France. The leading journalists in France are the political journalists; they get the strategies for elections, and the side stories of politics, the 'off' stuff they can use but can't name the source.
>
> The way to the top of journalism is through political reporting. And we like opinionated journalism. Even now, there's not so much investigative reporting. The state still is powerful: remember that journalism began in France, with the Gazette,[24] in 1630, founded to give official news from the court.
>
> The secret services are reported on more now, because we like to criticise them. In France there is still a rather negative view of the secret services. But the job of finding out the details of what is done by whom to whom with what and why – that's rarer. I fear we are far too interested in personalities: we do need more of a journalism of explanation.

To illustrate the different takes on the secret services between France and the Anglo-Saxons, Deloire mentioned the popular series of 'OSS117' films: both the novels, by Jean Bruce, and the films predated the Bond novels and films by some years. However, the central character, Hubert Bonisseur de La Bath, though handsome and active, is also imperialist and sexist, a figure of mockery as well as of action. The films ended their run in the 1970s – but were revived in the 2000s, with the central agent played by Jean Dujardin, and the element of parody more obvious: Deloire said that 'he [the agent] was made to be ridiculous, he was never taken seriously: quite different from Bond, and the Anglo-Saxon approach generally'.

Deloire's strictures on the lack of investigative zeal among French journalists are less relevant now than they were. The signal event in contemporary times which has been responsible for a large shift in French journalism on security issues, was another affair, less internationally notorious than Dreyfus but more immediately transformative of the world of journalism. The Greenpeace ship *Rainbow Warrior*, safely docked in July 1985 in the port of Auckland, New Zealand's largest city, on its

North Island, was being prepared to disrupt French nuclear testing on the Morura Atoll in the French possession of New Caledonia. The previous year New Zealand had seen the election of the strongly anti-nuclear prime minister David Lange: opposition to the French strong commitment to nuclear power plants and its nuclear *force de frappe* was growing in France and South Pacific nations had loudly signalled their fears of nuclear contamination from the tests. The defence minister in the Mitterrand socialist government, the popular Charles Hernu whose close links with the military and intelligence had done much to bring the socialists to agree with the retention of nuclear weapons, was outraged by the domestic and especially foreign opposition.

The external security force, the DGSE, was dominated by the military and itself possessed a special strike force, staffed by paras and commandos. Its director was an Admiral, Pierre Lacoste – a much-decorated officer who had joined the Free French in North Africa during the war, and who rose rapidly through the post-war naval ranks to take several appointments in the cabinets of the pre-Mitterrand governments of the centre-right. Lacoste, armed as he later claimed with the explicit permission of both Hernu and Mitterrand, ordered a group of agents from the DGSE's Service Action unit to be sent to New Zealand. The first to arrive, the commando Lieutenant Christine-Huguette Cabon, passed herself off to the Greenpeace group as a keen ecologist, and in that guise reported back on the plans to stymie the Mururoa test. The group of agents decided to sink the ship.[25] On 10 July, in the night, two frogmen swam under the converted trawler and fixed two mines, one timed to go off after the other. When the first, smaller mine exploded, the crew – as had been intended by the DGSE operatives – left in a panic: but when the second large mine exploded, a photographer, who had returned to retrieve his camera, was killed.

The consequences were painful, long and drawn out. The agents were apprehended and the nature of the attack quickly became clear. France, reluctantly and very slowly, admitted the attack and paid compensation; the affair caused much mockery and soured relations between the two countries, including mutual embargoes of exports. French testing went ahead after a pause, and the commitment both to nuclear-powered energy and a nuclear *force de frappe* remain centrepieces of French politics, no longer now controversial in mainstream politics. The main political victim was Defence Minister Hernu, who resigned.

The government and the DGSE did try to cover up the affair, by putting out a stream of chaff to the friendly press, one line of which was to allege that the British secret services sank the ship in order to discredit France. But the cover-up was as clumsy as the main event: and neither the state nor the secret services could count on wholly pliant news media. A government-appointed commission chaired by Bernard Tricot, a senior civil servant much advanced in his career by General de Gaulle with appointments including that of secretary general of the Elysée, produced a report which affirmed that the DGSE agents did no more than monitor the *Rainbow Warrior* in Auckland – a report later revealed as being founded on a series of false declarations by the agents and senior officials whom he interviewed. Pascal Krop in the weekly *Evénement de Jeudi* and Jacques-Marie Bourget in another weekly *VSD* (both having since gone through several changes of name and editorial direction as their circulations fell: the latter is now a weekly TV guide), first cut through the government stories to reveal that the DGSE had been responsible. However, their stories, based on unnamed sources within the intelligence services, lacked the coup de grâce – the precise details of the action, and the name of the minister with whom the responsibility finally rested.

These were supplied by Edwy Plenel, one of the most prominent and controversial journalists of his generation and one who, both at *Le Monde* (where he was the managing editor) and later at the investigative website, Mediapart, which he founded in 2008, has done much to embed the investigative tradition in France. Plenel, with a source or sources deep inside the administration hostile to Hernu, discovered that the first two teams sent to Auckland had no equipment which would allow them to sink the *Rainbow Warrior*, and that there was a third team, which planted the mines. In a story in *Le Monde* co-written with Bertrand Le Gendre, he pointed the finger firmly at Hernu.[26]

Twenty years later, in July 2005, *Le Monde* published extracts from a note written by Admiral Lacoste, who had resigned with Hernu. In the note, dated 8 April 1986, Lacoste made it clear that he had consulted Mitterrand:

> I asked the president if he authorised me to set in motion the project of neutralisation which I had looked at on the request of M Hernu. He gave me his agreement in showing the importance he attached to nuclear tests. I didn't then go into greater detail, [since] the authorisation was sufficiently explicit ... [I would not be] thrown into such an operation without the personal authorisation of the President of the Republic.[27]

There is some ambiguity in Lacoste's note – the agreement was signalled rather than asserted – 'he gave me his agreement in showing the importance he attached to nuclear tests' (the French is 'm'a donné *son accord en manifestant l'importance* qu'il attachait aux essais nucléaires': emphasis added). This might mean either that he agreed, while at the same time showing how important nuclear tests were; or the agreement was assumed by Lacoste because he stressed that nuclear tests were important. In any case, Lacoste took it as authorisation.

Recalling the affair in a piece for Mediapart in January 2013,[28] Plenel wrote that 'the lie rested on the logic of a raison d'Etat which protected those primarily responsible for the operation, those who construct the political order: the Defence Minister in the first place and over and behind him, the President of the Republic himself. [The lie] was adopted by the institutions concerned on the view that even if we are guilty, the honour of the army demands that we are innocent.' That was exactly the response of both the senior officers in the army and the politicians of nearly a century before: honour trumps truth.

In a later interview[29] with *Paris Match* on the 30th anniversary of the sinking of the Greenpeace ship, Plenel told the journalist Charlotte Anfray that

> the truth is sometimes unbelievable: that's what we showed in the Greenpeace affair, when we showed the involvement of the presidency of Francois Mitterrand. The revelations of thirty years ago certainly prompted the collapse of the house of cards of official lies but, immediately afterwards, a lid was placed over it. There was neither a commission of enquiry nor a hearing. If we make an account of the year just passed, with the law on the military programme, the anti-terrorist law and the law on intelligence, we are aware of the challenge to our liberties … we will not be in a safer world, but a more dangerous one.

Natalie Nougayrede, the former chief editor of *Le Monde*, says that 'for the French secret services, the affair was a success. The opposition to the test was neutralised, and it went ahead'.

At least as averse as their British counterparts to openness and publicity (except that which they shaped themselves), the agencies opened up markedly in the 1990s, and now, like the other services shifting towards a SIGINT-dominated intelligence capability, they are spending more time in reaching out to journalists – including to Mediapart, which is the most assiduous in investigating their activities. Christophe Deloire of Reporters sans Frontières says that 'the secret services have changed a bit; some parts are more open in the last 20 years. The culture of civilians is beginning to take over from that of the military. In French there is the word "barbus" – a notion which came from the Gaullists: it was applied to the DGSE and it meant stupid, reactionary. They got fed up with this designation and so became more open, in order to cope with it.'

Plenel's high position in the French journalistic pantheon would have been impossible to obtain at another time, and probably in another country. The son of a senior administrator and educationist based in the French colony of Martinique, whose support for the independence movement had him recalled to Paris when Plenel was around 10, he grew up in a highly educated, politically engaged household – but chose to give up his place at the elite Sciences Po, instead spending more than a decade of his young manhood in the Marxist Ligue Communiste, one of the larger Trotskyist groups, in which he became a leading figure, writing regularly for the group's publication, *Rouge*.

In a long interview given in 1994,[30] when he had been appointed chief editor of *Le Monde*, he spoke of the Ligue in affectionate terms, saying that 'in its best period, the Ligue Communiste was a vast university, a place of learning, knowledge and apprenticeship. Perhaps I'm inclined to idealise it, but in my memory of it, I retain that impression of political and intellectual debate. Simply, it was, I have to admit, my real university.' In the same interview he said that, feeling increasingly distanced from far left militant politics, and having completed a short obligatory spell in the army, he applied for a job at *Le Monde* and was to his surprise accepted, with the only stipulation that he desist from activism (in fact, he continued to speak publicly on issues which concerned him like anti-imperialism and racism). For him, the value of *Le Monde* was 'that of a collective of independent journalists, masters of their paper, more so than an individual editor has for himself. I would claim its position is that of a countervailing power. Existing on the terrain of power, but a little on the edge, to one side, dissident, taking distance.'

Le Monde, he said, 'mixed professionalism and conviction, respect for facts and independence of spirit' – adding that 'from that point of view, even if this shocks some people, I still think that Trotskyism was a good school: a school of rejection'. What Plenel has taken from a political current which he has never attempted to disavow is no longer an ideology, but a style not just of scepticism, but of militant challenge of authority and a contemptuous attitude to the institutions of established political power – while at the same time ambitious to achieve high positions in journalism from which he could exercise a large power of his own. He shares much of the contempt which Glen Greenwald expresses for mainstream journalism – while, unlike Greenwald, passing much of his life in mainstream journalism.

That power has been most evident in his revelations, based in a network of contacts which crucially included a number of former comrades from the Ligue Communiste. Among the most useful of those was Jean-Paul Besset, a former journalist on *Rouge*, who became head of communication in the cabinet (which contained several other former Ligue-ists) of Laurent Fabius, then the prime minister, whose period in that post (1984–6) under the presidency of Mitterrand, covered the *Rainbow Warrior* affair. Mitterrand, however, was no fan, telling his foreign minister, Roland Dumas, that Plenel had persecuted him for a decade and that he believed the journalist was a foreign agent.

In the hothouses which are the national news media everywhere, competition for space, time, money and status ensure jealousies and badmouthing. Plenel – hard driving, with a reputation for seeking destruction of his enemies and cowing his staff – has considerable experience of that kind of attention and is always ready to return fire. He also made good use of contacts – gained (and never apparently lost) when he held the job, early in his *Le Monde* career, of police and security correspondent – to do some important stories, including:

- In the affair of the arrest of three Irish citizens in Vincennes charged with being Republican terrorists, Plenel revealed the planting of the arms and explosives by Captain Paul Barril, a commander of the presidential protection squad created by Christian Prouteau – who received a suspended sentence, while the case Barril brought against the newspaper collapsed.
- In the Bettencourt affair, he and his colleagues alleged that large sums had been paid to conservative politicians by the L'Oréal heiress Liliane Bettencourt – including to Nicolas Sarkozy. In lengthy court proceedings investigating the affair, Sarkozy was dropped from the investigations.
- In the Calhuzac affair, Jerome Calhuzac, a Socialist deputy made Junior Minister of the Budget, was accused by Plenel of keeping a secret foreign bank account for two decades, in order to avoid tax.

Calhuzac strongly denied the allegations, then confirmed the existence of the account; he lost his ministerial post, his parliamentary seat and his membership of the Socialist Party.

The last two of these were uncovered by Mediapart. Plenel left the paper in 2005 after a book, *La face cachée du Monde*,[31] ripped into the triumvirate leading *Le Monde* – Alain Minc, chairman of the supervisory board, Jean-Marie Colombani, the paper's CEO and Plenel, the editorial director, while he grew increasingly alienated from Colombani and Minc, as the circulation of the paper fell sharply. He concluded that the game was up for the written press: in his long interview (given while he was still at *Le Monde*), he said that

> *the press was dominant until the beginning of the 80s, from a professional and cultural point of view – even if it wasn't the largest influence on the public as a whole. And in this sense,* Le Monde *served as a reference for the whole profession. Now, this is a position we've lost; with the coming of a new televisual era, political and general journalism has been dethroned as a reference point for the deep structure of the profession.*
>
> *In my view, you don't need to look further than that for the real explanation, cultural and sociological, for the repeated crises in* Le Monde *for the past ten years. The paper's crisis isn't that of its own democratic structure: on the contrary, that has allowed it to overcome the difficulties inherent in maintaining its independence. It speaks, essentially, to the crisis of the journalistic model built up after the war, of which* Le Monde *was the flower. The stakes for us, working in the daily written press, are to now recreate the model in a context turned completely upside down, to once again be winners and not to gently sink further under the domination of the audio-visual media, their rhythms and practices.*[32]

Mediapart was his answer to the press crisis – and, unlike most other web-based start-ups, it turned a profit three years after its launch, of €500,000 with 60,000 subscribers. It has since continued to grow, making alliances with the photographic site Vu, and with Wikileaks. It has created its own 'leak box' and also a club for its subscribers, run largely by them.

Plenel was not the first to do something about the slow drowning of the press. Pierre Haski was deputy editor of *Libération*, a paper founded by the philosopher Jean Paul Sartre and the journalist Serge July in 1973, and for almost a decade the beacon of the far left in France and beyond. Now substantially more politically moderate, its largest shareholder is Edouard de Rothschild, who had headed a Rothschild family bank which he founded, left in 2004, and in 2005 invested €20m in *Libération*, the investment buying him a controlling stake. After many rows and plans – including one, aborted, to stop paper publication, publish only to the internet and transform the paper's offices into a cultural centre and café – a number of the senior journalists either left or were fired, including, in the first group, Haski, taking with him others interested in a new form of journalism.

Rue 89 (the name derives from two dates of liberation: the revolution of 1789, and the fall of the Berlin Wall in 1989), does do some revelatory journalism, but it is not its main aim. Haski said that 'we try not to get into the grey zone of espionage: most of it comes from the magistrates and the police, and you can't check if it's real'. Instead, Haski and his colleagues, all enthusiastic bloggers, believed in – as he puts it – 'the rise of the reader'. He says that

> around 25 per cent of our content comes from non-journalists; these people are writing about their lives. They have changed the definition of journalism. For example, after a large oil refinery in Normandy closed, we got a letter from one of workers. He wrote well – about what it is to lose a job he had much of his life, and to have a son who would not get one; this is what the internet has brought to journalism. The 'me' comes in.
>
> Another came from a man who drove cabs for Uber Pop before it was banned here [the service, which has drivers taking passengers in their own cars in their spare time, without any training, was banned in the summer, with the Constitutional Court upholding the decision in September]. He wrote, 'I want to make a better living and you are not going to stop me'. We got a lot of hostile comments: the man then responded as aggressively, saying, 'I wanted to tell people what real life is like'.

Rue 89 has not enjoyed the same success as Mediapart: in 2011 the struggling company was brought by the *Nouvel Observateur*, which continues to publish it.

Plenel is as much excoriated, or at least doubted, by his professional peers as he is admired: his career has been one of confrontations, quarrels both personal and principled and, as well as successful investigations, some allegations which he could not prove. But for those who seek to expose the many dark corners of politics, business, finance, institutions and foreign policy and practice, he and Mediapart have become – to use his word – a 'référent', a reference point and an inspiration. His style – owing much, as he has said, to the 'spirit' of Trotskyist politics – has angered the powerful, as investigations, especially if they are accurate, often do. His foundation, in middle age, of Mediapart, seems to have shown that revelatory journalism 'à l'Anglo-Saxone' has a better chance of succeeding financially in France than it has had in the US and the UK – where the most prominent sites, such as the US Politico and the UK's Centre for Investigative Journalism, rely on foundations for their existence – though the new news sites, such as Vice, BuzzFeed and Huffington Post, have investigative reporters, relying on more popular journalism to support their audience numbers.

* * *

Damien Leloup of *Le Monde* is one of a new breed of reporters, adept on the internet, able to navigate the new security world both as a reporter and as a web native. 'The most important thing now is to have a basic idea of how to encrypt. You must have at least a vague idea of how the network works, or you will never know what's happening. You will be like an economics correspondent who doesn't understand basic economics. This is a big problem in our profession: journalism schools are only just beginning to teach this kind of thing.'

He shares the frustration of many of those who attach a strong importance to the Snowden revelations, because of the apathy which he sees in the public.

> We've written a lot about it but the effect hasn't been large. The first revelations – on the hacking of the President's phone, part of Snowden's revelations[33] – did get a strong response but after that only some people were interested in further revelations: most people turned off. The readership for the articles from Snowden was much lower than for other articles on the website. After the Charlie Hebdo killings, the mood was very much for the police and the security services and the state. People thought, 'Spies spying? That's their job'. As for Hollande's phone – it was probably his personal phone which he uses all the time, to text journalists. His presidential phone is very strongly encrypted so probably they didn't get into that. No one has said that the presidential phone was tapped.

All the indications are that the much greater carnage caused by the Paris attacks in November have strengthened that public feeling.

Leloup believes, however, that too little attention is given to the malign effects of a heightened fear of terrorism. In a story[34] in his paper in December 2015, he cited several instances of arrests, in some cases of men with North African names, who had, usually when drunk, called out 'Vive Daech' (the Islamic State), or in one case 'je suis Salah Abdeslam' (Abdeslam was arrested in Brussels in March 2016, charged with a series of terrorist-related offences including murders and is on trial at the time of writing). He quoted Elizabeth Blisson, head of the magistrates' association, as saying that bringing an arrestee to court a day after arrest, as had become the norm, and charging them with support for terrorism because of such speech was a danger to civil liberties, since it gave no time to properly brief defence counsel and meant that the court risked being guided by emotion rather than reason.

Alonso agrees with Glen Greenwald, that 'we need to be hostile to the state. We have to be much more than sceptical, because we're being manipulated by the state. We can't trust them, especially now, because there's a huge difference between France and the UK and US: there isn't much of an investigative tradition here. But it's Mediapart that is making this change, because it both became the vehicle for investigations and it's successful.'

Mourning with Leloup that his work for *Libération* now rouses only narrow interest – 'most readers don't care: that's a fact, but the strength of journalism is to keep publishing, to put the stuff on the record' – Alonso says that 'the tools which the secret services use themselves change the nature of democracy. They want to have more control over the society – though I don't think they have a secret plan to rule, they are in the end loyal to the republic. But they do have their own agenda. Greater control can happen without conscious will of the system.'

For the radical part of French society – still more prominent and better represented in the establishment than in either the US or the UK – the state of emergency and the new laws are largely, in some cases wholly, unwelcome. William Bourdon is a prominent civil rights lawyer with offices opposite the Louvre and with a large clientele in Francophone Africa, who represented Snowden's legal interests in France. He says that

journalists are moderators of public opinion, and they recognise that there is a worldwide movement which affects the trust of citizens. This response of distrust on their part isn't confined to those who follow Snowden and Greenwald. The leaderships of many countries now put out a new propaganda of ethics which they claim to espouse – but which is a façade. This lack or loss of confidence affects the citizens and increases their distrust of private and public leadership. There is a link to be made between the terrorist threats manipulated by governments and companies. There is both a privatisation of public institutions and a public-isation of private companies. Public institutions and governments can do less now. So people are leaving the public sphere.

In November 2015, a bare week before the attacks, Bourdon took part in a debate, organised by *Le Monde*, with the former foreign minister Hubert Vedrine on the issue of leaking. Bourdon saw Assange and Snowden in the line of Antigone – in Greek drama, a daughter of Oedipus who, in mourning for her dead brother Polynices, breaks the law against doing so propounded by King Creon, holding that divine law sanctioning mourning has precedence over man-made law. Bourdon argued that the leaks of Assange and Snowden had transformed journalists into 'institutional sounders of alarm (*lanceurs d'alerte institutional*)'.[36] Vedrine, by contrast, argued that the state must keep an 'irreducible number of secrets', and that the demand for an 'immediate, total and absolute transparency' is a dangerous one to the state and its citizens.[37]

* * *

Most of the journalists who cover the secret services say that they changed in the 2000s, though some add that the changes were cosmetic, not real. Among the changes was a shift, which continues, away from military-led and -staffed organisations to ones led by civilians. One of these, who served as director of the external intelligence service, DGSE, for six-and-a-half years from 2002 to 2009, was Pierre Brochand, a former ambassador to Hungary, Israel and Portugal, a man who had never worked for the secret services before leading one of them. Seated in the lobby of a grand hotel in Cannes, the city in which he was born and to which he has retired, he says that

I was surprised to be asked, but I was a dedicated public servant and so accepted.

As to the relations with the media, as soon as I took up my post at the DGSE, I realised there was something dangerously wrong. Coming from the outside, I probably had a clearer picture of the situation than those inside.

As a matter of fact, we were facing a sort of vicious circle.

On the one hand, for various reasons, partly historical, the public image of the DGSE left much to be desired. Which was regrettable not only in itself, but also because it had a direct impact on our work. If you think about it, the sole real asset of an intelligence service is its credibility, which stems from trust, which, in turn is correlated to reputation. And, in our times, reputation is still made, to a large extent, by what the mainstream media say about you.

At the time, the service was totally cut off from these circles. It had become a silent fortress, still traumatised by disastrous past experiences [the Ben Barka[38] *and* Rainbow Warrior *affairs ...]. Then, the media were only seen as a source of trouble and mischief, and, as a consequence, were kept at arm's length. The prevailing attitude was a sort of anxious paralysis, not too dissimilar to a mongoose tetanised by a snake and waiting to be eaten.*

But, on the other hand, to be honest, this defiance was not without justification. The paranoia that goes traditionally with the trade of intelligence has nowadays more legitimate reasons to feed itself: in our societies as they are, i.e. individualistic democracies, the motto has become 'liberty, equality, transparency, morality'. Transparency being, in a way, the condition for protecting liberty and equality, since information is power, and, if it is hidden from the people, both liberty and equality are supposed to be in danger. 'Morality' is a corollary, inasmuch as notions like 'raison d'Etat', 'secret d'Etat' or 'mensonge d'Etat', 'realpolitik' in general (which, by the way, are at the core of the workings of an intelligence service) are similarly looked down upon as menaces.

The national state, which was previously 'above' civil society, has gone 'under': it is no longer 'in the driver's seat', everything it does coming under the close scrutiny of the 'controllers' (judges, journalists, pollsters, advocacy NGOs, whistleblowers, etc. ...) and what remains out of reach from their constant oversight being, by definition, highly suspicious.

More generally, it is not too far-fetched to recognise that the value system which guides the activities of secret services is in almost total opposition to the current dominant set of values: opacity vs transparency, discretion vs noise, clandestinity vs openness, anonymous dedication vs narcissism, 'esprit de corps' vs individuality, loyalty vs volatility, duties vs rights, hierarchy vs horizontality, obedience vs independence, sacrifice vs life's pleasures, etc. ... On the whole, the services have become anachronistic islands of traditions in an ocean of hyper modernity, of which the media, among others are the self-appointed guardians.

The secret services see themselves as an endangered species and, as a consequence, feel threatened, while prejudices still regard them as threatening.

I realised that this status quo was untenable, since, in spite or maybe because of its very low profile towards the press, the DGSE was too attractive a target to remain ignored. As a result, the only news about it was negative or foolish fantasy or both.

In this context, the only option available was to react and adapt: since we could not change the environment within which we operated, we had to adjust to it, but in a way that ultimately would be more beneficial than detrimental.

We started by analysing the various facets of the problem the media were posing to us.

We found out that there were at least four dimensions to be taken into account. On the potentially negative side, the media could be considered as 'adversaries' and 'competitors'. On the other side, potentially positive, they could be envisaged as 'interlocutors' and even 'partners'. The strategy we set forth was to tackle these different aspects, in order to maximise the positive and minimise the negative.

Doing that, we were also keen to capitalise on the new background offered by the rise of jihadist terrorism (including hostage taking) and the multiplication of foreign crises in which our military was involved or about to be involved.

This is a crucial point. Because while our contemporaries want transparency, morality and so forth and, as a result, are eager to keep the state on a tight leash, they are also extremely concerned with their security (it is easy to demonstrate that individualism goes with an increased fear of dying, but this is another story ...).

So, starting from the end of 2002, we initiated a policy of progressive opening, becoming little by little more proactive towards the media, not only accepting but seeking contacts with their representatives on an 'off' basis, except when 'on' was specifically authorised.

In the first stage, only two persons were allowed to interface with journalists. I met them one on one (for the most prestigious) or invited groups of them for long lunches 'à bâtons rompus' (which meant freely raising any subjects or questions). While one of my closest collaborators, although not identified as a spokesman, was available 24/24, 7/7, in order to answer queries or pass on messages. I also, for the first time ever, gave (rare) interviews on the record and wrote articles of a general nature, while, also for the first time, we created a site on the net with recruiting in mind. We even opened the doors of our premises and let some of our members be interviewed for an unprecedented programme on national television.

The idea was to build long-term relationships based upon mutual trust. Which implied, on our side, to never lie, except by omission, and, on the other side, not to breach that trust. Otherwise the relationship would be immediately severed.

As to 'adversaries', i.e. investigative journalists looking for a scoop or some spicy stories, which would put intelligence activities in an unfavourable light, we tried to show them we were not the monsters they expected us to be, but devoted professionals, doing their best in a difficult world. Since these people were mostly interested in the inside workings of the service, we went as far as security allowed in order to explain the 'why', 'what' and 'how' of our trade, releasing once in a while tidbits of sexy information they could publish without inconvenience for us, but of great value to them, since it gave them an opportunity to maintain their reputation of insiders ...

The media as 'competitors' were another matter, more important, although often ignored.

It is a fact that people in government (our 'customers') function in a world of immediacy, where they are informed of and have to react to events without delay. That is why they get their firsthand information from the media, which, according to me, give a somewhat distorted vision of the real world, either because they have their own agenda or because they skew the facts with emotions and wishful thinking, not to mention ideology.

But we realised that the first impression our leaders got from the media was there to stay. Since we could not compete in terms of rapidity (i.e. being the first to announce an event that had actually taken place), we reacted by launching two new kinds of products. One, exposing reasonable anticipations about the evolution of crises and situations of interest, in order to try to stay ahead of 'breaking news', and hopefully making it appear as not a total surprise. ... The other one was aimed at unmasking any element of disinformation that could contaminate the information feed of our government.

That was not easy, since intelligence services are used to working with patience and not being perturbed by the chaos of daily occurrences. So we had to force ourselves to dive into this mess and produce on very short notice, based on our expertise and knowledge, papers completing with, connecting, contradicting news reports when it seemed necessary, in order to enable our authorities to see the world as it is and not as they wish it to be. The intention was to decode what remained 'behind the curtain' without complacency, nor euphemism or emotion, but with rationality, objectivity and bluntness.

Then, in the last instance, we took the view that journalists could become 'interlocutors' and even 'partners', while of course respecting each other's independence.

Since we were dealing with the same matters and material (what's going on in the world and what are the threats affecting us), it appeared fruitful to exchange views on subjects of mutual interest. We invited journalists to specific briefings and some of them were also ready to share impressions after their trips in the field.

When trust was established over time, we could go even further and arrange meetings for them with our liaison officers in embassies. And, in return, it was not rare that journalists spontaneously produced articles or films giving a reasonably good image of the DGSE.

On the whole, the outcome of all this had been extremely satisfactory. We were certainly helped by the context, i.e. the direct threat to national security, which started emerging at the beginning of the twenty-first century and the nature of these threat which put intelligence on the front line. The absence of internal scandals or obvious blunders during all those years was also a big point in our favour, contributing to the increase reputation of professionalism of our service. Not to mention the gratitude towards the DGSE for having played the leading role in the liberation of journalists taken hostage in Iraq in 2004 and 2005.

This turning around of the relationship between the DGSE and the media was the basis upon which our successors could go further, since now the service has a designated spokesman. In addition, a new popular TV series shows its agents in action in a very positive way ...

* * *

The politicisation of the French secret services, and the temptation presented to ministers and officials to use sympathetic agents within them to pursue their own agendas, is probably not over but seems to have lessened. However, since the time of de Gaulle, the DGSE has acquired a reputation for spying on its industrial and technological competitors: indeed, a former head of the DGSE, Pierre Marion, said that 'this espionage activity is an essential way for France to keep abreast of international commerce and technology. Of course, it was directed against the United States as well as others. You must remember that while we are allies in defence matters, we are also economic competitors in the world.' Marion, who was head of the French aviation company Aerospatiale in North America for a decade, had been appointed under Mitterrand but clashed with him several times, specifically on the President's private security team – and thus was in office only for 18 months, in 1981–2, was sure that commercial espionage does still continue.[39]

The internal and external secret services have been extensively de-militarised, and are now seen by their peers in the US, the UK and elsewhere as among the best in the world – particularly strong in the Middle East, and in parts of Africa. Both the French state and the agencies have been sceptical of the massive build-up of the security complex in the US: but since the chilling experiences in Paris in 2015 – *Charlie Hebdo* in January and the series of attacks in November – and in 2016, the attack in Nice and the murder of a priest near Rouen, both in July, they have become converts to a 'war on terror' strategy. These attacks have had the effect of drawing the French agencies closer to their UK and US equivalents: though whether this will mean a widening of the membership of the 'Five Eyes' is doubtful.

At least as significant a change has been wrought on French journalism which, reacting to scandals and seeking to develop a more active policy of investigation into the more hidden areas of the French state and corporate life, has been and is responsible for much of the more informed coverage which the news media now mount.

* * *

How could the French agencies open up more?

Both French and foreign security officials and commentators claim that the French agencies, once a byword for rivalry and refusal to cooperate with each other, are now working together relatively well – impelled, especially in 2015, by the attacks of January and November. One (foreign and anonymous) observer argues, however, that 'more should be done', and that fiefdoms within the services often remain closely guarded.

Similarly, the tendency to personalise intelligence round the figure of the president will be hard to eradicate; though there is general agreement that the intelligence group which President Mitterrand kept about himself, at least in part to deflect press inquiries, has been copied by his successors. However, the power of the presidency means the temptation is always available, especially in foreign affairs and military interventions: the French president is the Commander-in-Chief of the armed forces, he or she can dissolve the National Assembly, but is not responsible to the parliament. Defence, foreign policy and intelligence matters are part of the president's so-called *domaine reservé*.

Some of this could be addressed by better oversight. France, for much of the contemporary period, had no parliamentary oversight of the intelligence agencies of any kind. Proposals and pressure, especially from the socialist and communist left and particularly after the *Rainbow Warrior* incident, to establish an oversight committee was met with the refusal of the foreign and interior ministries to divulge secrets, and a reluctance on the part of successive presidents to dilute their power and freedom of action in the intelligence area. A law, promised by President Sarkozy during his campaign, was finally passed in 2007 to establish a Parliamentary Intelligence Committee with the aim of assisting senators and deputies 'to follow the general activity and the means of the specialized services', while at the same time preserving their secrecy.[40] The committee has the right to interview heads of the agencies and other officials, but no rights on the appointment of agency directors, nor the right to conduct investigations.

Charlotte Lepri, the author of the French case study in the EU study on national intelligence agencies, writes that

> ultimately, the committee has not enhanced Parliament's information on intelligence issues: the overall knowledge of MPs regarding intelligence activities has not improved: members of the committee do not communicate with the rest of the parliament and do not teach other MPs about intelligence. Because of the lack of contents in the committee's reports, the press has paid little attention to the functioning of the committee DPR and its work remains largely unnoticed.[41]

French political culture has been more resistant than in most democracies to oversight bodies, and the indifference of the parliament and of the news media is thus not a surprise. But it is a serious affair nonetheless – since in the wake of terrorist attacks and public anxiety, the powers of the secret services have greatly increased.

The Internal Security Code gives power to the intelligence and other agencies (such as customs) to intercept communications on such issues as national independence, territorial sovereignty and national security, the prevention of terrorism and organised crime and the protection of France's scientific and economic potential.[42]

These powers were increased in 2013, when the Military Planning Law amended the Code to allow access to personal communications and metadata, including content of phone conversations and other communications, held by the communications companies. They were increased further in 2015 by a bill reforming intelligence surveillance, legalising existing practice by the agencies and increasing surveillance powers. The bill, which has been highly contentious, allows surveillance technology to be installed in all communications companies to give the services the right to analyse the data when the prime minister requires identification of persons of interest. It also allows the services to locate individuals of interest within a given area – though it would also allow the surveillance of individuals not the target of the searches. The metadata collected may be kept for five years from when the data is decrypted – meaning that encrypted information could be kept indefinitely.[43]

None of these measures would require judicial authorisation. The law does provide for an expanded Commission for the Control of Intelligence Techniques, with 13 members, of whom six are members of parliament; the recommendations, are, however, not binding.

The laws are generally stronger and the oversight mechanisms weaker than elsewhere, the latter not so much by their structure as by the facts of French political life, whereby most power resides in the executive, little in parliament, and where the news media, though much more alert to security and intelligence issues than before, is still somewhat detached from day-to-day holding to account.

It is here that both structures and approaches should change. It is clear that, after the shocks of 2015, the national leaders, the politicians in general and the public are impatient with barriers to the fullest deployment of intelligence against a significant terrorist threat. However, a case should be made for the need for greater scrutiny of those who do surveillance: Privacy International has expressed strong concern that 'electronic surveillance by French intelligence agencies and other bodies is overly broad, does not require prior judicial authorisation and it is not subject to effective oversight'.[44] Were this to continue, the risks of public disaffection in both the political class and the intelligence services would be high.

France is not part of the 'Five Eyes', an exclusively Anglo-Saxon information-sharing system – but could have been. In 2009, the then newly appointed Director of US National Intelligence, Admiral Dennis Blair, began talks with Bernard Bajolet, the presidential security adviser, about the possibility of bringing France in to the club.[45] This was in the context of President Sarkozy's strongly pro-American posture: such an agreement would mean that France would have access to, above all, much US intelligence; and that the others would have to cease spying on France (and vice versa) – since that is the rule (though not formally set down in writing).

Blair overreached himself in pushing the idea, annoyed Obama in doing so and with other missteps was forced to resign. However, the possibility of French membership should not be confined to a failed effort at a particular time. All of the Western agencies, which had been strongly different in their areas of interest and work, have been brought closer together by a common terrorist threat.

The strengthening of France's security services and their particular areas of expertise in the Middle East and in Francophone Africa means they would be a valuable addition. The bad communications between the French and the Belgian agencies which contributed to the initially confused response to the March 2016 attacks on Brussels airport (as well as the weakness of the Belgian services themselves) highlighted the need for better coordination and sharing.

The risks, as seen from inside the services, are large. French culture, both in the secret services and in politics, is more different from the Anglo-Saxon countries than they are from each other. The strongest link between the Americans and the British grew out of close wartime collaboration, at a time when the UK was the more experienced and larger intelligence partner. The fact that the British intelligence chiefs were immediately received into the inner councils of the US equivalents after 9/11 shows the instinctive closeness of the two systems.

There are strong barriers. But the present terrorist threat, the rising dangers of cyber warfare, the increasing enmity of Russia and the exposure of France to further large attacks are also strong – arguably stronger – reasons for a dispassionate investigation of the possibility.

Conclusion: More Light to Lighten the Darkness

> Surveillance has achieved very important goals, has found very important facts that have served American security ... [but] increasingly we are living behind one-way mirrors in which the government knows more and more about us and we know less and less about what the government is doing.
>
> (Barton Gellman, *Washington Post*, NPR interview, September 2013)

The dilemma round which this book has circled – that journalism professes to hold power to account, but cannot hold to any detailed account the secret services, whose power is now greater than at any time since the depths of the Cold War – cannot be resolved. It remains a necessary tension. The very large latent power the services have to subvert democratic politics and civil society relies for its restraint on the staff and leadership of these agencies, and their adherence to the norms of democratic life, including submission to elected authority and to the law. But though not resolvable, they can be lessened.

Those impatient with the general support for the intelligence services, and for the government's handling of them, believe that the attitude amounts to complacency or, in David Davis's view, intellectual laziness. They are too dismissive of an experience which has seen little to fear in the agencies' activities, and much to be thankful for: but the critics are right that the debate should be more active. The role, scope and challenges which the agencies now have are much changed, and the majority know little of what these changes mean.

It would thus be a public good if debate could be stimulated and the media were persuaded to make the issues surrounding the preservation of security more prominent. The services, politicians and officials, the security institutes which study and propose change in their practice, the

215

commentators and reporters who provide most of what the public knows about their activities, and members of these publics themselves with an interest in them, are inevitably and rightly drawn deeper and deeper into a debate on their place and powers. In the Cold War, the putative enemy was external, the Soviet bloc. Now, the putative enemies are within, or relatively easy entrants to, the states which are targets. That has changed, and will continue to change, the relationship between agencies and the public, and between the agencies and the mediating institutions, of which the media, because of their wide diffusion, are the most important.

* * *

The secret services are among the largest challenges for journalism in democratic states. The growth in their capacity to collect data, the resources they command and the trust citizens have that they will keep them safe from the effects of terrorism mean they are some of the most consequential institutions of the modern state. If, as many in these services and those close to them believe, jihadist terrorist groups may acquire and use or threaten to use weapons of mass destruction, then a large part of the fate of nations rests on their shoulders: their role is thus potentially existential.

Even if that does not happen their role is now central. A world whose level of development depends on a series of vulnerable networks – the internet itself, energy supply, trade routes, financial exchange, migration patterns, water and food availability, media – demands a level of protection against attack which in turn depends ever more heavily on good intelligence.

Central – and secret: the intelligence agencies must keep many secrets if they are to retain the ability to act. These secrets embrace their personnel, their operations, ongoing, past and planned; their targets; and their strategies. With the belief in their indispensability – a belief which, with differing degrees of intensity, remains general, certainly among the political classes everywhere and to a large extent among publics – goes at least an implicit assent to their need for secrecy.

All of the agencies needed to 'retool' after the ending of the Cold War around 1990, though the beginning of what the journalist Edward Lucas has designated a 'New Cold War'[1] has reversed that to an extent, with Russian and Ukrainian speakers again prized hires. The peace dividend was small and brief: jihadist terrorism was already evident as the Cold War melted. Osama bin Laden was working out how to create al Qaeda in the 1990s from the disparate groups who came out of the anti-Soviet war in Afghanistan in the late 1980s, fired with a vision of replacing the regimes in the Muslim states with a purer Islamic administration. In the post-9/11 wars, 'from 2001–2011 around 250,000 people were killed [in a] series of conflicts exacerbated, catalyzed or provoked by the strikes on New York and Washington ... from 2011 to 2015 the total was even greater ... armed conflicts had led to 49,000 fatalities across the world in 2010 [while] 180,000 people had died in forty-two conflicts in 2014.'[2] A small minority of these fatalities were in Western states and no single incident approached that of the destruction of the Twin Towers: but by the 2010s, bombings and shootings in Europe and North America were relatively common occurrences.

The scale of the terrorist challenge and the fact that the organisations promoting it – especially IS – work across all states has meant that the Western agencies have become more similar in their day-to-day activities than before, when, apart from the common Soviet threat, they were dealing with differing challenges – whether Irish Republican terrorism, or North African terrorist groups, or domestic gun crime linked to native extremist groups or individuals. It also means that the impetus to share information is greater – and raises the issue of closer collaboration through formal mechanisms.

This book is written on the assumption, based on the reasons above, that the secret services are more important now than they have been since the hotter periods of the Cold War. It also depends on the assumption that the three services which form the main part of the book are quite securely under the control of democratic and generally liberal states. It is not my judgment – though it is of several of those interviewed in this book – that the democratic fabrics and civil societies of any of these are presently threatened by the new legislation and expanded police and secret service powers of the decades of the 2000s and 2010s: France, the UK and the US have done most in the world to develop and embed both democratic institutions and lively, often contrarian civil societies. Only a deep and sustained period of economic decline and a heightening of the terrorist threat could begin to carve into that heritage and present practice – and, of course, that is possible, but not actual. One of the reasons why it is not, is that journalism in all of these is strong, and many of the effects of the internet, though deeply uncomfortable for my trade, newspapers, will strengthen it further.

The main claim of journalism as a democratic actor is that it provides citizens with much of what they need to enrich and inform their civic life.

It does so by being part of the process of giving 'accounts', reports as full and accurate as possible of the main issues of politics, society and the economy, a process which the internet has hugely assisted. And it probes behind the curtains which every kind of power reflexively puts over many of its activities, and tries to illuminate that which is not made public but which bears upon public, and even private, life. It often does so badly, or not at all; as often, its imagined audience is inattentive or absent. Yet emerging from journalism come, in most democratic societies, narratives which inform and reveal, issues which often are not put in the public domain by any other means.

The dilemma with which mainstream journalism in democracies has lived and must continue to live is that the secret state is beyond its power to hold to account as it does politics, business, economic management or the arts. Its accounts are nearly always retrospective, a retrospection sometimes measured in decades. In the political process, in the activities of corporations, in the policies and actions of foreign states, as well as in the reporting of culture or sport, journalism can report and comment on day-by-day events, give judgements as to the stakes in these events and whether or not the actions taken are succeeding or failing. In the intelligence area such close engagement is out of the question. At the heart of the modern state is a power which, though no longer wholly screened off from the journalistic gaze and thus more often fictionalised than accounted for, cannot be open to real-time inspection. Though the journalistic effort mobilised behind tracking the agencies' work varies greatly from country to country, as well as among the three countries examined here, they cannot be held to account as other – including much less consequential – institutions are.

* * *

The 'new radicals' behind Wikileaks and the NSA revelations, and their supporters, propose a new model of journalism: one which goes beyond scepticism into determined net-based guerrilla raids on secret information, especially that held by the state and its various departments, and the intelligence agencies. Though strongest in the US – and the US is usually their main target – this new model journalism has supporters everywhere.

The journalism adumbrated by the new radicals on the security beat, however, has not yet been given a clearly defined form. Julian Assange's writing is not programmatic: his default position is to see the authorities of the world – including the mainstream news organisations – as engaged in, or at best prone to, the suppression of information, rather than interested in its publication. Redaction in order to safeguard names, organisations or operations is usually for him a compromise, not a principle – as his dump of all of the diplomatic cables, unredacted, shows.

Glen Greenwald, who wrote for the *Guardian* and for Slate before working with Snowden, sees 'career' journalists as subservient to governments and commercial pressures. He believes most of them recoil from what he sees as a truth by which all journalists must live and work – that the state power structures are now so badly compromised by the apparatuses they have constructed to secretly spy on their own citizens that they can no longer be reported objectively, but must be confronted aggressively.

But these are comments within interviews and scattered writings, not a programme. Assange has never confronted the problem of what his brand of journalism would look like; how it would operate day by day, or what its relationship with governments would be. Greenwald is more down-to-earth and works within an internet journal. But neither has he given a sketch of what his journalism, were it to become the dominant mode – as he appears to wish it to be – would look like.

Mainstream reporting cultivates men and women of power, and their lieutenants, in order to understand the major effects their institutions will have on societies. The new radicals see these figures as lost causes; instead, they cultivate those within the institutions who for whatever reason will reveal their secrets, especially their 'guilty' secrets – one such being the effective block put on any publicising of the bulk collection programmes by the US's NSA, and the UK's GCHQ.

The heroes – or in Chelsea Manning's case, the martyr – of this approach are not usually part of the power structure, but people whose disagreement with the direction and policies of their institution takes the form of leaking vast quantities of information both to the new radicals and the mainstream press, so that it can be deployed with as much force as possible.

The *Washington Post*'s Barton Gellman, who was chosen by Snowden to handle some of his material (and with whom Greenwald quarrelled), differs[3] quite sharply from the new radicals with whom he has worked. He does fear that 'increasingly we are living behind one-way mirrors in which the government knows more and more about us and we know less and less about what the government is doing'. And he thinks that publication of some of the Snowden material is good for democracy:

> one of [the commitments of government] ... is to secure the national defense. It's not the only interest we have and there has to be a balance, and the balance has not been debated by an informed public because there was an absolute dearth of information. And what we're seeing now, what a lot of Americans say they appreciate, is enough transparency to enable Congress and the American public to decide where they want to draw the lines.[5]

But he does not believe that America has become an Orwellian dystopia as both Assange and Greenwald do. On the bulk collection of data, Gellman says that 'I see no evidence that the government is assembling these tools in order to spy on political opponents or corruptly to serve some private interest, or things that you worry about with the Big Brother analogy'. He also thinks that 'surveillance has achieved very important goals, has found very important facts that have served American security. It's not all ... in the field of counterterrorism, but we care a lot about the spread of nuclear weapons; we care a lot about certain activities that are undertaken by foreign governments. So I am absolutely not making the claim that this stuff [the NSA operations] does not serve American security.'[6]

The contrast between Gellman on the one hand and the new radicals on the other is that they see an absolute good in absolute transparency for states, absolute privacy for themselves. He sees journalism as a push and pull between publication and the retention of information by authorities. They see a utopia; he sees a continuing tussle, already centuries old. Gellman, for all his strongly proactive reporting, is of a piece with other mainstream investigative reporters, some of which have been featured above. For them, leaked documents are subjects for examination, redaction and above all judgement as to whether or not they should be published according to what are ultimately democratic-statist criteria (even if, as is usual, the officials of the state do not agree with the criteria employed).

The logical extrapolation from the position of the new radicals – unclear as it is – is not a stable basis for journalism in a democratic state. Indeed, at least in Assange's case, they do not believe that the states which are the object of their revelations *are* democratic, or if formally so, that the word has little real meaning. Journalism in a democratic state has to closely observe, report on, investigate and criticise the political order, but insofar as it remains democratic and encourages a civil society to flourish in freedom, journalism has to cede the prime responsibility for guiding society to the elected institutions, which will reflect many of the weaknesses of the societies they govern. That the institutions of elective democracy are under strain and face a myriad of challenges is patently the case: but the twentieth century taught, among much else, that an attempt to leap from a muddle into a utopia produces tyranny. Journalism in a democracy is constrained by the democratic rules: indeed, it is itself a political and democratic act.

The radicals have gathered round the leaks to Wikileaks and by Edward Snowden. In April 2016, some 11.5 million documents were leaked from the Panamanian law firm Mossack Fonseca, which revealed the lengths to which some of the wealthiest people in the world went to hide their wealth from the demands of the taxation authorities in their own countries. Apart from the company's own protestations that it had committed no illegal act and that the criminals were those who had hacked into their computers, the revelations attracted no opprobrium. Those caught in various acts, were for example, then prime minister David Cameron who held £30,000 in an offshore investment fund, sold when he became prime minister in 2010; the prime minister of Iceland, Sigmundur Gunnlaugsson, who had not declared an offshore company owned with his wife when he became an MP (he later resigned); and the head of the world football institution FIFA, Gianni Infantino, was shown by some of the documents to be potentially involved in deals with figures under investigation in a series of probes into football fraud when he was head of legal services at UEFA, the European football governing body. President Putin, through a spokesman, let it be known that he saw this as another example of 'Putinophobia' in the West – and that the allegations against many in his close circle were part of an information war against him, 'the curatorial work of the US State Department itself'.[7] By contrast, President Obama took the opportunity in an unscheduled appearance before the White House press, to describe the Panama revelations as 'important stuff … a lot of these loopholes come at the expense of middle-class families, because that lost revenue has to be made up somewhere. Alternatively, it means that we're not investing as much as we should in schools, in making college more affordable, in putting people back to work rebuilding our roads, our bridges, our infrastructure, creating more opportunities for our children.'[8]

This was an exact reversal of the roles the two presidents played in the Snowden leaks. Then, Obama praised the NSA, 'staffed by patriots laboring in obscurity' and dismissed Snowden – 'I'm not going to dwell on Mr. Snowden's actions or his motivations ... [but the] sensational way in which these disclosures have come out have often shed more heat than light.'[9]

By contrast, Putin has granted Snowden what seems like an indefinite leave to stay in Russia: and in their *The Red Web*, Andrei Soldatov and Irina Borogan give a vivid and detailed account of a press conference Snowden gave, in July 2013, to a room packed with reporters in Moscow's Sheremetyevo airport, where he had been held in limbo for some weeks. On the testimony of Russian reporters and heads of civil rights NGOs there, the conference had been organised by the Russian domestic security service, the FSB, and was led by the lawyer Anatoly Kucherena, a member of the FSB's Public Council, founded in 2007 to promote the organisation's image. They comment that the press conference 'was a sign that Putin was not going to keep his distance from Snowden but rather would attempt to co-opt him for his own purposes'. Tanya Lokshina, head of the Human Rights Watch office in Moscow, who attended the press conference, said later that 'it was obvious that the comrades from the intelligence agencies gathered a group of people who made up all the participants in the event. And they arranged the meeting, probably to legitimize the decision already made that he would be granted temporary asylum.'[10]

Ironically, the two men at the centre of the two great security leaks – Julian Assange and Edward Snowden – have both taken refuge in states which have a poor record on press freedom. Assange is in the Ecuadorian Embassy in London. Both Freedom House and Reporters sans Frontières believe Ecuador is not free, and that Russia is even less free – the environment of both seen as having worsened under President Corea of Ecuador and President Putin of Russia.

* * *

There is no question that the agencies, everywhere, have lifted some of the veils that were wound around them. In the case of the US, a greater openness of the institutions was much more deeply embedded in the culture than in Europe. In the case of the UK and France, a distrust of journalism which limited contacts to a handful of trusted individuals has been replaced by a cautious laying out of some low-value cards, and carefully choreographed public relations exercises, such as a tour of the GCHQ.

They have also – they claim – ceased to recruit journalists as secret agents. The practice of recruitment in the US was proclaimed wrong in the report of the Church Committee in 1975/6: 20 years later, it was found still to be in existence and was banned in law in 1997. Few doubt, however, that in extreme circumstances the CIA would use a reporter for espionage purposes. In the UK, the intelligence services say that they no longer do it though there is no legal bar. The French say the same, but nor is there a law against it.

Yet the Wikileaks and Snowden revelations have shone a harsh light on the manoeuvres of the agencies and the governments which public relations will not address. As some senior intelligence officials admit, the attempt to keep secret a huge increase in the collection of data was bound to be discovered. The good reason for doing so – not alerting hostile groups to the surveillance – is too thin, since it is clear by now that these groups will factor in the certainty of close observation into their activities. To fool the public but not the enemy is a bad outcome.

The complexity and scope of the agencies require a public account made of them which is a significant event in the political and journalistic calendar. This might be a day's debate in the legislatures, with as much material presented as possible; an annual report by a senior figure in an ombudsman role with a substantial and expert staff, representing the public to the agencies and vice versa; events which would be likely to prompt large coverage in the news media, which would themselves wish to both host the debates and question the main actors. The aim would be to provide a forum for display and debate, an opportunity to present criticism, fears and objections as well as clarification of activities and assertions of democratic procedure. The public, as well as a selection of journalists, should have the ability to see the face, if not the internal organs, of the intelligence services they fund and on which they rely.

That can be hard and hazardous for the agencies; but their centrality to the modern democratic state makes it imperative that they, and their political overseers, do not automatically default to a refusal to countenance any further openness because of the risks.

If the dangers could be contained while the increased openness was genuine, then there is plenty about secret service work that can and should be exposed to public scrutiny. This could include, for example, the protocols governing the operations of the services, and the rules for the surveillance of the public. The mistakes made by all the main agencies on Iraqi possession of WMD should not be allowed to occur again: it would be good to have this explained and debated by figures from the intelligence world, as well as politicians and former high officials.

Nor should this be limited to the agencies. The relationships between politicians, officials and the secret services should also be explained and open to debate – the more so, since the politicians and ministers are themselves elected, and directly accountable to the electorate, in this as well as the rest.

Journalists who cover security also have particular responsibilities. The attitude of the best of them is one of determined investigation, with a strong sense of limits, both those imposed by their news organisations and by themselves. To cover services in which people take great risks for a nation's security is to learn respect for the craft: respect does not preclude sharp observation, questioning and revelation of abuse.

The way in which intelligence is reported has, in the 2000s, become more polemically conditioned than ever before. The view that the modern security state is a danger to and an oppressor of its citizens, using the terrorist threat to extend its control over them, has passed into journalism as a spur, especially to younger reporters, to reveal and expose the workings of the secret services in dramatic and highly critical ways. In less stark terms, many in the mainstream media and in politics believe in some version of a 'slippery slope' – that with increased powers and with more sophisticated technology comes the danger of the services, in coalition with authoritarian political forces, closing off in the future democratic possibilities and constricting civil society and human rights.

Those who believe such fears are fanciful, in the view of John McLaughlin, the former deputy and acting director of the CIA and David Omand, the former head of GCHQ, who see in the services men and women dedicated to the preservation, not the narrowing, of democracy and the protection, not the shrinking of human rights. Yet they concede that the inability of the US and UK agencies and governments to explain what was being done in collecting and storing communications data in bulk was a bad mistake, and its exposure by Snowden, though not justified in the terms under which he did it, was both inevitable and may have a generally positive effect. Snowden taught one salutary lesson: that to engage in as momentous an act as bulk collection of the metadata of everyone's communications without making it clear why was worse than a crime (it was probably legal). It was a huge mistake, harming democratic practice in the name of preserving democracy.

It would be well if the impetus for a new relationship between the services, the government and the news media could be prompted by reformers on both sides. Such an approach demands understanding between two trades which, as said at the beginning of this book, are both similar and wholly different. They are, however, committed in their different ways to preserving democratic life: it should be a platform for at least discussion on how best, and how far, to cooperate.

* * *

This book has been generally admiring of US journalism, especially on security issues: though much of that admiration is based on the practice of newspaper and magazine journalism, since US television, which does cover secretive intelligence services, is less impressive in analysis and documentaries on the subject. The reason for the admiration is that those papers, magazines and now websites which command sufficient resources see investigation into the nature of the intelligence world as high on the agenda, and prosecute these investigations with care and at length. That is far from absent in the UK, and broadcasting, notably the BBC's Radio 4, often covers the issues well. But there are gaps in the coverage, especially now that the subject has become more salient and more a subject for public interest and concern. This is even more the case in France, which these proposals also cover.

The intelligence area should now be seen as a central one for journalism. This is the case even if the objection – that the reactions of politicians and thus of the news media are panicky and overdone – is wholly or partly right. If it is so, the news media must not stop at a passive transmission of politicians' hype, but interrogate it and argue for a calmer more purposeful response.

It is central because of the presumed seriousness of the terrorists' ambitions; their possible acquisition of WMD; the attraction they have for some, especially the young, largely within the Muslim communities of all three states under review, especially France and the UK; the effect terrorist acts have on relations between host, settled and recent immigrant populations; the expansion of the intelligence services and the passing of new laws; and the powers granted to the police and secret services.

The weight and scope of the new and much refurbished security state has only been partly recognised in the UK and in France. It is the case that coverage has been expanded and it is also the case that the intelligence services are now more open. Heads of the service – including the once deeply uncommunicative GCHQ – give speeches and reporters are invited in for briefings. Pierre Brochand takes credit for beginning that practice in the DGSE. An official history (cutting off before the 1960s) has been published of MI6, on John Scarlett's initiative. These moves, slight when compared to other centres of power, are genuinely seen by the services as significant moves.

On the services' side, this new openness should be built on further. Wider briefings on issues of current interest and urgency should be part of the repertoire; background information on longer lasting issues, such as (a random selection) the state of play in Ukraine; the expansion of Chinese influence in Africa; the state of energy security in the world. The phenomenon which Stephen Grey noticed – that the US services brief impartially, no matter how tough the reporting of individual journalists has been – should be copied in the UK and France, where the assumption remains that some journalists are beyond the pale.

On the journalists' side, there is a need for more thorough analysis and better knowledge, both of the nature of the world of the services and of the main issues in the world where they are engaged. In the same way as government departments, banks, corporations and various institutions mount seminars to clarify difficult issues, so the services, perhaps in collaboration with security and defence institutes, could run seminars in areas where they believe there is a lack of knowledge and understanding.

The capacity of, and appetite for, investigations in the news media in both France and the UK is less than in the US, in this area as in others. It is a difficult beat, and good results can take a long time and be expensive to secure. But there are few more important parts of the journalistic spectrum in which to work. In all cases – France, the UK and the US – what both the news media and the public interest require is a double assumption: that operational secrets must be inviolable and that the public has a right to know as much as possible. These two requirements will always conflict but they should conflict fruitfully, in favour of greater understanding.

Notes

Preface

1 http://www.dailymail.co.uk/news/article-3027073/Last-Week-Tonight-host-John-Oliver-grills-Edward-Snowden-leaking-documents-knew-harmful.html.
2 Philip Bobbitt, *Terror and Consent* (Allen Lane, 2008).

Chapter 1   Fictions Before Facts

1 Michael Howard, 'Cowboys, Playboys and Other Spies', *New York Times*, 16 Feb. 1986.
2 Quoted in review of Sidney Blumenthal, *The Clinton Wars* (Farrar, Strauss and Giroux, 2003) by Joseph Lelyveld, *New York Review of Books*, 29 May 2003, 'In Clinton's Court'.
3 Tim Weiner, *The Legacy of Ashes* (Doubleday, 2007), 25.
4 See Park Honan's biography of Marlowe, which makes clear the biographer's view in the title: *Christopher Marlowe, Poet and Spy* (OUP, 2005).
5 http://www.electroniclibrary21.ru/literature/nabokov/14.shtml.
6 Andrew Boyle, *The Riddle of Erskine Childers* (Hutchinson, 1977), 108.
7 Christopher Andrew, *Her Majesty's Secret Service* (Viking Press, 1986), 37–56.
8 W. Somerset Maugham, *Ashenden* (Vintage Books, 2000), ix.
9 Ibid. 4.
10 Tim Crook, *The Secret Lives of a Secret Agent* (Kultura Press, 2010).
11 http://www.independent.co.uk/news/people/profiles/writer-lover-soldier-spy-the-strange-and-secretive-life-of-alexander-wilson-2100874.html.
12 http://www.theguardian.com/books/2011/nov/18/mackenzie-memoirs-banned-republished.
13 http://www.tandfonline.com/doi/abs/10.1080/0161-118891862819?journalCode=ucry20.
14 Keith Jeffery, *MI6: The History of the Secret Intelligence Service, 1909–1949* (Bloomsbury, 2010).
15 The use of the word as a description of 'the whole matrix of official and social relations within which power is exercised' was first coined (at least in the British context) by Henry Fairlie in the *Spectator*, 23 Sept. 1955.

16 Richard Davenport-Hines, *An English Affair: Sex, Class and Power in the Age of Profumo* (Harper Collins, 2013, Kindle edition), loc. 3037.
17 Ibid. loc. 3039.
18 *Sunday Mirror*, 23 June 1963.
19 Howard, 'Cowboys'.
20 Davenport-Hines, *An English Affair* (Harper Press, 2013, Kindle edition).
21 Ibid., loc. 3090.
22 http://www.economist.com/blogs/blighty/2014/08/obituary.
23 The Ecu de France does not survive: in a tribute, the wine and restaurant writer Andrew Stevenson recalls it as (with Le Boulestin) 'one of the last of the grandes dames of classic French cuisine in London'. And that 'when L'Ecu finally closed its doors, MI5 had to nip and remove all their microphones hidden in the banquettes, and that when they did so, they found all the KGB microphones in there too'. http://www.andrewstevenson.com/londonrestaurantreminiscences.htm.
24 http://www.theguardian.com/commentisfree/2011/jul/01/ian-jack-chapman-pincher-fleet-street.
25 See Ben Pimlott, *Harold Wilson* (Harper Collins, 1992), 440–3.
26 https://www.theguardian.com/commentisfree/2011/jul/01/ian-jack-chapman-pincher-fleet-street.
27 MI5, now the Secret Service, was recognised in law in 1989; MI6, now the Secret Intelligence Service, together with the signals intelligence agency Government Communications Headquarters, GCHQ, in 1994.
28 Chapman Pincher, *The Secret Offensive* (Sidgwick & Jackson, 1985), 7–8.
29 Douglas Porch, *The French Secret Services* (Macmillan, 1996), 23.
30 Ibid.
31 Piers Paul Read, *The Dreyfus Affair* (Bloomsbury Paperback, 2013), 266.
32 Text of 'J'accuse': http://tempsreel.nouvelobs.com/societe/20060712.OBS4922/j-accuse-par-emile-zola.html.
33 Read, *Dreyfus Affair*, 217.
34 Philippe Hayez, 'Renseignement: The New French Intelligence Policy', *International Journal of Intelligence and Counter Intelligence,* 23 (2010): 474–86.
35 Jean-Claude Cousseran and Philippe Hayez, *Renseigner les democraties, Renseigner en democratie* (Odile Jacob, 2015), commentary at https://www.nuffield.ox.ac.uk/Research/OIG/Documents/hayez2.pdf.
36 Porch, *French Secret Services*, 38.
37 http://africanrhetoric.org/pdf/H%20%20%20AYOR%203_1%20Dénécé%20and%20Arboit.pdf.
38 Dan Lomas, 'The Defence of the Realm and Nothing Else', *Intelligence and National Security* (June 2014), 793–816.
39 Porch, *French Secret Services*, 380.
40 Alistair Horne, *A Savage War of Peace* (NYRB Classics, 2006), 237–8.
41 Ibid. 17.
42 https://www.cia.gov/library/center-for-the-study-of-intelligence/csi-publications/csi-studies/studies/vol46no3/article10.html.

43 http://personal.ashland.edu/~jmoser1/trimmingham.htm.

44 Stephen Ambrose, in *Reporting World War II: American Journalism 1938–1946* (The American Library, 1995), xvii.

45 https://archive.org/stream/freeandresponsib029216mbp/freeandres ponsib029216mbp_djvu.txt.

46 Hutchins Committee Report, 4, https://archive.org/details/freeandresponsib029216 mbp.

47 Ibid. 20.

48 Ibid. 21.

49 Constitution of the United States, 13, https://www.gpo.gov/fdsys/pkg/CDOC-110hdoc50/pdf/CDOC-110hdoc50.pdf.

50 This account of the Cuban invasion is mainly drawn from an autumn 1967 article in the *Columbia University Forum* by two former staffers on *The Nation* magazine: http://jfk.hood.edu/Collection/Weisberg%20Subject%20Index%20Files/C%20Disk/Cuba%20Bay%20of%20Pigs/Item%2010.pdf.

51 *Columbia University Forum* (Autumn 1967).

52 Ibid.

53 Ibid.

54 http://www.latinamericanstudies.org/cuba-news/040761cu.htm.

55 Ibid.

56 *Columbia University Forum* (Autumn 1967).

57 Gordon Carera, *Intercept* (Weidenfeld & Nicolson, 2013), 206–7.

58 Peter Hennessy, *The Secret State* (Penguin, 2nd edition, 2003).

59 Ibid. 365.

60 Hennessy, *Secret State*, 367.

Chapter 2   Losing and Finding the Plot

1 http://www.seattlepi.com/local/article/Demand-solid-news-Rather-urges-1193799.php.

2 'Buying the War', YouTube, https://www.youtube.com/watch?v=0KzYL6e3sV0.

3 http://www.nytimes.com/2015/05/18/opinion/paul-krugman-errors-and-lies.html?_r=0.

4 http://edition.cnn.com/2004/ALLPOLITICS/10/08/factcheck.

5 Michael Massing, 'Now They Tell Us', *New York Review of Books*, http://www.nybooks.com/articles/archives/2004/feb/26/now-they-tell-us.

6 http://www.realclearpolitics.com/articles/2015/04/08/judith_millers_story_setting_the_record_straight_126181.html.

7 http://www.nytimes.com/1995/01/29/books/gordon-generals.html?pagewanted=all.

8 http://www.nytimes.com/2006/03/28/books/28nayl.html?_r=0.

9 http://www.nybooks.com/articles/archives/2004/feb/26/now-they-tell-us.

10 Massing, 'Now They Tell Us'.

11 Ibid.

12 http://www.washingtonpost.com/wp-srv/nation/transcripts/powelltext_020503.html.

13 http://www.nybooks.com/articles/archives/2004/feb/26/now-they-tell-us.

14 http://www.nybooks.com/articles/archives/2004/mar/25/now-they-tell-us-an-exchange.
15 http://www.nybooks.com/articles/2004/04/08/iraq-now-they-tell-us-an-exchange/.
16 Massing, ibid.
17 http://www.nytimes.com/2003/02/08/opinion/the-i-can-t-believe-i-m-a-hawk-club.html?pagewanted=all.
18 http://www.nytimes.com/2004/05/26/world/from-the-editors-the-times-and-iraq.html.
19 Ibid.
20 Judith Miller, *The Story* (Simon & Schuster, 2015), 211.
21 Ibid. 165.
22 John Walcott, IF Stone Medal acceptance speech, http://nieman.harvard.edu/events/2008-i-f-stone-medal-for-journalistic-independence.
23 Ibid.
24 In *At the Center of the Storm*, former CIA director George Tenet wrote, in some exasperation 'Let me say it again: CIA found absolutely no linkage between Saddam and 9/11 … the vice president [Dick Cheney] and others pushed us hard on this issue, and our answers never satisfied him or some of our other "regular customers". Tenet, *At the Center of the Storm* (Harper Perennial, 2008), 242.
25 Saddam intermittently displayed a devout image and called on Mohammed before he was executed.
26 Barack Obama speech, Chicago, 2 Oct. 2002, http://www.npr.org/templates/story/story.php?storyId=99591469.
27 Senator Hilary Clinton, speech, US Senate, 10 October 2002.
28 *New York Times*, 20 July 1984.
29 Schudson, 'Trout or Hamburger', in *The Power of News* (Harvard University Press, 1995).
30 Thomas Patterson, *Out of Order* (Random House, 1994).
31 http://www.people-press.org/2014/12/15/about-half-see-cia-interrogation-methods-as-justified.
32 http://www.esquire.com/news-politics/politics/news/a37933/spies-have-feelings-too.
33 https://www.cpj.org/attacks96/sreports/cia.html.
34 http://www.nytimes.com/2001/10/07/weekinreview/07WEIN.html?pagewanted=2
35 Ibid.
36 Ibid.
37 Tim Weiner, *The Legacy of Ashes* (Doubleday, 2007).
38 As, for example, in his own paper: http://www.nytimes.com/2007/07/22/books/review/Thomas-t.html?_r=1.
39 http://www.mensjournal.com/magazine/cofer-black-out-of-the-shadows-20131120.
40 Bob Woodward, *Bush at War* (Simon & Schuster, 2003), 53.
41 Jane Mayer, *The Dark Side* (Doubleday, 2008), 41. In *A Few Good Men*, Jack Nicholson plays the commander of – ironically – Guantanamo Base in Cuba

(the film is set more than a decade before it had acquired the duties and reputation it now has), who lied to a military court in order to protect what he saw as the reputation of the Marine Corps.

42 Weiner, 'To Fight in the Shadows'.

43 Scott Shane, *Objective Troy* (Tim Duggan Books, 2015), 135.

44 Weiner, *Legacy of Ashes*, xiii.

45 Ibid.

46 http://www.washingtonpost.com/wp-dyn/content/article/2007/07/19/AR2007071902217.html.

47 http://www.washingtondecoded.com/site/2007/09/sins-of-omissio.html.

48 https://www.cia.gov/library/center-for-the-study-of-intelligence/csi-publications/csi-studies/studies/vol51no3/legacy-of-ashes-the-history-of-cia.html.

49 https://web.archive.org/web/20141209165504/http://www.intelligence.senate.gov/study2014/sscistudy1.pdf.

50 Ibid. 20.

51 Ibid. 4.

52 http://www.theatlantic.com/politics/archive/2014/12/John-Mccain-Speech-Senate-Republican-CIA-Torture-Report/383589/.

53 http://www.washingtonpost.com/wp-dyn/content/article/2006/06/09/AR2006060901356.html.

54 Ibid.

55 Ibid.

56 http://www.historycommons.org/timeline.jsp?hr_general_topic_areas=hr_media&timeline=torture,_rendition,_and_other_abuses_against_captives_in_iraq,_afghanistan,_and_elsewhere&printerfriendly=true.

57 http://www.washingtonpost.com/wp-dyn/content/article/2005/11/01/AR2005110101644.html.

58 Dana Priest, *The Mission* (W. W. Norton, 2003), 18.

59 http://www.pulitzer.org/cms/sites/default/files/content/washpost_tsa_item1.pdf.

60 Ibid.

61 Dana Priest and William Arkin, *Top Secret America: The Rise of the New American Security State* (Little Brown, 2011).

62 Jane Mayer, *The Dark Side* (Doubleday, 2008).

63 Ibid. 7.

64 Ibid. 220.

65 Ibid. 247.

66 Jack Goldsmith, *The Terror Presidency* (W. W. Norton, 2009), 215.

67 This is no longer true. In November 2009, Major Nidal Hasan, an army psychiatrist turned jihadist, killed 13 and wounded 30 in Fort Hood, Texas; in May 2010, a bomb planted in a car in New York's Times Square by the Pakistani Naisal Sahzad failed to go off; and in April 2013, a bomb in a pressure cooker planted among spectators of the Boston Marathon by two Chechen brothers Dzhokar and Tamerlan Tsarnaev exploded, killing three and wounding more than 200 others. In December 2015, a married couple, Syed Rizwan Farook and

Tashfeen Malik, US citizens of Pakistani origin, killed 22 of their colleagues in the public health department of San Bernardino, California; and in June 2016, a man pledging allegiance to IS killed 50 people in a gay night club in Orlando, Florida.

68 Mark Mazzetti, *The Way of the Knife* (Penguin Press, 2013), 3, 14.

69 http://www.nytimes.com/2015/04/13/us/terrorism-case-renews-debate-over-drone-hits.html.

70 Scott Shane, *Objective Troy* (Tim Duggan Books, 2015).

71 Ibid. 161.

72 Scott Shane, *Dismantling Utopia: How Information Ended the Soviet Union* (Ivan Dee, 1994).

73 Shane, *Objective Troy*, 177.

74 http://www.pbs.org/wgbh/pages/frontline/shows/faith/interviews/albacete.html.

75 Shane, *Objective Troy*, 202.

76 https://www.thebureauinvestigates.com/2015/09/02/monthly-drone-report-august-2015-32-us-strikes-hit-afghanistan-alone.

77 http://www.nytimes.com/2015/04/24/world/asia/drone-strikes-reveal-uncomfortable-truth-us-is-often-unsure-about-who-will-die.html.

78 Ibid.

79 http://www.nytimes.com/2015/08/30/magazine/the-lessons-of-anwar-al-awlaki.html.

80 https://www.whitehouse.gov/the-press-office/remarks-president-acceptance-nobel-peace-prize.

81 https://www.washingtonpost.com/blogs/monkey-cage/wp/2015/03/16/has-obama-delivered-the-most-transparent-administration-in-history.

82 https://theintercept.com/2015/02/18/destroyed-by-the-espionage-act.

83 Maass, WNYC interview, 20 Mar. 2015, http://www.wnyc.org/story/stephen-kims-leak/#transcript.

84 http://www.nytimes.com/2013/07/21/us/politics/math-behind-leak-crackdown-153-cases-4-years-0-indictments.html.

85 https://theintercept.com/2015/02/18/destroyed-by-the-espionage-act/.

86 Maass, WNYC interview.

87 https://www.washingtonpost.com/news/post-politics/wp/2013/05/16/obama-no-apologies-for-leaks-investigation.

88 http://www.nytimes.com/2015/02/10/us/former-cia-officer-released-after-nearly-two-years-in-prison-for-leak-case.html.

89 https://www.whitehouse.gov/the-press-office/2011/10/07/executive-order-13587-structural-reforms-improve-security-classified-net.

90 http://fas.org/irp/dni/icd/icd-119.pdf.

91 http://www.nytimes.com/2012/02/12/sunday-review/a-high-tech-war-on-leaks.html?_r=0.

92 www.fas.org/sgp/foia/tenet499.html.

93 Steven Aftergood, 'An Inquiry into the Dynamics of Government Secrecy', *Harvard Civil Rights-Civil Liberties Law Review*, 48(2) (Summer 2013): 511–30.

94 Tenet, *Center of the Storm*, 241.

95   Ibid. 242–3.
96   Jose R. Rodriguez, *Hard Measures* (Threshold Editions, Simon & Schuster, 2012).
97   Ibid. 71.
98   http://www.newyorker.com/magazine/2016/03/07/michael-hayden-comes-out-of-the-shadows.
99   Ibid.
100 http://www.theatlantic.com/politics/archive/2011/08/powell-cheneys-book-is-full-of-cheap-shots/244275/.
101 Tenet, *Center of the Storm*, 18.
102 http://www.ozy.com/2016/how-an-ex-cia-chief-would-brief-trump-on-foreign-policy/68206?utm_source=dd&utm_medium=email&utm_campaign=03042016&variable=ef30fc3ba46ebdafb0127c40f212a610.
103 http://foreignpolicy.com/2013/06/17/the-real-reason-youre-mad-at-the-nsa/.
104 Thttp://www.pbs.org/newshour/bb/international-jan-june99-blair_doctrine4-23/.
105 Samantha Power, *A Problem from Hell* (Basic Books, 2002).
106 http://www.newyorker.com/magazine/2014/12/22/land-possible.
107 https://fas.org/irp/offdocs/wmd_report.pdf.
108 https://fas.org/irp/world/uk/butler071404.pdf.
109 http://www.nytimes.com/2016/07/07/world/europe/chilcot-report.html.
110 Priest and Arkin, 'Top Secret America'.
111 http://coursesa.matrix.msu.edu/~hst306/documents/indust.html.
112 http://blogs.reuters.com/david-rohde/2013/06/11/the-intelligence-industrial-complex/.
113 https://www.whitehouse.gov/the-press-office/2016/04/01/remarks-president-obama-and-prime-minister-rutte-opening-session-nuclear.
114 https://www.foreignaffairs.com/articles/2016-03-29/coming-isis-al-qaeda-merger.
115 http://www.spectator.co.uk/2016/04/how-our-politicans-and-media-are-helping-terrorists-win.
116 https://www.fbi.gov/news/speeches/going-dark-are-technology-privacy-and-public-safety-on-a-collision-course.
117 https://www.apple.com/privacy.
118 http://www.nytimes.com/2016/03/29/technology/apple-iphone-fbi-justice-department-case.html?_r=0.
119 http://www.nytimes.com/2016/03/01/technology/apple-wins-ruling-in-new-york-iphone-hacking-order.html.
120 http://www.gchq.gov.uk/press_and_media/news_and_features/Pages/Director-dispels-encryption-myths-in-MIT-speech.aspx.

Chapter 3   Down with the State and its Servile Hacks!

1   Julian Assange et al., *Cypherpunks: Freedom and the Future of the Internet* (OR Books, 2013, Kindle Edition), loc. 1887.
2   http://www.wsj.com/articles/SB95326824311657269.

3 http://www.ft.com/cms/s/0/bf638156-a366-11e5-bc70-7ff6d4fd203a.
html#axzz3uZHKInRl.

4 David Plouffe, seminar at the Institute of Public Policy and Research, London,
December 2015.

5 Paul Starr, *The Creation of the Media* (Basic Books, 2015).

6 https://newrepublic.com/article/64252/goodbye-the-age-newspapers-
hello-new-era-corruption.

7 The Washington Post Company lost $15m in the second quarter of 2013:
bought by Jeff Bezos, owner of Amazon, in August of that year, it has not
been required, as a wholly owned private company, to file a declaration.
The Guardian Media Group lost £45.3m in fiscal year ending March 2015.
Le Monde lost €6m in 2014. In all cases the papers' managements forecast a
reduction in losses in the succeeding years.

8 http://www.newyorker.com/magazine/2005/02/14/fear-and-favor.

9 http://www.ft.com/cms/s/0/8843ca9e-70f5-11e5-9b9e-690fdae72044.
html#axzz3ytkaO9J1.

10 Some on the left believe that the press in democracies fulfils the same function
as the state-controlled news media – the legitimation of the system – only
more cunningly disguised. This is the belief behind Noam Chomsky and
Edward Herman's famous equation of *Pravda* (in its Soviet incarnation, as the
Communist Party's most authoritative daily organ) and the *New York Times* in
their book, *Manufacturing Consent* (Pantheon, 2002).

11 http://journalism.about.com/od/ethicsprofessionalism/a/whfoxnews.htm.

12 http://www.newyorker.com/magazine/2015/12/14/a-house-divided.

13 https://cdt.org/blog/'going-dark'-versus-a-'golden-age-for-surveillance'.

14 http://archive.atomicmpc.com.au/archives.asp?s=1&c=1&t=24724.

15 Misha Glenny, *Dark Market* (Bodley Head, 2011), 35.

16 Henry Porter, *The Dying Light* (Orion, 2009).

17 Pete Eggers, *The Circle* (Penguin, 2013).

18 Ibid. 384.

19 http://www.ft.com/cms/s/0/8843ca9e-70f5-11e5-9b9e-690fdae72044.html#
axzz3ytkaO9J1.

20 Helmut Schmidt said that 'Hitler will never be forgotten, but what he did will
only be relegated to the background if something even more terrible happens,
something even worse. I wouldn't like this to happen. But as long as it doesn't,
Hitler will be remembered.' http://www.nytimes.com/1984/09/16/magazine/a-talk-
with-helmut-schmidt.html?pagewanted=all.

21 A. Jacobsen, *The Pentagon's Brain* (Little, Brown & Co., 2015).

22 M. Mitchell Waldrop, *The Dream Machine* (Viking Penguin, 2001).

23 http://time.com/75484/putin-the-internet-is-a-cia-project/.

24 Jamie Bartlett, *The Dark Net* (Heinemann, 2014), 6.

25 Steven Levy, *Crypto* (Penguin Books, 2001), 15.

26 Ibid. 57.

27 https://s3.amazonaws.com/s3.documentcloud.org/documents/238963/huge-
c-i-a-operation-reported-in-u-s-against.pdf.

28 http://www.nytimes.com/2005/12/25/weekinreview/the-agency-that-could-be-big-brother.html.

29 Levy, *Crypto*, 106.

30 http://www.newyorker.com/books/page-turner/the-n-s-a-s-chief-chronicler.

31 http://www.nytimes.com/2005/12/16/politics/bush-lets-us-spy-on-callers-without-courts.html.

32 http://www.newyorker.com/magazine/2015/10/12/the-network-man.

33 Bartlett, *Dark Net*.

34 Levy, *Crypto*.

35 'Eric Hughes: A Cypherpunk's Manifesto', http://www.activism.net/cypherpunk/manifesto.html.

36 http://www.libertarian.co.uk/lapubs/scien/scien009.pdf.

37 The law which prompted Barlow's manifesto fell foul of a number of constitutional safeguards – especially the Supreme Court – was vigorously opposed by the American Civil Liberties Union and was ultimately eviscerated by the institutions of the physical and governing world which Barlow had enjoined to make themselves scarce.

38 Glenny, *Dark Market*.

39 Bartlett, *Dark Net*, chapter 3.

40 Assange et al., *Cypherpunks*.

41 Ibid. loc. 73.

42 Ibid. loc. 66.

43 Ibid. loc. 1945.

44 Ibid. from Assange's final statement, loc. 1923–end.

45 Julian Assange, *Julian Assange: The Unauthorised Autobiography* (Canongate, 2011).

46 http://www.lrb.co.uk/v36/n05/andrew-ohagan/ghosting.

47 Most of Wikileaks' revelations, and all of the files taken from the NSA, do damage to, or at least embarrass, Western governments and security services. With the exception of an early 2007 report on 'the looting of Kenya under President Moi', the focus of Wikileaks has been the West, and especially the US, though the content of the diplomatic cables which was the site's biggest haul also embarrassed or angered foreign states (and reflected quite well on US diplomats). Authoritarian societies have powerful secret police forces and would deal harshly with leakers.

48 http://www.employmentlawwatch.com/2015/02/articles/employment-france/whistleblower-protection-around-the-world.

49 Bob Woodward and Carl Bernstein, *All the President's Men* (Simon & Schuster, 1974).

50 *New York Times Co. v. United States*, 403 US at 714–20.

51 Ibid. 403 US717.

52 http://www.vanityfair.com/news/2011/02/the-guardian-201102.

53 https://wikileaks.org/Transcript-Meeting-Assange-Schmidt.html.

54 Manning, statement to court martial, https://www.theguardian.com/world/2013/mar/01/bradley-manning-wikileaks-statement-full-text.

55 Ibid.

56 Luke Harding, *The Snowden Files* (Guardian Faber Publishing, 2014).

57 http://arstechnica.co.uk.

58 edwardsnowden.com/2014/06/25/edward-snowden-speaks-to-the-council-of-europe-on-improving-the-protection-of-whistleblowers/.

59 Harding, *Snowden Files*.

60 Sherry Turkle, *Life on the Screen* (Simon & Schuster, 1997), 263.

61 http://www.npr.org/2013/09/11/221359323/reporter-had-to-decide-if-snowden-leaks-were-the-real-thing.

62 Ibid.

63 Glen Greenwald, *No Place to Hide* (Penguin, 2015), 53.

64 https://www.washingtonpost.com/world/national-security/in-nsa-intercepted-data-those-not-targeted-far-outnumber-the-foreigners-who-are/2014/07/05/8139adf8-045a-11e4-8572-4b1b969b6322_story.html.

65 https://www.opendemocracy.net/john-lloyd/full-monty-journalism-assange-greenwald-and-snowden.

66 https://www.theguardian.com/commentisfree/2013/oct/14/independent-epitaph-establishment-journalism.

67 Greenwald, *No Place to Hide*, 87.

68 http://www.nytimes.com/2013/10/28/opinion/a-conversation-in-lieu-of-a-column.html.

69 http://www.lrb.co.uk/v36/n05/andrew-ohagan/ghosting.

70 http://www.nytimes.com/2006/07/01/opinion/01keller.html?_r=0.

71 http://www.huffingtonpost.com/2014/05/16/glenn-greenwald-new-york-times_n_5337486.html.

72 https://theintercept.com/2014/06/06/encouraging-words-dean-baquet-weasel-words-james-clapper.

73 Jay Rosen, 'Why Pierre Omidyar Decided to Join Forces with Glenn Greenwald for a New Venture in News', http://pressthink.org/2013/10/why-pierre-omidyar-decided-to-join-forces-with-glenn-greenwald-for-a-new-venture-in-news.

74 Glenn Greenwald et al., 'The Inside Story of Matt Taibbi's Departure from First Look Media', https://theintercept.com/2014/10/30/inside-story-matt-taibbis-departure-first-look-media/.

75 Rosen, 'Why Pierre Omidyar'.

76 Greenwald et al., 'Inside Story'.

77 http://www.vanityfair.com/news/2015/01/first-look-media-pierre-omidyar.

78 Wolfgang Sofsky, *Privacy: A Manifesto* (Princeton University Press, 2008), 21.

79 Ibid.

Chapter 4   The Breaking of Freedom's Back?

1 Robert Dover and Michael Goodman (eds), *Spinning Intelligence* (Hurst & Co., 2009).

2 Ibid. 177.

3 Harold Evans, *My Paper Chase* (Abacus, 2010).

4 Philip Knightley, *The First Casualty* (Johns Hopkins UP, 2002). Quoted in Evans, *Paper Chase*, 6.

5 Evans, *Paper Chase*.

6 http://www.stephengrey.com/2004/05/americas-gulag/.

7 Stephen Grey, *Ghost Plane* (C. Hurst & Co., 2006).

8 Ibid. 192–3.

9 Jason Burke, *The New Threat from Islamic Militancy* (Bodley Head, 2015, Kindle edition), loc. 73.

10 Ibid. loc. 90.

11 http://foreignpolicy.com/2009/10/27/think-again-al-qaeda-4.

12 Ibid.

13 Ibid.

14 Jason Burke, *Think Again: Al Qaeda* (Simon & Schuster, 2004), 2.

15 http://www.ft.com/cms/s/0/e47d9e72-2be4-11df-8033-00144feabdc0.html#axzz3syDKYsrq.

16 http://www.bbc.co.uk/news/uk-14750998.

17 http://www.theguardian.com/commentisfree/2013/jun/08/torture-britain-reputation-david-cameron.

18 http://www.theguardian.com/law/interactive/2011/aug/04/mi6-torture-interrogation-policy-document.

19 http://www.theguardian.com/world/2010/oct/28/mi6-chief-torture-john-sawers.

20 http://www.dailymail.co.uk/news/article-2872153/Britain-pays-400-000-silence-Libyan-dissident-demanding-1million-damages-claims-delivered-Gaddafi-s-torturers-MI6.html.

21 Stephen Grey, *The New Spymasters* (Penguin, 2013, Kindle edition), loc. 5317.

22 http://www.theguardian.com/uk-news/2014/jan/17/barack-obama-surveillance-pledge-gulf-with-uk.

23 http://www.theguardian.com/uk-news/2014/may/09/westminster-may-have-to-concede-edward-snowden-had-a-point.

24 http://www.theguardian.com/uk-news/2014/jan/28/gchq-mass-surveillance-spying-law-lawyer.

25 http://www.theguardian.com/media/2014/jan/17/alan-rusbridger-nsa-snowden-revelations.

26 BBC Press office. The number of journalists in BBC news and English regions in September 2014 was 6,000; there have been several cuts since then, thus 5,400 is itself an estimate. http://www.bbc.co.uk/pressoffice/keyfacts/stories/news.shtml.

27 http://www.telegraph.co.uk/men/active/mens-health/11247597/Frank-Gardner-I-will-never-forgive-the-terrorists-who-did-this-to-me.html.

28 Gordon Corera, *Intercept* (Weidenfeld and Nicholson, 2015), 389.

29 Gordon Corera, *The Art of Betrayal* (Weidenfeld & Nicolson, 2011).

30 http://www.mensjournal.com/magazine/kidnapped-in-syria-anthony-loyds-harrowing-story-20141017.

31 Mark Urban, *Task Force Black* (Abacus Paperback, 2011).

32 General McChrystal, one of the most admired US military commanders of his time, had a military career destroyed by the press. A reporter from the

US weekly *Rolling Stone*, Michael Hastings, was permitted to 'embed' with McChrystal's command in Afghanistan, and in a 2010 profile, 'The Runaway General' reported, sometimes in direct quotes, on the general's and his aides' dismissive view of Obama, their commander-in-chief – and even more of the vice president, Joe Biden ('Biden – who's he?' Hastings quotes McChrystal as saying). In another passage, informed by one of McChrystal's (unnamed) aides, Hasting writes that, on their first meeting, in a gathering of senior generals at the White House, 'McChrystal thought Obama looked 'uncomfortable and intimidated' by the roomful of military brass. Their first one-on-one meeting took place in the Oval Office four months later, after McChrystal got the Afghanistan job, and it didn't go much better. 'It was a 10-minute photo op', says an adviser to McChrystal. 'Obama clearly didn't know anything about him, who he was. Here's the guy who's going to run his fucking war, but he didn't seem very engaged. The Boss [McChrystal] was pretty disappointed.' The profile, skilfully woven, is also a more or less explicit critique of McChrystal's belief in a 'surge', an aggressive taking of the fight to the enemy with a greatly augmented force, reluctantly agreed by Obama. The day after the story appeared, McChrystal, proclaiming in a statement his respect for the President, resigned – to become a visiting professor at Yale, found a consulting group and join the boards of several companies, mainly in the arms industry. Hastings died in Los Angeles in June 2013 when his Mercedes hit a tree at high speed at 4.00 am, and burst into flames: the crash came when he was working on a story about the Snowden leaks, and had told colleagues at BuzzFeed, where he was then employed, that he wanted to 'go off the radar' for some time because of the sensitivity of the story. Though there was no evidence that the crash was other than an accident, there was much speculation, mainly on blogs (http://jonathanturley.org/2013/07/20/what-happened-to-michael-hastings), that Hastings had been assassinated by one of the powers-that-be and McChrystal was interviewed by the police on the issue.

33 Mark Urban, *UK Eyes Alpha* (Faber & Faber, 1996).
34 Ibid. 267.
35 Mark Urban, *The Edge* (Little, Brown, 2015).
36 http://www.telegraph.co.uk/culture/books/bookreviews/11541639/The-Edge-by-Mark-Urban.html.
37 Cathy Massiter was an MI5 officer detailed to spy on the Campaign for Nuclear Disarmament from 1981 to 1983, but resigned from the service. In a Channel 4 documentary she said that she had come to believe that the organisation posed no threat to UK security. Though never charged, she was involved in a court case brought by the National Council for Civil Liberties, whose two leading members – Harriet Harman, the legal officer, and Patricia Hewitt, the general secretary (both later senior Labour cabinet ministers in the Blair governments) – were under surveillance in the early 1980s, a period when the agency's 'F' branch spied on left-wing trade unionists, politicians (not only Communists) and activists. Massiter's (very full) revelations included allegations that MI5 had been tasked to spy on left wingers for political reasons, rather than on grounds of national security: a newspaper story quoted her as alleging that

material gathered by MI5 was passed on to a counter propaganda unit set up by Mr [Michael] Heseltine [then Defence Secretary] in March 1983 to combat the CND's unilateralist line. The unit is known as DS19. Instructed by her superior Ms. Massiter passed on nonclassified information on any extreme left-wing affiliations of CND leaders. The passing of information from MI5, a security organisation, to DSI9, a political body may be seen as a direct breach of MI5's own code of conduct, known as the Maxwell Fyfe directive. It states that it is essential that 'the Security Service should be kept absolutely free from any political bias 'or influence.' Cathy Massiter said: 'It did begin to seem to me that what the Security Service was being asked to do was to provide information on a party political issue'.

(Patricia Morgan, 'The MI5 spy who had a conscience',
Courier Mail, 11 May 1985.)

38 Edward Lucas, *The New Cold War* (Bloomsbury, 2009).

39 http://www.amazon.co.uk/The-Snowden-Operation-Greatest-Intelligence-ebook/dp/B00I0W61OY.

40 Ibid. Kindle edition, loc. 807.

41 http://www.pressgazette.co.uk/economists-edward-lucas-claims-russian-radio-silence-over-invasion-crimea-was-due-snowden.

42 https://www.lawfareblog.com/interview-dean-baquet-executive-editor-new-york-times-publication-decisions-about-intelligence.

43 http://sites.cardiff.ac.uk/dcssproject/files/2015/08/UK-Public-Opinion-Review-180615.pdf.

44 http://www.thetimes.co.uk/tto/news/uk/defence/article4597803.ece (pay wall; published 28 Oct. 2015).

45 Ben Macintyre, *A Spy among Friends: Kin Philby and the Great Betrayal* (Broadway Books, 2015).

46 Macintyre, 'GCHQ Lifts the Lid'.

47 Ibid.

48 Ibid.

49 http://www.theguardian.com/books/2015/dec/01/shami-chakrabarti-criticises-orwellian-political-language-paris-attacks.

50 http://www.cps.gov.uk/news/articles/coming_out_of_the_shadows.

51 Moore had already sought to bury other bad news on 11 September 1991, the day of the attack on the World Trade Center.

52 http://www.thetimes.co.uk/tto/news/politics/article2027791.ece.

53 http://www.theguardian.com/world/2013/jun/17/defence-d-bbc-media-censor-surveillance-security.

54 http://www.abovetopsecret.com/forum/thread979767/pg1.

55 http://www.thesundaytimes.co.uk/sto/news/uk_news/National/article1568673.ece. In June 2015, the *Sunday Times* story – which stated that 'Russia and China have cracked the top-secret cache of files stolen by the fugitive US whistleblower Edward Snowden, forcing MI6 to pull agents out of live operations in hostile countries, according to senior officials in Downing Street, the Home Office and the security services' – was heavily criticised by the *Guardian* and other liberal media for lacking evidence and sources. Ryan Gallagher, who

writes on security issues for The Intercept and other publications, wrote (http://
notes.rjgallagher.co.uk/2015/06/sunday-times-snowden-china-russia-
questions.html):

> All in all, for me the Sunday Times story raises more questions than it
> answers, and more importantly it contains some pretty dubious claims,
> contradictions, and inaccuracies. The most astonishing thing about it is
> the total lack of scepticism it shows for these grand government assertions,
> made behind a veil of anonymity. This sort of credulous regurgitation of
> government statements is antithetical to good journalism.

The alteration to which Davis refers was to the assertion in the story that David
Miranda, Glen Greenwald's partner held at Heathrow Airport for some hours
and his laptop temporarily confiscated, had been visiting Snowden in Moscow:
he had been visiting Laura Poitras in Berlin, as the correction stated.

56 In March 2015 Isabella Sankey, director of policy at Liberty, told the ISC that
'Some things might happen that could have been prevented if you took all of the
most oppressive, restrictive and privacy-infringing measures. That is the price you
pay to live in a free society.' The statement drew some hostile stories (http://www.
dailymail.co.uk/news/article-2992642/Even-collecting-data-stops-terror-plots-
s-wrong-says-Liberty-Human-rights-group-criticised-unacceptable-comments.
html). Hazel Blears, a Labour member of the committee, criticised her sharply for
the statement. Sankey later said that 'There is absolutely no excuse for terrorism
and society must take all proportional steps to deal with it – but the real story here
is that, despite their best efforts, the committee has been unable to present any
evidence that mass surveillance of innocents' calls and emails is saving any lives.'

57 http://www.theguardian.com/world/2014/nov/06/intelligence-agencies-
lawyer-client-abdel-hakim-belhaj-mi5-mi6-gchq.

58 In 1983, the Sunday Times published excerpts from Hitler's diaries, which
had been syndicated to the paper (with others) by the weekly magazine
Stern, which had bought them. The Times asked for the six volumes to be
authenticated by the distinguished historian Hugh Trevor Roper, who was
one of its independent directors: Trevor Roper said they were genuine. They
soon were exposed as a fake.

59 The Wikipedia definition of Tempora (https://en.wikipedia.org/wiki/Tempora) is
that it is

> the code word for a formerly secret computer system that is used by the British
> GCHQ. This system is used to buffer most Internet communications that are
> extracted from fibre optic cables, so these can be processed and searched at a
> later time. It was tested since 2008 and became operational in the autumn of
> 2011. Tempora uses intercepts on the fibre-optic cables that make up the
> backbone of the Internet to gain access to large amounts of Internet users'
> personal data, without any individual suspicion or targeting. The intercepts
> are placed in the United Kingdom and overseas, with the knowledge of
> companies owning either the cables or landing stations.

60 http://www.theguardian.com/commentisfree/2015/nov/27/david-cameron-
syria-macho-foolish-labour-jeremy-corbyn.

61 https://www.theguardian.com/media/2014/aug/20/-sp-bbc-report-future-charter-renewal.

62 http://www.theguardian.com/world/2015/nov/04/theresa-may-surveillance-measures-edward-snowden.

63 Human Rights Watch (HRW), a much larger organisation than Liberty and with a worldwide reach, is certainly tough on what it believes to be breaches of human rights by governments everywhere: recent (November/December 2015) statements finger Brazil, Egypt, the UK and France as well as the US for bringing in repressive legislation. What Carlile means is that it is prepared to give credit at times to governments which do, as HRW would see it, the right thing, such as commending President Obama for getting a step nearer to closing the Guantanamo prison where terrorist suspects are held, sometimes for years, without trial (https://www.hrw.org/news/2015/10/23/us-veto-step-closing-guantanamo). Liberty rarely does so, attack being its default position.

64 Richard Aldrich, *GCHQ* (Harper Collins, 2010), 495.

65 David Omand, *Securing the State* (OUP, 2014), 7.

66 https://www.gchq.gov.uk/press-release/director-gchq's-valedictory-speech.

67 Alan Judd, *Inside Enemy* (Simon & Schuster, 2015).

68 http://news.bbc.co.uk/nol/shared/bsp/hi/pdfs/14_07_04_butler.pdf.

69 http://www.theguardian.com/world/2015/nov/03/former-reviewer-of-anti-terror-laws-co-owns-consultancy-with-ex-mi6-chief.

70 http://www.standard.co.uk/news/uk/chilcot-report-tony-blair-blamed-for-totally-disastrous-and-unneccesary-iraq-war-a3289206.html.

71 Keith Jeffery, *MI6: The History of the Secret Intelligence Service, 1909–1949* (Bloomsbury, 2010).

72 http://www.theguardian.com/politics/2015/nov/08/david-davis-liberty-draft-investigatory-powers-bill-holes.

Chapter 5   Le jour de guerre est arrivé

1 'Between democracy and [secret] intelligence, history teaches us that the relationship has not always been placid'. http://discours.vie-publique.fr/notices/103001970.html.

2 http://www.history.ac.uk/reviews/review/562.

3 http://edition.cnn.com/2015/11/16/world/paris-attacks.

4 Chris Harris with Agence France-Presse, Euronews, 16 Apr. 2015.

5 http://www.lemonde.fr/politique/article/2015/12/14/un-etat-sans-garde-fous-comme-le-reve-le-fn_4831275_823448.html.

6 http://www.atlantico.fr/decryptage/sondage-choc-attirance-francais-pour-gouvernement-technocratique-non-elu-ou-autoritaire-jerome-fourquet-christophe-voogd-vincent-2418641.html.

7 Anja Becker, 'The Spy Who Couldn't Possibly Be French', *Journal of Intelligence History*, 1(1) (June 2001): 68–87.

8 Ibid.

9 Jean-Claude Cousseran and Philippe Hayez, *Renseigner les democraties, renseigner en democratie* (Odile Jacob, 2015).

10 http://www.nytimes.com/1985/10/06/world/greenpeace-ship-reaches-test-site.html.

11 http://www.lemonde.fr/politique/article/2009/10/05/les-declarations-du-general-philippe-rondot-et-de-dominique-de-villepin-divergent_1249610_823448.html.

12 http://prdchroniques.blog.lemonde.fr/2011/05/11/clearstream-le-general-rondot-et-lart-du-portrait.

13 http://www.liberation.fr/medias/1996/01/08/france-2-22h45-l-affaire-des-irlandais-de-vincennes-documentaire-de-pierre-pean-et-christophe-nick-i_160665.

14 http://www.telegraph.co.uk/news/worldnews/nicolas-sarkozy/8739805/Sarkozys-France-wiretaps-brown-envelopes-and-never-any-regrets.html.

15 http://www.independent.co.uk/news/uk/politics/the-truth-about-churchills-spy-chief-and-the-zinoviev-letter-419180.html.

16 http://www.rtl.fr/actu/societe-faits-divers/l-heure-du-crime-jeudi-10-avril-2014-l-affaire-des-micros-du-canard-enchaine-7771230671.

17 http://www.liberation.fr/france/2010/09/25/les-micros-du-canard-enterres_681570

18 Becker, 'The Spy', 72.

19 http://www.sciencespo.fr/psia/users/philippehayez.

20 Christophe Dubois and Christophe Deloire, *Les Islamistes sont déjà là* (Albin Michel, 2004).

21 Christophe Dubois and Christophe Deloire, *Sexus Politicus* (Albin Michel, 2006).

22 http://www.nytimes.com/2006/10/16/world/europe/16iht-france.3180613.html?pagewanted=all.

23 Dubois and Deloire, *Sexus Politicus*.

24 *The Gazette*, founded in 1630 or 1631 by Theophraste Renaudot, with the support of Cardinal Richelieu, continued until 1915. It gave approved news of the court, and foreign news. It was not the first newspaper to appear: the *Mercure Francois* was published from 1605, but appeared only once a year and died in the 1640s.

25 http://www.lemonde.fr/idees/article/2015/06/29/edwy-plenel-raconte-l-affaire-greenpeace_4663675_3232.html.

26 *Le Monde*, 17 septembre 1985.

27 http://tempsreel.nouvelobs.com/societe/20050710.OBS3013/francois-mitterrand-aurait-donne-son-accord.html.

28 https://blogs.mediapart.fr/edwy-plenel/blog/030113/laffaire-greenpeace-reponse-aux-questions-dun-abonne.

29 http://www.parismatch.com/Actu/Environnement/Edwy-Plenel-combat-toujours-la-raison-d-Etat-797028.

30 http://www.mei-info.com/wp-content/uploads/2014/02/MEI_02_01.pdf.

31 Pierre Péan and Philippe Cohen, *La face cachée du Monde* (Mille et Une Nuits, 2003).

32 Ibid.

33 One of the Snowden revelations was that the NSA was, or had been, hacking into the mobile phone used by President François Hollande: this was reported in France first by the daily *Libération* and then Mediapart. The response of the French government was more irritation than either astonishment or fury.

34 http://www.lemonde.fr/attaques-a-paris/article/2015/12/18/dans-le-grand-fourre-tout-de-l-apologie-du-terrorisme_4834349_4809495.html.

35 http://www.liberation.fr/france/2015/12/22/mesures-extraordinaires-bilan-ordinaire_1422350.

36 http://www.lemonde.fr/idees/article/2015/11/07/a-quoi-servent-les-lanceurs-d-alerte_4805264_3232.html?xtmc=vedrine&xtcr=1.

37 Ibid.

38 Mehdi Ben Barka was an opposition politician in Morocco, exiled in 1962 when accused of plotting against King Hassan II, and thereafter active in internationalist left circles. He was captured from a street in Paris in 1965, and was never seen again: several theories circulate. In 2009 warrants were issued in Paris for the arrest of Moroccan officials deemed to have been complicit in his capture and probable murder but were quickly withdrawn, leaving the family to allege that this was 'a scandal of scandals', and reviving theories that the DGSE (then named the SDECE) was involved (http://www.telegraph.co.uk/news/worldnews/europe/france/6339205/French-secret-services-accused-of-link-to-murder-of-Ben-Barka.html).

39 http://www.hanford.gov/files.cfm/frenchesp.pdf.

40 http://www.europarl.europa.eu/document/activities/cont/201109/20110927A TT27674/20110927ATT27674EN.pdf.

41 Ibid.

42 Ibid.

43 http://www.lefigaro.fr/vox/societe/2015/04/14/31003-20150414ARTFIG00255-loi-sur-le-renseignement-douce-france-beau-pays-de-la-surveillance.php.

44 https://www.privacyinternational.org/sites/default/files/PI%20submission%20France.pdf.

45 https://next.ft.com/content/08e7f266-0d8e-31b5-a829-e817bdb2efb5.

Conclusion: More Light to Lighten the Darkness

1 Edward Lucas, *The New Cold War* (Bloomsbury, 2009).

2 Jason Burke, *The New Threat From Islamic Militancy* (Bodley Head, 2015).

3 Fresh Air, 'Reporter had to Decide if Snowden Leaks were the Real Thing', http://www.npr.org/2013/09/11/221359323/reporter-had-to-decide-if-snowden-leaks-were-the-real-thing.

4 http://www.economist.com/news/international/21696506-mossack-fonseca-leak-shakes-ukraine-more-russia-russia-finds-little-say-about-panama.

5 Fresh Air, 'Reporter had to Decide'.

6 Ibid.

7 http://www.theguardian.com/news/2016/apr/05/justice-department-panama-papers-mossack-fonseca-us-investigation.

8   https://www.whitehouse.gov/the-press-office/2016/04/05/remarks-president-economy-0.

9   http://www.usnews.com/news/articles/2014/01/17/obama-praises-nsa-trashes-edward-snowden.

10 Andrei Soldatov and Irina Borogan, *The Red Web* (Public Affairs, 2015), 207–8.

Index

BOOKS

Journalism and the NSA Revelations: Privacy, Security and the Press
Risto Kunelius, Heikki Heikkilä, Adrienne Russell and
Dmitry Yagodin (eds)
ISBN: 978 1 78453 675 6 (HB); 978 1 78453 676 3 (PB)

Journalism in an Age of Terror: Covering and Uncovering the Secret State
John Lloyd
ISBN: 978 1 78453 790 6 (HB); 978 1 78453 708 1 (PB)

Media, Revolution and Politics in Egypt: The Story of an Uprising
Abdalla F. Hassan
ISBN: 978 1 78453 217 8 (HB); 978 1 78453 218 5 (PB)

*The Euro Crisis in the Media: Journalistic Coverage of Economic Crisis and
European Institutions*
Robert G. Picard (ed.)
ISBN: 978 1 78453 059 4 (HB); 978 1 78453 060 0 (PB)

Local Journalism: The Decline of Newspapers and the Rise of Digital Media
Rasmus Kleis Nielsen (ed.)
ISBN: 978 1 78453 320 5 (HB); 978 1 78453 321 2 (PB)

The Ethics of Journalism: Individual, Institutional and Cultural Influences
Wendy N. Wyatt (ed.)
ISBN: 978 1 78076 673 7 (HB); 978 1 78076 674 4 (PB)

*Political Journalism in Transition: Western Europe in a
Comparative Perspective*
Raymond Kuhn and Rasmus Kleis Nielsen (eds)
ISBN: 978 1 78076 677 5 (HB); 978 1 78076 678 2 (PB)

*Transparency in Politics and the Media: Accountability and
Open Government*
Nigel Bowles, James T. Hamilton and David A. L. Levy (eds)
ISBN: 978 1 78076 675 1 (HB); 978 1 78076 676 8 (PB)

Media and Public Shaming: Drawing the Boundaries of Disclosure
Julian Petley (ed.)
ISBN: 978 1 78076 586 0 (HB); 978 1 78076 587 7 (PB)